A TEXT BOOK OF

BUILDING DESIGN AND DRAWING

For
Semester II

SECOND YEAR DEGREE COURSES IN
CIVIL ENGINEERING

As Per New Revised Syllabus of
North Maharashtra University, Jalgaon,
June 2013-2014

A. D. Pawar
M. E. (Civil) Construction & Management
Assistant Professor, NICMAR, PUNE Campus
Formerly, SKN - Sinhgad Institute of Technology & Science,
Kusgaon (Bk), Lonavala,

Mrs. V. S. Limaye
M. Tech. (Civil), M.P.M.
Associate Professor of Civil Deptt.,
Sinhgad College of Engineering,
Vadgoan (Bk.) PUNE

N3084

BUILDING DESIGN AND DRAWING (SEM. II CIVIL, NMU) ISBN 978-93-83971-25-1

Second Edition : February 2016
© : Authors

The text of this publication, or any part thereof, should not be reproduced or transmitted in any form or stored in any computer storage system or device for distribution including photocopy, recording, taping or information retrieval system or reproduced on any disc, tape, perforated media or other information storage device etc., without the written permission of Authors with whom the rights are reserved. Breach of this condition is liable for legal action.

Every effort has been made to avoid errors or omissions in this publication. In spite of this, errors may have crept in. Any mistake, error or discrepancy so noted and shall be brought to our notice shall be taken care of in the next edition. It is notified that neither the publisher nor the authors or seller shall be responsible for any damage or loss of action to any one, of any kind, in any manner, therefrom.

Published By :
NIRALI PRAKASHAN
Abhyudaya Pragati, 1312, Shivaji Nagar
Off J.M. Road, PUNE – 411005
Tel - (020) 25512336/37/39, Fax - (020) 25511379
Email : niralipune@pragationline.com

Printed By :
REPRO INDIA LTD,
Mumbai.

☞ **DISTRIBUTION CENTRES**

PUNE
Nirali Prakashan : 119, Budhwar Peth, Jogeshwari Mandir Lane, Pune 411002, Maharashtra
Tel : (020) 2445 2044, 66022708, Fax : (020) 2445 1538
Email : bookorder@pragationline.com, niralilocal@pragationline.com

Nirali Prakashan : S. No. 28/27, Dhyari, Near Pari Company, Pune 411041
Tel : (020) 24690204 Fax : (020) 24690316
Email : dhyari@pragationline.com, bookorder@pragationline.com

MUMBAI
Nirali Prakashan : 385, S.V.P. Road, Rasdhara Co-op. Hsg. Society Ltd.,
Girgaum, Mumbai 400004, Maharashtra
Tel : (022) 2385 6339 / 2386 9976, Fax : (022) 2386 9976
Email : niralimumbai@pragationline.com

☞ **DISTRIBUTION BRANCHES**

JALGAON
Nirali Prakashan : 34, V. V. Golani Market, Navi Peth, Jalgaon 425001,
Maharashtra, Tel : (0257) 222 0395, Mob : 94234 91860

KOLHAPUR
Nirali Prakashan : New Mahadvar Road, Kedar Plaza, 1st Floor Opp. IDBI Bank
Kolhapur 416 012, Maharashtra. Mob : 9850046155

NAGPUR
Pratibha Book Distributors : Above Maratha Mandir, Shop No. 3, First Floor,
Rani Jhanshi Square, Sitabuldi, Nagpur 440012, Maharashtra
Tel : (0712) 254 7129

DELHI
Nirali Prakashan : 4593/21, Basement, Aggarwal Lane 15, Ansari Road, Daryaganj
Near Times of India Building, New Delhi 110002
Mob : 08505972553

BENGALURU
Pragati Book House : House No. 1, Sanjeevappa Lane, Avenue Road Cross,
Opp. Rice Church, Bengaluru – 560002.
Tel : (080) 64513344, 64513355,Mob : 9880582331, 9845021552
Email:bharatsavla@yahoo.com

CHENNAI
Pragati Books : 9/1, Montieth Road, Behind Taas Mahal, Egmore,
Chennai 600008 Tamil Nadu, Tel : (044) 6518 3535,
Mob : 94440 01782 / 98450 21552 / 98805 82331,
Email : bharatsavla@yahoo.com

niralipune@pragationline.com | www.pragationline.com

Also find us on www.facebook.com/niralibooks

Dedicated To ...
   Our Beloved Parents

... **Authors**

PREFACE

It gives us immense pleasure to present this book on **"Building Design and Drawing"**.

The book is written mainly for the second year students of Civil Engineering of North Maharashtra University, Jalgoan for the subject **"Building Design and Drawing"**.

The text book has been thoroughly prepared according to Five Units as per revised curriculum of 2013. An attempt is made to give due justice to the use of plans in building design and drawing activities. The authors with their professional and academic experience have taken all efforts to present the text in lucid manner. The theoretical matter has been explained with number of diagrams and illustrations supported by solved examples and Appendices of Several Plans.

Nirali Prakashan put the book, what we thought into reality. Our sincere thanks to Shri. Dineshbhai Furia, Shri, Jignesh Furia and Shri. M. P. Munde. The books could be completed in time, due to sincere and hard work of Nirali Prakashan's staff namely Mr. Akbar Shaikh, Mrs. Roshan Khan and Miss Chaitali Takale. We thanks them all.

We also thankful to **Mr. Pruthviraj M. More**, Branch Manager, Jalgaon office for his valuable help and efforts for promotion of our books.

Valuable suggestions from our esteemed readers to improve the text will be most welcome and highly appreciated.

January 2014   **Authors**

Pune

SYLLABUS

UNIT I   (08 Hours, 16 marks)

1. **Introduction**

   Building definition and types of building as per occupancy, Principles of Planning of Residential Buildings, Plan Sanctioning Procedure, Building Bye Laws and its necessity.

2. **Ventilation and Air-conditioning of Buildings**

   Ventilation: Necessity of Ventilation, Functional requirements, Systems of Ventilation and their choice, Movement of Wind through building, Wind Effect etc.

   Air-conditioning: Classification, Comfort and Comfort Conditions, Principles and System of Comfort, Object and Necessity of Air-conditioning.

3. **Fire Protection:** Fire Load, Fire safety, Grading of occupancy by Fire Load, Considerations in Fire Protection, Fire Resistant Construction and Wall Openings, Fire Escape Elements.

4. **Building Services:** Its importance, Constructional requirements for different building services- like electrical, Tele Communication Service and Plumbing Services : Layout of Water Supply and Drainage System, One Pipe and Two Pipe System, Storage and Disposal arrangement, Septic tank, Garbage disposal arrangements, Solar water heater.

UNIT II   (07 Hours, 16 marks)

(a) Planning and Designing of Residential Buildings (Load Bearing or Frame Structure).

(b) **Working Drawings:** Importance and use of all types of working drawings at site.

UNIT III   (08 Hours, 16 marks)

(a) Planning and Designing of Apartment Houses (Flats) (Framed Structure only).

(b) **Perspective Drawings:** One Point and Two Point Perspective Drawings.

UNIT IV   (08 Hours, 16 marks)

(a) Planning and Designing of Educational Buildings, Hostel Buildings, Library Buildings, Restaurants, Hotels/Lodging-Boarding, Building and Primary Health Centers/Hospitals (Frame Structure only)

UNIT V   (08 Hours, 16 marks)

(1) Planning and Designing of Bus Stand Buildings, Commercial Complex Buildings, Bank Buildings, Post Office Buildings, Community/Marriage Halls, Factory Buildings (Frame Structure only)

   Note: Theory Questions shall be asked on Unit I.

(2) Only Drawing Questions shall be asked to Draw on Drawing Sheets from Units II, III, IV and V.

CONTENTS

UNIT I

1. INTRODUCTION TO BUILDING DRAWING   1.1 – 1.14
    1.1   Concept of an Integrated Built Environment   1.1
    1.2   Principles of Planning   1.2
    1.3   Building Rules and Bye-Laws   1.9
         1.3.1   Minimum Sizes for Different Components in a Residential Building   1.9
         1.3.2   Space and Floor Area Requirements per Head for Ventilation   1.10
         1.3.3   Building Line   1.10
         1.3.4   Control Line   1.10
         1.3.5   Plinth Height   1.11
         1.3.6   Height of Rooms   1.11
         1.3.7   Open Space Requirements   1.11
         1.3.8   Regulations to Decide the Height of a Building   1.11
         1.3.9   Bye-Laws for Lighting   1.12
         1.3.10 Built-Up Area   1.12
         1.3.11 F.A.R. (Floor Area Ratio) or F.S.I. (Floor Space Index) and State its Necessity   1.13
         •   Important Points   1.13
         •   Questions   1.14

2. VENTILATION   2.1 – 2.22
    2.1   Introduction   2.1
    2.2   Comfort Factors for Ventilation   2.2
    2.3   Systems of Ventilation   2.5
    2.4   Air conditioning   2.11
    2.5   Comfort Air conditioning   2.12
    2.6   The Cooling Load   2.15
    2.7   Components of Air Conditioning System   2.17
    2.8   Air Distribution System   2.20
    2.9   Systems of Air conditioning   2.20
         •   Important Points   2.21
         •   Questions   2.21

3. FIRE PROTECTION   3.1 – 3.22
    3.1   Introduction   3.1
         3.1.1   Fire Safety   3.2
    3.2   Classification of Buildings Based on Occupancy   3.2
    3.3   Fire Load   3.3
    3.4   Factors affecting Fire Development   3.5
    3.5   Pattern of Fire   3.5
    3.6   Fire Severity   3.6
    3.7   Fire Resistance   3.7
    3.8   Some Common Construction Materials   3.9

3.9	Fire Resistant Construction	3.9
3.10	Means of Escape	3.18
3.11	Fire Detecting Systems	3.21
3.12	Fire Extinguishing Systems	3.21
	• Important Points	3.22
	• Questions	3.22

4. BUILDING SERVICES   4.1 – 4.32

4.1	Constructional requirements for different Building Services	4.1
	4.1.1 Electrical Services	4.1
	4.1.2 Switch Room	4.2
	4.1.3 Energy Meters	4.2
	4.1.4 Layout and Installation of Wiring	4.2
	4.1.5 Telecommunication Services	4.3
	4.1.6 Entertainment Services	4.4
	4.1.7 Air Handling, Conditioning and Air Heating	4.4
	4.1.8 Vertical Circulation: Lifts and Escalators	4.5
4.2	Solar Water Heating System	4.10
4.3	Plumbing Services	4.16
4.4	Water Supply Requirements for Buildings	4.16
4.5	Storage of Water	4.18
4.6	Layout of Water Supply and Drainage System	4.20
4.7	Plumbing System for Waste Water	4.21
	• Important Points	4.32
	• Questions	4.32

UNIT II

5. PLANNING AND RESIDENTIAL BUILDINGS   5.1 – 5.36

5.1	Introduction	5.1
5.2	Site Selection	5.2
5.3	Types of Structure	5.2
	5.3.1 Comparison Between Different Types of Structures	5.3
5.4	Arrangement of Rooms for Residential Buildings	5.4
5.5	Size of Rooms for Residential Buildings	5.8
5.6	Planning of a Residential Complex	5.9
	• Important Points	5.12
	• Questions	5.12

6. WORKING DRAWING   6.1 – 6.34

6.1	Introduction	6.1
6.2	Types of Drawings	6.1
6.3	Use of I.S. Specifications	6.2
6.4	Graphical Symbols	6.4
6.5	Scales	6.8
6.6	Title Block	6.8
6.7	Line - Plan	6.10

6.8	Development of Line – Plan	6.11
6.9	Plan	6.11
6.10	Elevation	6.12
6.11	Sections	6.13
6.12	Schedule of Doors and Windows	6.18
6.13	Area Statement	6.20
6.14	Abstract From I.S. - 962 – 1967	6.22
	6.14.1 Size of Drawing Sheets	6.22
	6.14.2 Size of Drawing Boards	6.23
	6.14.3 Margins	6.23
	6.14.4 Title Block	6.23
	6.14.5 Numbering of Drawing Sheet	6.24
	6.14.6 Reproduction of Drawings	6.24
	6.14.7 Folding of Prints	6.24
	6.14.8 Reinforced Concrete Work	6.26
	6.14.9 Colouring the Plan	6.26
6.15	Detailed Drawings	6.27
6.16	Methods of Preparing detailed Drawings	6.28
	6.16.1 Drawing Foundation Plan	6.28
6.17	Roof Plan and Terrace Floor Plan	6.29
	6.17.1 Roof Plan for Pitched Roof	6.30
	6.17.2 Roof Plan for Flat Roof	6.31
6.18	Site Plan	6.31
6.19	Other Details	6.33
	• Important Points	6.34
	• Questions	6.34

UNIT III

7. PLANNING OF APARTMENT — 7.1 – 7.22

7.1	Introduction	7.1
7.2	Minimum Floor Area and Height of Rooms	7.2
7.3	Arrangement of Rooms in Apartments	7.2
7.4	Additional Drawings for Reference	7.5
	• Important Points	7.22
	• Questions	7.22

8. PERSPECTIVE DRAWING — 8.1 – 8.22

8.1	Introduction	8.1
8.2	Important terms in Perspective Drawings	8.2
8.3	Principles of Perspective	8.3
8.4	Types of Perspective	8.6
	8.4.1 Based on Position of Object with Respect to Picture Plane	8.6
	8.4.2 Based on Number of Vanishing Points	8.7
	8.4.3 Shades and Shadows in Perspective Drawings	8.8
8.5	Method of Drawing One Point Perspective	8.8
8.6	Method of Drawing Two Point Perspective	8.9
	• Questions	8.18

UNIT IV

9. PLANNING AND DESIGNING OF PUBLIC BUILDINGS - I   9.1 – 9.18
- 9.1 Planning of Public Buildings   9.1
- 9.2 Types of Buildings   9.1
- 9.3 Group B: Educational Buildings   9.2
- 9.4 Group C: Institutional Buildings   9.7
- 9.5 Hotels and Restaurants   9.11
  - 9.5.1 Hotels   9.11
  - 9.5.2 Restaurants   9.11
- 9.6 Group E: Business Buildings   9.12
- 9.7 Hostel Building   9.15
  - Important Points   9.17
  - Questions   9.17

UNIT V

10. PLANNING AND DESIGNING OF PUBLIC BUILDINGS - II   10.1 – 10.20
- 10.1 Industrial Buildings   10.1
  - 10.1.1 Data Required for Steel Fabrication Shop   10.7
  - 10.1.2 Data Required for Vehicle Service Centre   10.8
  - 10.1.3 Data Required for P.V.C. Pipe Unit   10.9
  - 10.1.4 Prestressed Concrete Pole Factory   10.10
- 10.2 General Buildings   10.12
- 10.3 General Guidelines and some common units which are needed in Public Buildings   10.16
  - Important Points   10.18
  - Questions   10.19

UNIVERSITY QUESTION PAPERS   UQP.1 – UQP.10

Chapter 1
INTRODUCTION TO BUILDING DRAWING

1.1 CONCEPT OF AN INTEGRATED BUILT ENVIRONMENT

Planning deals with the development of plan composition to facilitate in purely practical ways the purpose of the building. Sizes are decided according to accommodation, and rooms are grouped in their functional sequence. For instance, factory buildings are planned according to their functional sequence and plans are made very simple. Location of structural members is determined so as not to disturb the function or its sequence and they are constructed to their correct size according to the structural design. This is the planning of a building or a structure.

The planner, before he actually begins planning, has to consider the requirements of accommodation. Site location and condition definitely indicate the layout and design of a building as well as the location of its entrance and exit etc.

Selection of the site depends mainly on the general scope or purpose of the building and the extent of essential privacy. Financial aspects decide ownership and costs. Besides, there are certain important factors given below:

1. Services rendered to the community such as police and fire protection,
2. Clearing of waste from the streets and society,
3. Availability of water and gas,
4. Electricity and drainage,
5. Amenities such as schools, hospitals, libraries, recreation centres and post office,
6. Shopping facilities, and
7. Means of transport.

There are certain adverse elements listed below which may compel to reject the particular building site:

1. Immediate neighbourhood of rivers carrying heavy floods in monsoon;
2. Reclaimed soils, lands subject to subsidence or continuous settlement;
3. Smoke and obnoxious odours due to industrial vicinity; and
4. Noise.

Adverse effects of noise are not immediately noticeable. In fact, a quiet environment is an amenity. People get used to regular and continuous types of noises such as of local trains and noise due to heavy traffic thoroughfares. It is the occasional noises which are really disturbing such as factory sirens, whistles of loco-engines, aeroplanes flying at low altitudes. The relation of a site with its environment and the site itself would influence the moulding of the planner's scheme. He has to consider whether the proposed building would stand isolated amidst a vast field of agricultural lands or closely clustered around by a busy thoroughfare. The topographical features of the site with natural and artificial surroundings are to be taken into account while planning and designing a building. Also geophysical conditions, position of ground water table and vegetation should be considered.

1.2 PRINCIPLES OF PLANNING

The factors or principles to be considered in planning a building are:
1. Aspect
2. Prospect
3. Grouping
4. Privacy
5. Roominess
6. Furniture requirement
7. Sanitation
8. Circulation
9. Elegance
10. Economy.

1. Aspect: Aspect means the peculiarity of the arrangement of doors and windows in the external walls of a building which allows the occupants to enjoy the natural gifts such as sunshine, breeze, scenery etc. The external appearance of the building is obviously dependent upon the position of the doors and windows in the external walls; however, aspect should not be confused with the appearance of the building.

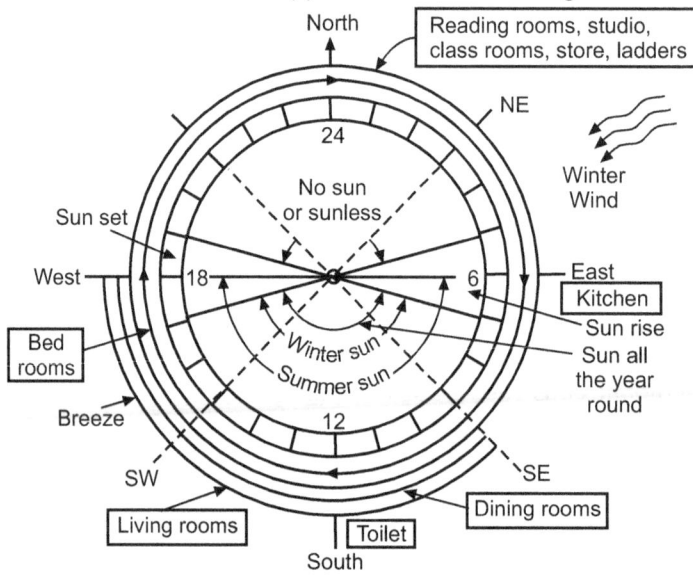

Fig. 1.1: Sun diagram

Residential buildings should have aspect of a particular direction. When a room gets light, air and breeze etc. from a particular direction, the room is said to have aspect of that direction. A kitchen in the household has eastern aspect, so that the morning sun would refresh and purify the air and the kitchen would remain cool during the latter part of the day. The living rooms may have southern or south east aspect as the sun is towards south during cooler days and the living rooms with the south aspect will be benefited by the sunshine when it is desired in winter. Bedrooms have west or south west aspect as the breeze in the summer prevails from that side. A verandah, a gallery should be provided to protect the structure from the hot afternoon sun so that there will not be much heat radiations during the night. As we live in the north hemisphere, direct rays do not enter from the north. There is no glare. Therefore, reading rooms should have north aspect.

Aspect provides comfort and is also important from the hygienic point of view as well. The sun's rays are potential destroyers of organic poison and impart a cheerful air to room. The rooms should get enough sunlight and air as this, apart from creating a cheerful atmosphere, is also good from the hygienic point of view. Windows are provided to fulfil these requirements.

2. Prospect: Prospect means both revealing some notable pleasant or redeeming feature and also the concealment of some undesirable views in the given outlook.

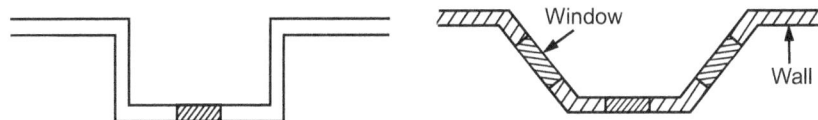

Fig. 1.2: Projecting windows for better prospect

Prospect refers to the view as seen of the outside from the windows in general and doors in external walls. It is determined by the view as desired from certain rooms of the house, viz. view of the garden or of a nearby hill. At the same time, it is naturally intended to conceal some undesirable views. It will be observed that sometimes aspect and prospect consideration may be at variance with each other.

However, a good layout should not be distorted for the sake of a good prospect.

3. Grouping: Every apartment in the building has got some definite function or functions i.e. there is some sort of sequence.

In a residential building:

(a) Living room should be next to verandah. It should be away from the kitchen to avoid smell and smoke.

(b) Dining room should be close to the kitchen.

(c) Kitchen should be so arranged that the housewife can easily approach the entrance without invading any rooms. A window should be provided in such a way that she can easily keep watch at the entrance of the house and also on the children playing in the house.

(d) Main bed rooms should be so placed that there is an independent and separate access from each bedroom to the sanitary units directly.

(e) Staircase must be approachable from maximum number of rooms.

(f) Passage areas must be minimum, well ventilated and with sufficient light.

4. Privacy: This is one of the important principles in the planning of buildings of all types in general and residential building in particular.

Privacy needs consideration in two ways. One way, it is privacy of one part from the other and secondly, it is the privacy of all parts together as a whole from the neighbouring buildings, public streets and by ways.

Proper grouping of all rooms in their correlation is of prime importance to secure internal privacy. Further the position of doors and mode of their hanging also considerably affects the internal privacy. All the units in the building should have an independent access. For example, an independent access should be provided to every bedroom without disturbing the other units of the house. Great skill lies in grouping various rooms and positioning them while planning.

The proper position of the doors and the way in which shutters are hung are very important in securing privacy. Privacy means, one unit in the building should not disturb another unit, therefore, separate access should be provided to each unit so that better privacy can be achieved. Proper positions of windows, doors at the entry, are very important in securing privacy. The desirable and undesirable ways of positioning doors and hanging shutters should be fixed judiciously.

Privacy is of two types:

1. Privacy in the whole building with reference to the surrounding buildings and roads. This can be achieved by screening the entrances (front and back), planning of trees and creepers etc.

2. Privacy in different rooms, i.e. bedrooms, bathrooms, kitchen etc. This is achieved by the correct positioning of doors and the openings of shutters. The shutters should open in such a way that a person entering the room will get the minimum view. A large portion of the details of the bedroom (such as beds in a bedroom) should not be visible at a glance. For maximum privacy, single shutters are better than double shutters. Provision of frosted glass for windows provides more privacy than plain glass. Louvres for shutters provide ventilation as well as privacy.

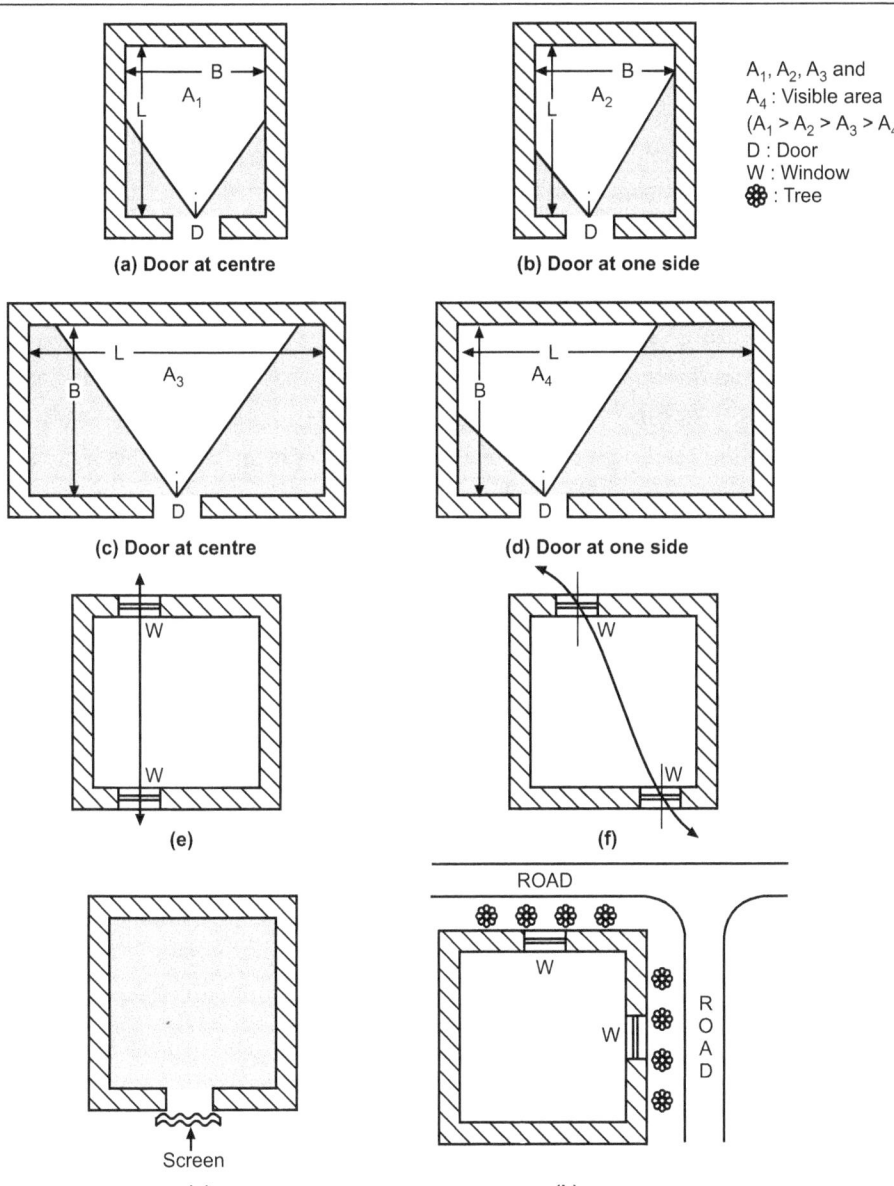

Fig. a, b, c and d: Privacy by positioning of door

Fig. e, f: Privacy by positioning of window

Fig. g: Privacy by providing screen

Fig. h: Privacy by tree plantation

Fig. 1.3: Illustrating privacy

5. **Roominess:** Roominess refers to the effect produced by deriving the maximum benefit from the minimum dimensions of a room. It means the accomplishment of economy of space, at the same time avoiding cramping of the plan. Besides, the size, shape of certain rooms creates some desirable and undesirable impressions regarding roominess. A square room relatively appears smaller than a rectangular room of the same area. Small rooms should also not be made inordinately high, as they tend to produce a cavernous effect. Such rooms appear relatively smaller than their actual sizes. Further the positioning of the doors in particular, and windows and cupboards in general, also affects the roominess. Skill is essential in making use of the accommodation provided by suitable arrangements of the rooms, by locating the doors and passages in such a way that the utility, liveability, privacy and the exterior appearance are not adversely affected.

A simple illustration can be given by comparing a square room with a rectangular room:

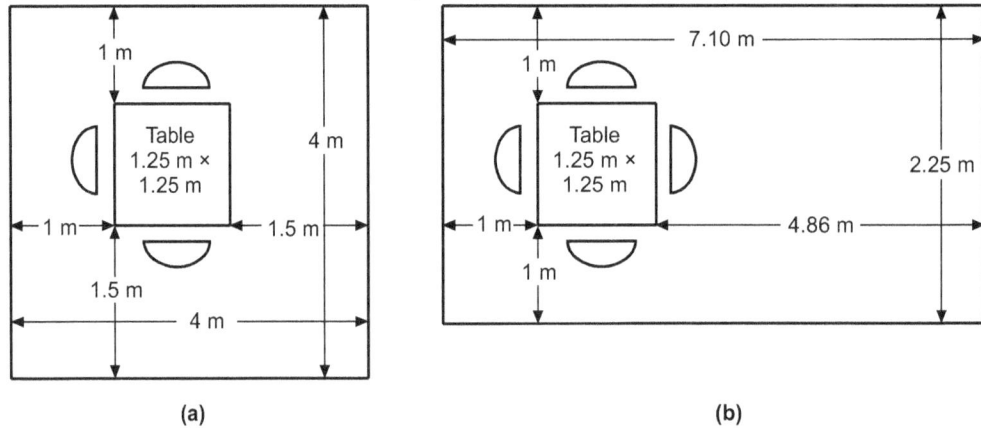

Fig. 1.4: Illustrating roominess

The dimension of the room should be arranged in such a way that maximum advantage is obtained from the maximum dimensions required for the functions expected from the room.

The following observations should be noted:
(a) If the length of the room exceeds 1.5 times the width, it will produce a cramped effect. Better proportion of length to width is 1.2 to 1.5.
(b) **Shape:** A square room relatively appears smaller than a rectangular room of the same area. It is also smaller with respect of utility as compared to a rectangular shaped room.
(c) **Height:** Small rooms should not be made too high because they tend to produce a cave like effect, such rooms appear smaller than their actual sizes.
(d) Position of doors, windows, cupboards, lofts and their level as well as colour treatment of flooring walls, ceilings etc. are all responsible for creating the effect of space. Light colours will create the effect of more space as compared to dark colours.

6. Furniture requirement: The success of function planning is revealed, in turn, in the plans showing detailed furniture arrangement in the various rooms, e.g. the arrangements of sofas, chairs, tables, carpets, television and other decorative pieces in the living room, chairs and dining table in the dining room, cupboards and the refrigerator in the kitchen, beds, easy chairs and dressing table etc. in the bed rooms.

The furniture should be arranged to give maximum area for movement, convenience regarding opening of doors, windows and cupboards. Positioning of beds should give privacy, sufficient light for reading and comfortable breeze during the night.

The whole set up must be fully comfortable and it should not create any clumsy or cramped feeling. In case of library buildings, hostels, schools, cinema theatres etc. the furniture arrangement plans are necessary to fix the sizes of the units with reference to the number of persons to be accommodated. The sizes and shapes of the machines should be taken into account while deciding the factory building units.

Although, mechanically treated air in the form of air conditioning and well controlled heating provides a man made climate within apartments in western countries, there is no substitute for sunshine and natural breeze. In low rent housing, where there will rarely be air conditioning, breezes and exposure become extremely important in locating units for comfortable living.

Every room intended for human habitation shall be exposed to an interior or exterior open air space of the width or dimensions of an open verandah.

Every such exterior or interior open air space unless the latter is a street, needs to be maintained for the benefit of such buildings exclusively and has to be entirely within the owners premises. All such open spaces whether exterior or interior shall be open to the sky and no choice of roof, or whether shade more than 0.75 m wide shall overhang over such open spaces.

Generally a domestic building shall have a front yard of at least 3 m width or minimum 45 m from the centre line of the street. In case of a building, 4.5 m minimum wide space should be left open in front of the building and should form an inseparable part of the site. Similarly, every residential building should have a yard of an average width of 4.5 m and at no place should the yard measure less than 3 m. If a building on its rear abuts to a street the rear space may be considered up to the opposite edge of the street. Accordingly, a minimum side space of 1.5 m is required. However, if any habitable room not receiving its light and air from either front or rear is abutting side space, then, its width should not be less than 3 m. If it is a kitchen, then, the width may be somewhat less, i.e. upto 1.8 m.

7. Sanitation: Lighting, ventilation, general cleaning and sanitary cleanliness are major parameters in sanitation.

Uniform distribution of light is necessary for sanitation particularly in schools, workshops and industries etc. An accommodation (room) should get light, as long as it is available, in the day time. Hence, the windows are designed as vertical rather than horizontal. Generally minimum window area for proper lighting is $1/10^{th}$ of floor area; however it may be increased to some more extent in school buildings, dormitories, factories etc. to $1/5^{th}$ of floor area.

Very good lighting promotes hygienic condition for the accommodated person, which increases the working capacity, accuracy, safety and finally pleasing environment for working.

Good ventilation is an important factor for comfort in a building. Poor ventilation or lack of fresh air into the building produces headache, sleepiness, tiredness and less concentration on work. There are two types of ventilation (1) Natural ventilation and (2) Artificial (Mechanical) ventilation. In natural ventilation, the fresh air is supplied into the building through windows and ventilators, whereas in mechanical ventilation, the fresh air is supplied through fans and air blowers. Good ventilation is generally achieved by proper placement of doors, windows and ventilators.

General cleaning is the responsibility of the occupants, any waste (solid/liquid) generated should be disposed-off immediately so that it should not decompose in the building. The floors should be as far as possible with non-absorbent surface and should be smooth with proper slope to facilitate the easy drain out of wash water.

8. Circulation: Circulation in a building means "access" or internal thorough space. It is of two types:

- **(a) Horizontal Circulation:** It means access to the rooms on the same floor. It is achieved by provision of passages, corridors, halls and lobbies.
- **(b) Vertical Circulation:** It means access to the rooms on different floors. It is achieved by the provision of stairs, staircases and electric lifts.

For better results, the points given below should be considered in planning the building:

(i) All passages should be short, straight, well lighted and well ventilated. Narrow, much widening and semi dark passages should be avoided.

(ii) The entrances, hallways corridors should create a sense of invitation to go from one room to the other. They are transitional places and they should be carefully planned. They should not have an old tunnel like appearance.

(iii) Privacy should not be disturbed in moving from one room to another.

(iv) All the sanitary services on the same floor must have an independent access from every room through a lobby. This increases the usefulness of the building.

(v) Stairs should be easily accessible from the entrance as well as rooms on the floors. It should have strong hand rails preferably on both sides. It should satisfy the minimum requirements regarding width, rise, tread, landing, light and ventilation.

9. Elegance: Elegance is related to the effect produced by elevation, which depends upon the proportion of width, height, doors and windows, as also the choice of materials. The visualization of elevation should always be kept in mind while preparing a plan. Utility is the main consideration, keeping in mind the cost. Architectural design and composition should be studied in detail as a whole for achieving success in creating an elegant structure.

10. Economy: Economy is one of the dominating factors in building, planning and construction. To overcome this limitation, we can use most of the raw materials available nearby. Thus, along with cost of materials, transportation cost is also minimized.

Integrated Approach in Built Environment:

One should remember that all considerations such as usefulness and feeling for aesthetics etc. are interrelated and integrated. As one approaches a particular building, the location of the building with reference to its surroundings like hills, trees, valleys, rivers, lakes, and vegetation should be in proportion to the solids and shadows, colour scheme, texture of the construction material, etc. This creates a visual impact on the observer. The success of a design is dependent on all the details, considerations regarding functions, regulations and bye-laws of the sanctioning authority.

1.3 BUILDING RULES AND BYE-LAWS

The knowledge of the regulations and bye-laws which influence the building design needs to be considered as a sound basis for a professional engineer and the teacher and the students of engineering colleges also. A well planned and architecturally designed layout may have to be abandoned because the design does not adhere to the laws. The statutory requirements in one or other respects with all liberties in planning and designing, and the architect has to shape and trim this layout, if need be, so as to make the resulting plan to the mark of the rules and regulations enforced by the concerned authorities. Uncontrolled growth leads to slum areas with no facilities such as water supply, drainage, electricity and roads. If at all roads or pathways are there, they are very narrow and occupied by the slum dwellers. All these lead to fire, unsanitary condition and health hazards. For proper growth of a city, building regulations and bye-laws are must.

1.3.1 Minimum Sizes for Different Components in a Residential Building

Requirements of individual rooms and apartments according to their sizes are discussed here along with the principles of planning and essentials of certain types of buildings from the point of view of health and standards of living and ventilation. Certain absolute minimum rules about area are fixed and are given below:

1. Every habitable room should not have an area less than 9.5 sq.m with a minimum width of 2.4 m.
2. If such a room is a kitchen, its floor area should not be less than 5.6 sq.m and preferably 9 to 10 sq.m when it is to be used for dining also.
3. A kitchen cum dining hall should not have an area smaller than 18 sq.m.
4. The area of a living room of a double room tenement should not be less than 14 sq.m.
5. The area of a bathroom (minimum width 1.2 m) = 1.8 sq.m.
6. Area of W.C. (minimum width 0.9 m) = 1.18 sq.m.
7. Area of store room = 3 sq.m.
8. Area of a room general = 9.5 sq.m.

1.3.2 Space and Floor Area Requirements per Head for Ventilation

The space and floor area for:

Residential building	for a single person 5 m^2
Factories	22.6 m^3 per person
Hospital wards	15 m^2 or 56 m^3 per bed

1.3.3 Building Line

The position of the building frontage is decided by the category of the city zone in which the site of the proposed building is lying. Town planning authorities mark down the present width and future widening of each street and road. A minimum distance, either from the boundary of a road or its centre line is prescribed for the line of the frontage.

Sometimes there is a line to which generally all the buildings or any of them does not project beyond. This line is termed as 'General Building Line' and no building or its portion is allowed to be constructed in front of this line. However, the rule of the general building line is released if the general line of existing buildings is too deep or more than 15 m back from the roadway.

Distances of Building Lines:

Types of road	In open and Agricultural country		Along approaches		In actual limits	
	Building line (m)	Control line (m)	Building line (m)	Control line (m)	Building line (m)	Control line (m)
National and State Highways	30	56	18	30	30	45
Major district roads	24	45	9	15	15	24
Other district roads	15	24	6	9	9	25
Village roads	12	18	6	9	9	25

1.3.4 Control Line

Certain kinds of buildings such as cinemas, commercial concerns, factories, which attract large number of vehicles, should be set back a distance further apart from the building line. The line which accounts for this extra margin is known as the *control line*. Generally, in urban and industrial areas, the distance of the control line is taken as one and a half times that of the building line which is invariably measured from the centre of the roadway.

1.3.5 Plinth Height

It should be 0.9 m in height in case of a residential building. It varies according to the floor area of the building. It is 1 m in height in case of large buildings.

1.3.6 Height of Rooms

From the point of view of height and ventilation, certain absolute minimum restrictions about areas are laid down. The height of such rooms in every part should not be less than 2.75 m measured from the surface of the floor to the lowest point of the ceiling, provided that the minimum head room at any point in the room should not be less than 2.4 m. Whether the room is a living room, bedroom or kitchen, the above rules are applicable to all.

1.3.7 Open Space Requirements

Open space kept around the building depends upon air and light requirements for buildings of residential type. Every residential building should have an average width of 4.5 m and at no place the measure should be less than 3 m. If a building on its rear abuts to a street the rear space may be considered upto the opposite edge of the street. Accordingly, a minimum side space of 1.5 m is required. However, if any habitable room not receiving its light and air from either front or rear is abutting side space, then, its width should not be less than 3 m. If it is a kitchen, then, the width may be somewhat less, be i.e. up to 1.8 m.

1.3.8 Regulations to Decide the Height of a Building

1. The height of a building is decided by two factors, either by the width of the street on which it fronts, or the minimum width of rear space.
2. The height of the building is measured upto the beam in case of pitched roof and up to the surface of the roof in case of flat roof.
3. In case of pitched roof, the pitch is not expected to exceed 15 m, or the height of parapet by 1 m in case of flat roof.
4. No plinth or any part of a building or outhouse shall be less than 30 cm (60 cms. according to some authorities) above the determined level of the central part of the abutting street or footpath, or the highest part of a service lane or any portion of the ground within 3 m distance of such a building.
5. A table below gives a typical example of building heights with respect to street widths.

Sr. No.	Width of Street	Height of Building
1.	Upto 8 m	Not more than 1.5 times the width of the street.
2.	8 m to 12 m	Not more than 12 m.
3.	Above 12 m	Not more than the width of the street and not more than 21 m.

6. The height of the buildings with respect to the rear space is fixed by two imaginary lines : the horizontal line and the diagonal line.
7. The horizontal line is drawn at right angles to the road, through the centre of the front line. The location of this horizontal line is taken at the higher point along the line.
8. The diagonal line is drawn in the direction of the building from where the horizontal line meets the rear boundary.
9. No part of the building is allowed to project beyond the diagonal line except for fixed parts such as smoke chimneys, turrets etc.

1.3.9 Bye-Laws for Lighting

1. For light, a clear window area in the wall abutting to the air space either directly or through an open verandah or gallery should not be less than one tenth of the floor area of the room for dry, hot climate (hot arid) and one sixth for wet, hot climate (hot humid).
2. The aggregate area of the door and window openings should not be less than one seventh of the room.
3. However, for the apartments where doors need not be closed for the sake of privacy or security, aggregate area of openings may be provided either by windows or doors.
4. This becomes a possibility in the case of living rooms and dining halls where such rooms have an open verandah or gallery.
5. In addition to the above means of light, every such room should have a ventilator of at least 0.3 sq.m. in an area near the top of each of the two walls of such rooms and these ventilators should be preferably placed opposite to each other for thorough ventilation. When this is not possible, then ventilators should be placed at least in the adjoining walls.
6. Generally, the aggregate area of such ventilators is provided at the rate of 0.1 sq.m. for every 10 cubic meters of space of such rooms.

1.3.10 Built-Up Area

When restrictions regarding the open spaces around the building are observed, the built up area of any building is automatically checked. However, according to the zoning of the city area, there are regulations which demand more area to be left open on the site. Recent recommendations in this regard are given below:

1. In market area, the constructed area should not exceed 75% of the area of the site, provided sufficient space for parking etc. is available on the same site.
2. In an industrial area, the covered or built-up area shall not exceed 60% of the site area.
3. In residential area, the covered or built-up area shall not exceed 80% of the site area.

1.3.11 F.A.R. (Floor Area Ratio) or F.S.I. (Floor Space Index) and State its Necessity

Often in all the buildings, the maximum permissible covered area has a definite proportion with the actual area of plot. This is known as *floor area ratio*. In case of public and large buildings, the left round them is not only from the point of view of light and air considerations but there are other points which also receive consideration. Every room intended for human habitation shall abut an interior or exterior open air space of the width or dimensions. Specified or an open verandah abutting on to such exterior open space.

Floor Area Ratio (F.A.R.) is necessary for controlling the built-up area.

$$F.A.R = \frac{\text{Total covered area}}{\text{Plot Area}}$$

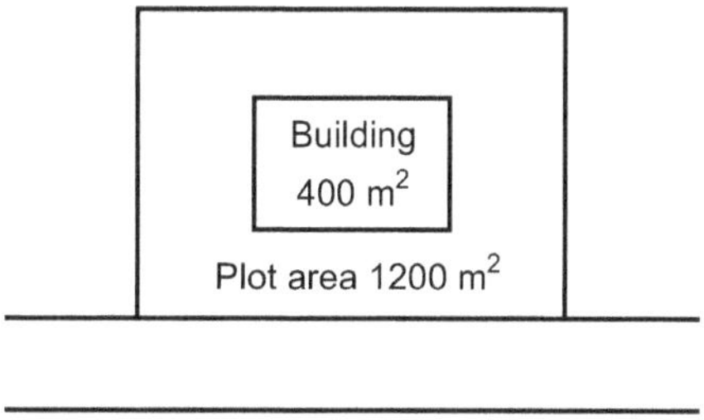

Building 400 m^2

Plot area 1200 m^2

Fig. 1.5

As per the bye-laws, the owner can construct the building in 1/3 area. In this way, it is controlled by taking 1/3 of the plot area.

E.g. Plot area = 1200 m^2

∴ Built-up area = 1/3 × 1200 = 400 m^2

Hence, to consume F.A.R. the building should be 3 storied.

G.F. 400 m^2 + F.F. 400 m^2 + S.F. 400 m^2 = 1200 sq.m.

Minimum height of each storey is 2.75 m.

IMPORTANT POINTS

- Necessity of Bye-laws and basic definitions used in projects.
- Area measurement of a building :
  1. Covered area 2. Plinth area 3. Floor area 4. Built-up area 5. Carpet area.
- Height of buildings for different rooms.
- Requirement of drainage and sanitation for different buildings.
- TDR its definition, eligibility, documents to be submitted for availing TDR.

QUESTIONS

1. What are the criteria for minimum area of plot?
2. What is F.A.R.? What are the areas exempted while calculating F.A.R.?
3. Why open spaces around any building should be left?
4. What is building line and control line?
5. What is FAR? State its necessity.
6. What is building line and control line? Explain their importance.
7. It is decided to plan a single storeyed hospital building. Enlist the essential amenities and areas for the different units. Explain also, with sketch, how you will apply principle of grouping, while preparing a flow diagram.
8. Enumerate the various area calculations in building and explain any one in detail.
9. Explain the necessity of building byelaws.
10. What is the difference between built-up area and carpet area?
11. Explain any one of the following:
    (i) Building line and control line OR (ii) Rules regarding height regulations of buildings.
12. Explain the following terms with sketches:
    (i) Building line (ii) Control line (iii) Marginal distances.
13. State the byelaws regarding road width and height of building.
14. What is Floor Area Ratio (FAR)? State which areas of construction are excluded while calculating floor area ratio.
15. Write a detailed note on building line and control line. Mention its distances for all types of roads.
16. Discuss the importance of built-up area, plinth area, and carpet area.
17. Explain the importance of orientation of building with respect to cardinal direction.
18. Explain with suitable sketches the following principles of planning:
    (i) Aspect (ii) Roominess (iii) Grouping (iv) Privacy (v) Sanitation (vi) Elegance
19. Explain principle of "circulation" and "aesthetic" you would use while planning commercial plaza in heart of city.
20. Enumerate various environmental and physical considerations in planning a building.
21. Write explanatory notes on:
    (i) Circulation (ii) Prospect (iii) Form (iv) Unity (v) Contrast
22. What do you understand by principles of planning a building? Prepare typical aspect diagram for the area where direction of prevailing breeze is from North - West.
23. What do you understand by the planning of man-made environment? Explain.
24. What do you understand by submission drawing? What is the necessity of it?
25. What are working drawings? Explain the importance of working drawings on site during execution.

■■■

Chapter 2
VENTILATION

2.1 INTRODUCTION

Our body produces heat continuously during its metabolic activity of converting the food we eat into living matter and energy required for doing work. Only some 20% of the energy produced is utilized by the body, the remaining 80% is to be dissipated as surplus heat from the system.

Heat may also be gained by the body from the environment by the following processes:

(i) Conduction by contact with warmer objects,

(ii) Absorption of heat from warmer enveloping air and,

(iii) Radiation by exposure to heat rays from the sun or hotter objects in the vicinity.

Dissipation of excess of heat, generated by metabolic activity and heat gained by the body, is very essential in order to maintain the intestinal temperature or deep body temperature constant around 37°C.

Excess body heat can be dissipated by conduction, convection, radiation and evaporation.

Heat loss by *conduction* depends upon the temperature gradient between the skin temperature and colder objects in contact with the skin.

Heat loss by *convection* is due to heat transmission from the body to the cooler air surrounding it. The heat loss increases with a faster rate of air movement around the body.

Heat loss by *radiation* is governed by the temperature difference between the skin and the objects surrounding it (but not touching it).

Heat loss by *evaporation* depends on the humidity of surrounding air and on the amount of body moisture available for evaporation. Low humidity of ambient air promotes a greater rate of evaporation.

To maintain the heat balance of the body, the excess of heat generated and gained by the body must be equal to the heat lost by the body.

In a hot environment, the heat acquired is more than the heat lost; blood circulation to the skin increases and skin temperature increases. If heat acquisition continues, the body sweats or perspires to prevent continued rise in skin temperature. In this condition, air movement close to the skin will reduce heat stress by dissipating heat from the body by evaporation of the sweat, particularly when the relative humidity is high and air temperature is near body temperature.

People consume oxygen, by inhaling air and exhale carbon dioxide. An average person, depending on his activity, inhales about 0.5 to 5 m^3/hr. In a closed environment, oxygen content is reduced and the carbon dioxide content is increased by man's presence. [Biologically the limit for comfortable existence is 0.5% CO_2 content by volume but a 0.15% increase is perceptible, because of the discomfort caused.]

The content of carbon dioxide in air rarely exceeds 0.5 to 1%. Body smells, fumes and vapours produced by a variety of processes such as combustion from the kitchen and other heating appliances, smoking etc., result in vitiating the air.

Hence, a supply of fresh air is required to supply oxygen to the human body and to maintain carbon dioxide concentration in the air within safe limits; for the control of odours, for the removal of products of combustion or other contaminants in air and to provide such a thermal environment as will assist in the maintenance of heat balance of the body in order to prevent discomfort and injury to health of the occupants.

Ventilation may be defined as 'the process of removing vitiated air from an enclosed space and supplying fresh air, either by natural or artificial means'.

2.2 COMFORT FACTORS FOR VENTILATION

Where no products of combustion or other contaminants are to be removed from air, the amount of fresh air required for dilution of inside air to prevent vitiation of air by body odours depends on the air space available per person and the degree of physical activity. The amount of air requirement increases with decrease in air space per person and it may vary from 20 to 30 m^3 per person per hour.

Requirement of air for different occupancies may be expressed in terms of air changes per hour which indicate the replacement of air in an occupancy by fresh air, expressed as the number of times such replacement is effected in an hour.

The following values of air changes are recommended by the National Building Code of India, based on maintenance of required levels of oxygen, carbon dioxide and other air quality parameters and for the control of body odours when no products of combustion or other contaminants are present in the air.

Table 2.1

Space to be ventilated	Air changes per hour
Assembly Halls / Auditoria	3 – 6
Bed Rooms / Living Rooms	3 – 6
Bath Rooms / Toilets	6 – 12
Cafes / Restaurants	12 – 15
Cinema halls / Theatres	6 – 9
Class Rooms	3 – 6
Factories (Medium metal work)	3 – 6
Garages	12 – 15
Hospital wards	3 – 6
Kitchen (Common)	6 – 9
Kitchen (Domestic)	3 – 6
Laboratories	3 – 6
Offices	3 – 6

Air change per hour: It is the volume of outside air allowed into a room in terms of the number of room volumes exchanged, in one hour.

Thermal comfort is that condition of thermal environment, in which a person can maintain a bodily heat balance at normal body temperature without perceptible sweating.

Air movement is necessary in hot and humid weather for body cooling. A certain minimum desirable wind speed is needed for achieving thermal comfort at different temperatures and relative humidities.

As per the National Building code of India, the following wind speeds are recommended:

Case 1: Applicable to sedentary work in offices and other places having no noticeable sources of heat gain.

Table 2.2: Desirable wind speeds in m/s for thermal comfort conditions

Dry bulb temperature in °C	Relative Humidity (percentage)						
	30	40	50	60	70	80	90
28	×	×	×	×	×	×	×
29	×	×	×	×	×	0.06	0.19
30	×	×	×	0.06	0.24	0.53	0.85
31	×	0.06	0.24	0.53	1.04	1.47	2.10
32	0.20	0.46	0.94	1.59	2.26	3.04	H
33	0.77	1.36	2.12	3.00	H	H	H
34	1.85	2.72	H	H	H	H	H
35	3.20	H	H	H	H	H	H

× - None, H - Higher than those acceptable in practice

Case 2: In somewhat warmer conditions such as in godowns and machine shops where work is of lighter intensity and higher temperatures can be tolerated without much discomfort, minimum wind speeds for just acceptable warm conditions are given in the following Table 2.3.

Table 2.3: Minimum wind speeds in m/s for just acceptable warm conditions

Dry bulb temperature in °C	Relative Humidity (percentage)						
	30	40	50	60	70	80	90
28	×	×	×	×	×	×	×
29	×	×	×	×	×	×	×
30	×	×	×	×	×	×	×
31	×	×	×	×	×	0.06	0.23
32	×	×	×	0.09	0.29	0.60	0.94
33	×	0.04	0.24	0.60	1.04	1.85	2.10
34	0.15	0.46	0.94	1.60	2.26	3.05	H
35	0.68	1.36	2.10	3.05	H	H	H
36	1.72	2.70	H	H	H	H	H

× - None, H - Higher than those acceptable in practice

For normal industrial working activity for a worker with light clothing, the wet-bulb temperature may not exceed 29°C and a minimum air velocity of 30 m/min. may be provided.

In relation to the dry bulb temperature, the wet bulb temperature of air in the work room, as far as practicable, should not exceed that given in the following Table 2.4.

Table 2.4

Dry bulb temperature in °C	Maximum wet bulb temperature in °C
30	29.0
35	28.5
40	28.0
45	27.5
50	27.0

The industry should not allow the thermal conditions to go beyond the above limits, for more than one hour continuously.

Efficiency decreases with rise in the dry bulb temperature for a given wet bulb temperature attained and efforts should be made to bring down the dry bulb temperature as much as possible. Long exposures to temperatures of 50°C dry bulb and 27°C wet bulb may prove dangerous.

[**Note: Dry bulb temperature:** It is the temperature of air, read on a thermometer, taken in such a way as to avoid errors due to radiation.

Wet bulb temperature: The steady temperature finally given by a thermometer having its bulb covered with gauge or muslin moistened with distilled water and placed in an air stream of not less than 4.5 m/s.]

2.3 SYSTEMS OF VENTILATION

I. Natural System

II. Mechanical System.

Natural Ventilation:

It is achieved by natural means through windows and ventilators.

Natural ventilation may be achieved by:

1. **Wind effect** which depends on the direction and velocity of wind outside and sizes and disposition of openings.
2. **Stack effect** arising from difference in air temperature or vapour pressure between inside and outside the room and the difference in height between the inlet and outlet openings.

1. Ventilation due to Wind Effect:

The general direction of prevailing winds is made use of, as far as possible, in the location of openings in buildings, for natural ventilation.

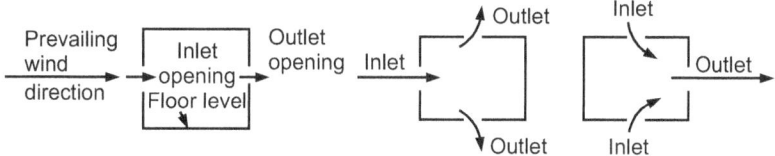

Fig. 2.1: Movement of wind through buildings

At the stage of planning itself, *orientation* of buildings with respect to the wind direction could gain some advantage in ventilation and removal of heat from inside buildings, so that the inside temperature is kept close to, if not lower than, the ambient temperature.

General Rules for Location of Windows:

1. Inlet openings in the building should be well distributed and should be located on the windward side at a low level and outlet openings should be located on the leeward side near the top, so that the incoming air passes over the occupants.

2. When outlets also serve as inlets, they should be at the same level.
3. Inlet openings should not, as far as possible, be obstructed by buildings, trees, signboards etc.
4. If inlet and outlet openings are of nearly equal areas, then greater flow per unit area of openings is obtained.
5. If only one wall of a room is exposed to the outer atmosphere, it is better to provide two small windows in the wall than to provide one large window.
6. As per the National Building Code of India, the minimum area of openings, excluding doors should not be less than,
   (a) One-tenth of the floor area for dry hot climate,
   (b) One-sixth of the floor area for wet hot climate,
   (c) One-eighth of the floor area for intermediate climate,
   (d) One-twelfth of the floor area for cold climate.

2. Ventilation due to Stack Effect:

Natural ventilation by stack effect occurs when air inside a building is at a different temperature than air outside. Thus, in heated buildings or in buildings wherein hot processes are carried out and in ordinary buildings during summer nights and pre-monsoon periods, the inside temperature is higher than that of outside, in which case, cool air will tend to enter through openings at low level and warm air will tend to leave through openings at high level. It would, therefore, be advantageous to provide ventilators as close to the ceiling as possible.

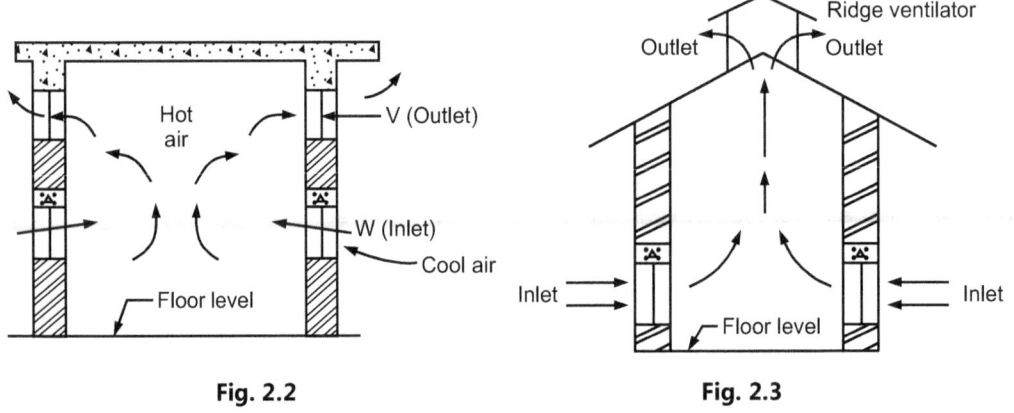

Fig. 2.2 Fig. 2.3

Calculation of Window Areas / Rate of Ventilation in Case of:

1. Ventilation due to Wind:

Based on the wind speed and angle of incidence of wind on the openings in buildings, the quantity of air through ventilating openings by wind action is given by,

$$Q = KAV$$

where,
- Q = Rate of air flow, in m³/h
- A = Free area of inlet openings, in m²
- V = Velocity of wind, in m/h
- K = Coefficient of effectiveness of openings.

The effectiveness of the openings, K, depends on the direction of the wind relative to the openings and on the ratio between the areas of inlet and outlet openings. It also depends on the ratios of larger openings to the smaller openings.

When inlet openings and outlet openings are equal in area,

Value of K = 0.6 for winds perpendicular to openings and K = 0.3 for winds at an angle less than 45° to the openings.

Example 2.1: Calculate the area of openings required for ventilating a living room of size 5 m × 4 m × 3 m in dry hot climate, if the wind is blowing at a velocity of 7.5 km/h perpendicular to the openings.

Solution: According to the table of number of air changes for different occupancies (Table 2.1) for a living room the number of air changes required is 3 to 6 per hour.

Assuming minimum 3 air changes/hour.

The volume of fresh outside air required in m³/h.

= (Number of air changes/h) × (Volume of the room in m³)

Hence, Q (m³/h) = 3/h × (5 m × 4 m × 3 m)

Also, $Q = KAV$, Q = 180 m³/h, V = 7,500 m/h and

Assuming K = 0.6 for winds perpendicular to openings,

180 m³/h = 0.6 × A × 7500 m/h

$$A = \frac{180 \text{ (m}^3\text{/h)}}{0.6 \times 7500 \text{ (m/h)}} = 0.04 \text{ m}^2 \text{ (minimum)}$$

As per National Building Code, for dry hot climate, the minimum area of opening,

$$= \left(\frac{1}{10}\right)^{th} \text{ of floor area}$$

$$= \frac{1}{10} \times (5 \times 4) \text{ m}^2 = 2 \text{ m}^2$$

Hence, required area of opening is 2 m².

(Here the local bye-laws should also be considered).

2. Ventilation due to Stack Effect:

Ventilation due to convection effects arising from temperature difference between inside and outside air is given by

$$Q = KA\sqrt{h(t_i - t_o)}$$

where,
- Q = The rate of air flow, in m³/h
- A = Free area of inlet openings, in m²
- h = Vertical distance between inlets and outlets, in m
- t_i = Average temperature of indoor air at height h, in °C
- t_o = Temperature of outdoor air, in °C
- K = Constant (usually 7) governed by the difference in elevation and temperature gradient between inlet and outlet openings

Example 2.2: The internal dimensions of a factory building are 30 m × 20 m × 10 m (height).

The number of air changes required per hour are 3, the indoor temperature is 36°C and outdoor temperature is 30°C. Find the area of openings required, if the distance between the inlet and outlet openings is 6 m.

Solution: Volume of fresh outside air required in m³/h

$$Q = (\text{Number of air changes/h}) \times (\text{Volume of the room in m}^3)$$

$$Q = \frac{3}{h} \times (30 \times 20 \times 10) \text{ m}^3 = 18{,}000 \text{ m}^3/\text{h}$$

Also

$$Q = 7 \times A \times \sqrt{h(t_i - t_o)}$$

i.e.

$$18{,}000 \text{ m}^3/\text{h} = 7 \times A \times \sqrt{6(36 - 30)}$$

Therefore free area of inlet openings,

$$A = \frac{18000}{7 \times 6}$$

$$= 429 \text{ m}^2$$

Ventilation of Industrial Buildings:

The volume of air required for ventilation of industrial buildings varies with the nature of manufacturing processes, height of buildings etc.

The supply of air from outside becomes necessary in an industrial building to remove contaminants as well as to remove heat generated.

The volume of air required for removal of heat should be calculated by using both sensible heat and latent heat.

(i) Volume of air required for removing sensible heat: Increase in sensible heat is said to occur, when there is a direct addition of heat in a building, given off by various sources; namely, the sun, manufacturing processes, machinery, occupants etc.

The volume of outside air to be provided for removing sensible heat is calculated from

$$Q_1 = \frac{2.9768 \, K_s}{t}$$

where,
Q_1 = Quantity of air, in m³/h
K_s = Sensible heat gained, in W
t = Allowable temperature rise, in °C.

Temperature rise refers mainly to the difference between the air temperatures at the outlet (roof exit) and at the inlet openings for outside air.

Table 2.5: Allowable temperature rise values for industrial buildings

Height of outlet opening, m	Temperature rise, °C
6	3 to 4.5
9	4.5 to 6.5
12	6.5 to 11

(ii) Volume of air required for removing latent heat: An increase in latent heat is said to take place when there is an increase in the humidity of the enclosure due to the addition of water vapour emitted by humans and from various manufacturing processes.

Therefore, if the latent heat gained from the manufacturing processes and occupants is known and a suitable value for the allowable rise in the vapour pressure is assumed, then the volume of air required for removing the latent heat is given by

$$Q_2 = \frac{4127.26 \times K_l}{h}$$

where,
Q_2 = Quantity of air, in m³/h
K_l = Latent heat gained, in W
h = Allowable vapour pressure difference, in mm of mercury.

In majority of cases, sensible heat gain will far exceed the latent heat gain.

Mechanical Ventilation:

When natural ventilation is not sufficient for providing the required thermal environment, mechanical ventilation may have to be resorted to.

Mechanical ventilation may be achieved by means of ceiling fans, exhaust fans, positive ventilation or a combination of exhaust and positive ventilation.

(i) Ceiling fans: These are generally provided in non-industrial occupancies and serve the purpose of creating air movement. They are, however, effective only over limited areas.

(ii) Exhaust/Vacuum system: It consists of mechanically removing the used air, thus creating a zone of low pressure and letting fresh air find its way in through grills and openings.

For removing used air, exhaust fans are provided in walls on one side of the building or in the attic and roof to draw large volumes of air through the building. These fans are usually of propeller type, since they operate against little or no resistance. Adequate inlet openings should be provided on the opposite walls to let the fresh air come inside the building.

(iii) Plenum system or positive ventilation: In this system, fresh air is supplied into a room by mechanical means and the used air is allowed to leave through the grills and ventilators.

Positive ventilation is provided by centrally located supply fans which are usually of the centrifugal type or sometimes axial flow type, since this application requires duct work with a wide range of satisfactory and quiet operation against high pressure. The air from such centrally located fans are supplied to individual rooms through these ducts. The ductwork should be air-tight and should be properly designed to allow smooth flow of air.

Unit ventilators may be provided for individual rooms and may be placed against the outside wall. Both the central system as well as unit ventilators, besides ventilating, may also carry out the function of cooling the incoming air by evaporation or the use of cooling coils.

(iv) A balanced system: It involves both supplying and removing of air by mechanical means. The exhaust system will remove ventilated air from inside and positive ventilation will supply fresh air from outside to replace the air driven out by the exhaust system. Hence, a balanced system has the advantage of providing better control conditions and better distribution of air over the entire area of occupancy, particularly in big buildings. This system consists of supplying sufficient volumes of air in proportion to heat load generated in the respective areas, at suitable velocities, at the required areas through duct work and by extracting used air in the return ducts in proportion to the supplied air quantities and recirculating the air or a part of it after properly mixing it with cool fresh air.

(v) Air conditioning: Air conditioning may be provided where the desired temperatures and humidities cannot be obtained by mere ventilation.

Air conditioning is the process of treating air so as to control simultaneously its temperature, humidity, purity and distribution to meet the requirements of the enclosed space.

2.4 AIR CONDITIONING

Necessity:

In rapidly developing cities, land area available for construction of houses is progressively reducing and the cost of construction, particularly in busy localities, is steadily increasing. It is no longer possible to construct independent houses, economically, conforming with specific conditions of aspects and orientation; in order to derive maximum benefits from natural light and ventilation. Also regional or local parameters such as temperature and humidity may be inclement and not contributory to creature comfort. Hence, in congested housing complexes and also in houses in regions of extremely hot, humid, cold or polluted environment, conditioning of air is desirable to maintain living comfort and well-being of inmates.

The following are the functions of a modern heating, ventilating and air conditioning system for a building:

1. Control of air temperature at desired values at all times by heating or cooling,
2. Control of air humidity (water vapour content) by humidification or dehumidification,
3. Control of air movement at a desirable velocity,
4. Introduction of outside air as required,
5. Control of air quality by removal of particles of dust and gaseous pollutants,
6. Control of sound produced by the air conditioning system itself.

Air conditioning is used for two purposes, for providing comfort to people in a living space or a working space or for control of a process. Comfort refers to supply of conditioned air that provides satisfaction to people in terms of creature comforts. Process control refers to air conditions, that are required to carry out or improve some operations of a process. For example, Textile industry requires dry bulb temperature of about $25°C$ and relative humidity of 50 - 85%. Rubber industry requires dry bulb temperature of $25° - 35°C$ and relative humidity of 25 - 50%.

2.5 COMFORT AIR CONDITIONING

Design Conditions: Cooling load calculations are usually based on inside and outdoor conditions of temperature and humidity.

Table 2.6: Inside design conditions for summer

Sr. No.	Optimum conditions		Maximum conditions	
	Dry bulb temp. °C	Wet bulb temp. °C	Dry bulb temp. °C	Wet bulb temp. °C
(1)	(2)	(3)	(4)	(5)
(i)	23.3	19.4	25.9	21.8
(ii)	23.9	18.4	26.1	21.6
(iii)	24.4	17.6	26.7	20.9
(iv)	25.0	16.8	27.2	20.1
(v)	25.6	16.0	27.8	19.4
(vi)	26.1	15.2	28.3	18.8
(vii)	–	–	28.9	18.1
(viii)	–	–	29.4	17.5

Table 2.7: Inside design conditions for winter

Sr. No.	Optimum conditions		Maximum conditions	
	Dry bulb temp. °C	Wet bulb temp. °C	Dry bulb temp. °C	Dry bulb temp. °C
(1)	(2)	(3)	(4)	(5)
(i)	21.4	17.8	18.3	15.0
(ii)	21.7	17.3	18.9	13.4
(iii)	22.2	16.4	19.4	12.0
(iv)	22.8	15.3	19.7	10.8
(v)	23.3	14.4	–	–
(vi)	23.6	13.4	–	–

Inside conditions are those that provide comfort (Table 2.6 and Table 2.7).

Outside design conditions are based on dry bulb and wet bulb temperatures for summer months for different cities in India, based on a 10 year data (Table 2.8). Based on the outside design conditions and required comfort conditions inside, the amount of heat to be removed and the change in humidity can be calculated. This would require a certain rate of movement of air (Table 2.9).

Comfort Factors for Air conditioning:

For comfort air conditioning, dry bulb and wet bulb temperatures may be adopted as given in the following Table 2.8.

Table 2.8: Outside design conditions for summer

City	Temperature, °C							
	Dry Bulb				Wet Bulb			
	1%	2.5%	5%	10%	1%	2.5%	5%	10%
Ahmedabad	42.8	41.7	40.7	39.5	27.6	27.2	26.9	26.4
Amritsar	42.5	41.5	40.3	38.4	27.9	26.9	26.3	25.3
Bhopal	41.7	40.8	39.8	38.5	25.3	24.8	24.4	23.8
Mumbai	34.5	33.8	33.6	32.8	28.4	28.0	27.8	27.4
Kolkatta	39.5	38.3	37.4	35.6	29.3	29.2	28.8	28.4
Coimbatore	36.7	35.9	34.9	33.7	28.3	27.4	26.7	25.9
Delhi	43.0	41.9	41.4	40.3	28.1	27.2	26.4	25.8
Hyderabad	39.5	38.7	37.9	36.7	25.3	24.4	23.9	23.5
Jodhpur	43.5	42.5	41.3	40.0	27.9	27.2	26.5	25.8
Lucknow	42.8	41.9	41.0	39.5	28.3	27.7	27.2	26.5
Chennai	39.2	37.8	36.9	35.5	28.5	28.2	27.8	27.4
Nagpur	42.9	42.0	41.1	39.9	27.5	26.2	25.6	25.1
Patna	42.4	41.1	39.9	38.3	28.1	27.8	27.4	27.1
Roorkee	42.5	41.4	40.6	39.2	27.8	26.9	26.1	25.6
Trivendrum	32.9	32.4	31.8	31.0	27.2	26.9	26.7	26.4
Vishakhapatnam	38.4	37.0	36.0	35.1	30.4	29.7	29.3	28.8

As far as possible, thermal shock of more than 11°C should be avoided.

Adequate movement of air should be provided in an air conditioned enclosure. Air velocities in the zone between floor level and 1.5 m level should be 0.25 m/s in the case of comfort air conditioning. Air velocity in excess of 0.5 m/s in this zone should be avoided.

The total minimum outside fresh air introduced into an enclosure by an air conditioning plant or unit is related to the number of occupants in the enclosure at any time, whether they are smokers or non-smokers and to the cubic contents of the enclosed space as per the following Table 2.9.

Table 2.9: Minimum fresh air requirements

Sr. No.	Applications	Smoking	Air requirement in m³/min.		Per m² of floor area
			Recommended	Minimum	
(1)	(2)	(3)	(4)	(5)	(6)
(i)	Apartments	Some	0.56	0.28	–
(ii)	Banking space	Occasional	0.28	0.21	–
(iii)	Board rooms	Very heavy	1.40	0.56	–
(iv)	Department stores	None	0.21	0.14	0.015
(v)	Directors rooms	Very heavy	1.40	0.84	–
(vi)	Drug stores	Considerable	0.28	0.21	–
(vii)	Factories	None	0.28	0.21	0.03
(viii)	Garages	–	–	–	0.30
(ix)	Hospitals:				
	(a) Operating rooms (all fresh air)	None	–	–	0.60
	(b) Private rooms	None	0.84	0.70	0.10
	(c) Wards	None	0.56	0.28	–
(x)	Hotel rooms	Heavy	0.84	0.70	0.10
(xi)	Kitchens:				
	(a) Restaurant	–	–	–	1.20
	(b) Residence	–	–	–	0.60
(xii)	Laboratories	Some	0.56	0.42	–
(xiii)	Meeting rooms	Very heavy	1.40	0.84	0.38
(xiv)	Offices:				
	(a) General	None	0.42	0.28	–
	(b) Private	Some	0.70	0.42	0.08
		Considerable	0.84	0.70	0.08
(xv)	Restaurants:				
	(a) Cafeteria	Considerable	0.34	0.28	–
	(b) Dining room	Considerable	0.42	0.34	–
(xvi)	Retail shop	None	0.28	0.21	–
(xvii)	Theatre	None	0.21	0.14	–
		Some	0.42	0.28	–
(xviii)	Toilets (exhaust)	–	–	–	0.60

The above table is to be used only when the contamination of the air in the conditioned enclosure results solely from respiratory and other physiological activities of occupants or due to their smoking.

2.6 THE COOLING LOAD

The interior of a building, gains heat from a number of sources. If the temperature and humidity of the rooms are to be maintained at a comfortable level, heat must be extracted to offset these heat gains. The net amount of heat that is removed is called the **cooling load**.

The gross room heat gain is the rate at which heat is being received in the room at any time. This heat gain is made up of the following components from many sources:

1. Conduction through exterior walls, roof and glass.
2. Conduction through interior partitions, ceilings and floors.
3. Solar radiation through glass.
4. Lighting.
5. People.
6. Equipment and furniture.
7. Heat from infiltration of outside air through openings.

Heat gains can be classified into two groups: Sensible and latent heat gains.

(a) Sensible heat gains result in increasing the air temperature.
(b) Latent heat gains are due to addition of water vapour, thus increasing humidity.

Items 1 through 4 are solely sensible heat gains, items 5 and 7 are partly sensible and partly latent, item 6 can be either sensible or latent or both depending on the type of equipment and the process carried out.

Procedure for Calculating Cooling Load for a Building:

1. Select inside and outside design temperatures from tables 2.6, 2.7 and 2.8.
2. Use building plans to measure dimensions of all surfaces through which there will be external heat gain for each room.
3. Calculate areas of all these surfaces.
4. Select heat transfer coefficient for each material.
5. Calculate the heat gain through structure i.e. through walls, roof, ceiling and floor by using the following equation

$$Q = U \times A \times ETD$$

where,
- Q = Sensible heat gain, in kcal/h
- U = Overall heat transfer coefficient between the adjacent and conditioned space, in kcal/h × m² × °C
- A = Area of the separating section concerned, in m²
- ETD = Equivalent temperature difference between outdoor and indoor, in °C

6. Calculate heat gain through glass.
   Radiant energy from the sun passes through transparent materials such as glass and becomes a heat gain to the room. Its value varies with time, orientation, shading and storage effect. The net heat gain can be found from the following equation

   $$Q = SHGF \times A \times SC \times CLF$$

   where,
   - Q = Net solar radiation heat gain through glass, in kcal/h
   - $SHGF$ = Solar heat gain factor, in kcal/h-m²
   - A = Area of glass, in m²
   - SC = Shade coefficient
   - CLF = Cooling load factor for glass

7. Calculate heat gain from people. This consists of two parts-sensible heat and latent heat resulting from respiration.
   Following equations may be used

   $$Q_S = q_s \times n \times CLF$$

   and

   $$Q_L = q_L \times n$$

   where,
   - Q_S = Sensible heat gain
   - Q_L = Latent heat gain
   - q_s = Sensible heat gain per person
   - q_L = Latent heat gain per person
   - n = Number of people
   - CLF = Cooling load factor for people

8. Heat gain from equipment may be found directly from the manufacturers.

9. Find the heat load from outdoor air and ventilation using the following equations.

   $$Q_S = V \times (t_o - t_i) \times \rho_a \times S_a$$

   and

   $$Q_L = V \times (W_s - W_i) \times \rho_a \times C$$

   where,
   - Q_S = Sensible heat gain
   - Q_L = Latent heat gain
   - V = Volume of outdoor air, in m³/h
   - t_o = Outdoor dry bulb temperature, in °C
   - t_i = Indoor dry bulb temperature, in °C
   - r_a = Density of air
   - S_a = Specific heat of dry air
   - W_s = Outdoor humidity ratio, kg of moisture per kg of dry air
   - W_i = Indoor humidity ratio, kg of moisture per kg of dry air
   - C = Constant approximating the average kilocalories released in condensing one kg of water vapour from air

10. Add heat gains due to supply ducts, leakage in ducts, heat gain due to supply fans etc.
11. Calculate required supply air conditions. All the heat gains must be offset by supplying air at a temperature and humidity low enough so that it can absorb these heat gains. The supply air takes care of removing both sensible and latent heat gains. In order to find the outside air load, psychrometric charts are used. The psychrometric chart is a graphical representation of the properties of atmospheric air.

2.7 COMPONENTS OF AIR CONDITIONING SYSTEM

Any air conditioning system has the following basic components:
1. Heating,
2. Humidifying,
3. Filtering and cleaning,
4. Circulating,
5. Dehumidifying and
6. Cooling.

Depending upon the season, there are two types of air conditioning systems - (a) winter air conditioning, and (b) summer air conditioning.

(a) Winter Air Conditioning:

In winter, if the air in a building is to be maintained at a comfortable temperature, heat must be furnished to the air in the rooms. This is because there is a continuous heat loss to the outdoor surroundings, that is at a lower temperature. If this loss of heat is not replenished, the room temperature will fall rapidly. Also if the air is very dry, certain amount of moisture will have to be added to the air. Therefore, during winter, heating and humidifying equipment is used.

Heating of air may be done by using radiators.

Humidifying devices provide a means of turning water into water vapour and mixing this vapour with air in the occupied space.

This can be done by many methods:
1. Exposing a large surface of water to air being humidified, or
2. Spraying atomised water into air being humidified.

The simplest spray system passes water directly from the city water system through spray nozzles which break the water up into very small droplets. The spray humidifiers are followed by elimination plates so arranged that when the air passes over these plates, the droplets of water are removed from air.

Humidification is important because, a dry atmosphere causes dry skin which may lead to dermititis in the form of flaking or scaling of the skin; breathing dryness and loss of moisture from hygroscopic materials such as wood, natural fibres and most foods.

A simple flow diagram of the operations carried out in the winter air conditioning system can be shown as follows:

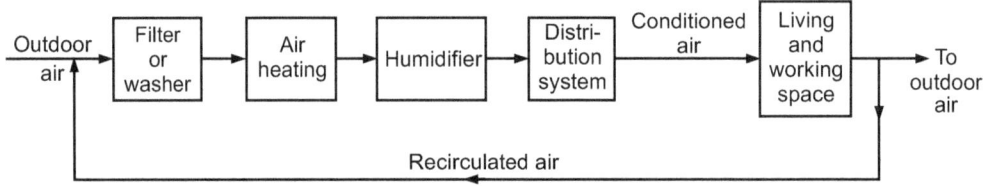

Fig. 2.4: Winter air conditioning

(b) Summer Air Conditioning:

In summer, in order to maintain the room air at a comfortable temperature, there must be continuous removal of heat from the room to offset the heat gains from the surroundings. The equipment that removes this heat is called a cooling system.

Cooling of air is done by several methods:

1. by mechanical refrigeration.
2. by using ice.

In mechanical refrigeration, air is passed over cooled surfaces of metal coils which contain a volatile refrigerant.

In ice system of air conditioning, cooling is done by melting ice, this is a practical method for theatres and public halls that have short operating houses and relatively high peak loads. Since, mechanical refrigeration equipment is expensive for short periods, ice can be used.

In a cooling cycle, the dry bulb temperature of the air is lowered. When this happens, the relative humidity increases. Some moisture must be removed to make this air comfortable. Excess humidity will cause condensation on window panes. Also, the rate of evaporation of perspiration being low, causes a wet and clammy feeling to the occupants. Very humid atmosphere also encourages the growth of several types of fungi and other micro-organisms. Therefore, dehumidification is carried out to remove the excess moisture.

Dehumidification may be done by two methods:

1. Dehydrating the air with chemicals or
2. Cooling the air below dew point, then removing the excess moisture by condensing it on a cool surface. The air is then reheated to the desired temperature with dry heat.

In general, air filtering and circulating equipment are the same for both winter and summer air conditioning.

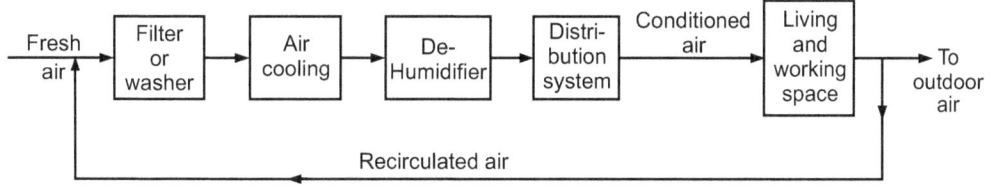

Fig. 2.5: Summer air conditioning

Air Cleaning:

Cleaning the air is a very important part of air conditioning.

Air contaminants include solids, liquids, gases and vapours. Efficient air conditioning systems will remove 75 to 95% of these contaminants.

Suspended solid particles are of the following three types:

(a) Dust which can have its origin in animal, vegetable or mineral matter.

(b) Fumes formed from materials that are ordinarily solids, but have been put into a gaseous state usually by an industrial or chemical process.

(c) Smoke caused by incomplete combination, consists of solid particles carried into the atmosphere by the gaseous products of combustion.

Liquid contaminants include the following:

(a) Mists: These small liquid particles are mechanically ejected into the air by splashing, mixing or atomizing.

(b) Fogs: These are small liquid particles formed by condensation.

Gaseous contaminants include carbon monoxide, sulphur oxides, nitrogen oxides and hydrocarbons.

The air cleaning devices must also be able to remove pollen, bacteria and moulds from the air.

Removal of solid contaminants can be done by using any of the following methods:

(i) centrifuging force for large particles,

(ii) washing the air for particles that can be wetted,

(iii) screens to block the larger particles.

(c) Adhesives: These are filters made of various fibres - glass, cotton, synthetic material and aluminium.

Fibres of adhesive filters are coated with adhesive liquid or oil. Air is forced to pass over these filters and the dust particles stick to the adhesive surface. When these filters get chocked with clogged dust over a period of time, they may either be washed and reused or replaced.

(d) Electrostatic precipitators: These electrically charge the particles and make them adhere to a surface of opposite charge.

To remove liquids, liquid absorbents can be used. These are chemicals that absorb or react with the liquid contaminant.

To remove gases and vapours, the following methods can be adopted:

- **(i) Condensation:** Cool the contaminant gas to its dew point and remove as a liquid.
- **(ii) Chemical reaction:** Pass the gas through a chemical which will remove the gas as a reaction product.
- **(iii) Dilution:** Mix the gas with air.
- **(iv) Adsorption:** Pass the gas over an adsorbent (e.g.: activated carbon).

2.8 AIR DISTRIBUTION SYSTEM

To deliver air to the conditioned space, air carriers are needed. These carriers are called ducts. They are made of steel, aluminium alloy or some non-combustible material such as clay or asbestos cement.

Ducts work on the principle of air pressure difference. Air will flow from a higher pressure area to a lower pressure area.

There are three types of ducts:
1. Conditioned air ducts,
2. Recirculating air ducts,
3. Fresh air ducts.

Ducts may be round, square or rectangular in cross-section.

They should be made substantially air-tight throughout and should have no openings other than those required for proper operation and maintenance of the system.

2.9 SYSTEMS OF AIR CONDITIONING

1. Room Air Conditioner:

It is also called unitary air conditioner and it is popular in moderate climates.

This consists of an encased assembly designed as a self contained unit, primarily for mounting in a window or through the wall or as a console. It consists of a compressor, heat exchangers and air handling system installed in one cabinet. It is designed essentially to provide free delivery of conditioned air to an enclosed space, room or zone. It includes a prime source of refrigeration for cooling and dehumidification and means for circulation and filtering of air. It also includes means for exhausting air. It may also include means for heating, humidifying or inducting fresh air. It is factory assembled. No ducts are needed for air distribution.

2. Packaged Air Conditioners:

Packaged air conditioning units come with all the needed equipments in a single cabinet and are suitable for offices, banks, shops, residences and some plants.

Window units are available upto a limited capacity. Large packaged units have ductwork for fully automatic room conditioning that is too large for one outlet.

3. Central Air Conditioning System:

A central air conditioning system has all the major items of equipment like filters, air washers, fans and refrigeration machinery in one centrally located space, removed from the area to be conditioned. The conditioned air is distributed to the desired spaces through a network of ductwork.

Advantages of a Central Air Conditioning System:

(i) The space occupied by the equipment need not be very valuable. The equipment can be located in the basement of a large building.

(ii) For a large conditioning load, the equipment may cost less.

(iii) The maintenance and inspection of a central system does not disturb the people in the conditioned areas.

(iv) The exhaust air can be returned and partly reused with obvious savings in heating and refrigeration.

IMPORTANT POINTS

- Types of ventilation and its two types:
  (a) Natural system
  (b) Mechanical system.
- Natural system in detail.
- Mechanical ventilation and its cooling types.
- Need for air conditioning for cooling with its comfort temperatures in different conditions.
- Ventilation need and factors affecting ventilation.
- Components of air conditioning system.
- Systems of air conditioning.

QUESTIONS

1. Explain with a neat diagram summer air-conditioning.
2. Explain with diagram winter air-conditioning.
3. Explain briefly the working principles of comfort air-conditioning.
4. Explain with sketches wind effects and stack effects.

5. What are the circumstances in which mechanical system of ventilation is adopted?
6. Explain in details Natural system of ventilation.
7. State different methods of mechanical ventilation. Explain only one in detail.
8. Explain with sketches various units of an air-conditioning system.
9. Differentiate between summer and winter air-conditioning.
10. Differentiate between:
    (a) Natural and Artificial ventilation.
    (b) Humidification and Dehumidification.

Chapter 3
FIRE PROTECTION

3.1 INTRODUCTION

Fire is an essential and integral part of our daily life but any misuse or accident in the use of fire can precipitate disaster.

Fires in buildings are nearly always man-made, resulting from error or negligence.

In olden times, dwellings were mostly timber - framed construction with thatched roofs, and within the walled townships overcrowding, narrow lanes, overhanging eaves and indiscriminate use of combustible materials provided all the necessary ingredients for the conflagarations which followed.

Towards the end of the nineteenth century, it was possible to construct large multi-storeyed buildings, the structural elements of which were of non-combustible materials. However, even today, inspite of using the most modern techniques of construction and fire resistant materials, fires still occur and cause a lot of damage to property and life.

Several rules and regulations have been drafted by government bodies to ensure the nature and quality of fire protection and safety accorded to a building.

The main purposes of fire safety legislation are:
1. To impose a level of fire safety, such that it is unlikely that people occupying a building would suffer injury in the event of an unwanted fire.
2. To protect the community at large from the consequences of a fire in an individual building.

Building regulations assume that if certain components of fire safety can be identified and suitable standards applied to particular building types, a satisfactory level of fire safety will be achieved.

It is assumed that if the purpose, for which buildings will be generally used, can be determined; then buildings used for a similar purpose can be classified as a particular building type. This method assumes that each building of a particular type will:
(i) have the same fire loading,
(ii) be of similar geometry,
(iii) experience a similar fire scenario and
(iv) be exposed to a fire of similar severity.

Hence, the standards for components of fire safety can be prescribed for building types.

Thus, building classification becomes a factor in risk determination.

3.1.1 Fire Safety

"Fire Safety is defined a person in or adjacent to a building will be exposed to an unacceptable fire hazard as a result of the design and construction of the building".

In simpler terms, fire safety is the reduction of the potential for harm to life as a result of fire in buildings. Although the potential for being killed or injured in a fire cannot be completely eliminated, fire safety in a building can be achieved through proven building design features intended to minimize the risk of harm to people from fire to the greatest extent possible. Designing a building to ensure minimal risk or to meet a prescribed level of safety from fire is more complex than just the simple consideration of what building materials will be used in construction of the building.

3.2 CLASSIFICATION OF BUILDINGS BASED ON OCCUPANCY

All buildings are classified according to the use or the character of occupancy into the following groups:

Group	
A	Residential
B	Educational
C	Institutional
D	Assembly
E	Business
F	Mercantile
G	Industrial
H	Storage
J	Hazardous

Group A: Residential Buildings:

These include any building in which sleeping accommodation is provided for normal residential purposes, with or without cooking or dining.

For example: residential houses, apartments, lodging and boarding houses, hotels, hostels, etc.

Group B: Educational Buildings:

These include buildings for schools, colleges or day care purposes involving assembly for instruction and education.

Group C: Institutional Buildings:

These include hospitals and sanatoria; homes for the aged, the convalescent and orphans; buildings for jails, prisons, mental hospitals etc.

Group D: Assembly Buildings:

These are buildings in which groups of people congregate or gather for amusement, recreation, social and religious activities and also for activities related to travel.

For example: theatres, assembly halls, auditoria, exhibition halls, museums, gymnasiums, restaurants, places of worship, dance halls, clubs, passenger stations and terminals of air, surface and marine public transportation services, stadia etc.

Group E: Business Buildings:
These are buildings which are used for transaction of business, for keeping of accounts and records, professional establishments, service facilities etc.

For example: city halls, town halls, court rooms, libraries, offices, banks, laboratories, research establishments etc.

Group F: Mercantile Buildings:
These are buildings which are used as shops, stores, market; for display and sale of merchandise.

Group G: Industrial Buildings:
These are buildings in which products or materials of all kinds are fabricated, assembled, manufactured or processed.

Group H: Storage Buildings:
These are buildings used primarily for the storage or sheltering of goods, wares or merchandise (except those that involve highly combustible materials or explosives), vehicles or animals. For example: warehouses, cold storage, truck and marine terminals, garages, grain elevators, barns and stables.

Group J: Hazardous Buildings:
These include buildings which are used for storage, handling, manufacture or processing of highly combustible or explosive materials or products which are liable to burn rapidly and/or produce poisonous fumes or explosions.

For example: storage under pressure of acetylene, hydrogen, natural gas, ammonia etc.

Storage and handling of highly inflammable materials or liquids, rocket propellants etc.

Manufacture of artificial flowers, synthetic leather, ammunition, explosives, fire crackers, match sticks etc.

3.3 FIRE LOAD

The term fire load is used to describe the heat energy which could be released per square metre of floor area of a compartment or storey by the combustion of the contents of the building and any combustible parts of the superstructure itself.

$$\text{Fire load} = \frac{M \times C}{A} \text{ in kJ/m}^2$$

where,
- M = Mass of combustible materials in the compartment or storey, in kg
- C = Calorific value of materials, in kJ/kg
- A = Floor area, in m^2.

Building regulations have adopted a grouping system, which is a grading of occupancies based on assumed fire loadings. The grouping of buildings is then used as a determinant in establishing the desirable fire-resisting characteristics of the elements of the structure of the building.

Thus, it is seen that the concept of fire loading attempts is to relate the combustible contents of a building to the potential severity of a fire in that building and consequently to the fire-resisting capabilities of the elements of the structure.

Broadly, the buildings are classified into the following three groups depending upon the fire load.

Building hazard classification	Fire load in kJ/m²
Low hazard group	0 - 49
Medium hazard group	50 - 100
High hazard group	> 100

Certain rules and regulations have been framed by government bodies, which direct that all the buildings must satisfy certain requirements which contribute individually and collectively, to the safety of life from fire, smoke, fumes and panic arising from fire.

The following are some of the general requirements:

(i) Every building must be restricted in its height above the ground level regarding the number of storeys, depending upon its occupancy and type of construction.

(ii) Open spaces around or inside a building must conform to the requirements of local development control rules and general building requirements.

(iii) For high rise buildings (height more than 15 m), the following additional requirements must be considered.

  (a) The width of the main street on which the building abuts should not be less than 12 m.

  (b) The road should not have a dead end.

  (c) Compulsory open spaces around the building must not be used as parking spaces.

  (d) Adequate passageways and clearances required for fire fighting vehicles to enter the premises must be provided at the entrance, the width of such an entrance should not be less than 4.5 m. If an arch or a covered gate is constructed; it should have a clear head room of not less than 5 m.

(iv) Fire detecting and extinguishing systems must be provided as per accepted standards according to the type of occupancy.

(v) All buildings depending upon the occupancy, use and height, should be protected by wet riser, wet riser-cum-down comer, automatic sprinkler installation, high pressure water spray or foam generating system etc. as per accepted standards.

(vi) Static water storage Tanks: A satisfactory supply of water for the purpose of fire fighting should always be available in the form of an underground static storage tank with its capacity specified for each building.

(vii) Automatic sprinklers can be installed in basements used as carparks; departmental stores, shops of area more than 750 m^2; godowns and warehouses on all floors of the buildings other than residential buildings, if the height of the building exceeds 45 m.

(viii) Air conditioning and ventilating systems should be so installed and maintained as to minimise the danger of fire, smoke or fumes spreading from one floor to another or from outside into any occupied building or structure.

(ix) For buildings over 15 m in height, fire lifts should be provided with a minimum capacity of 8 passengers and thus should be fully automated with emergency switches at ground level.

3.4 FACTORS AFFECTING FIRE DEVELOPMENT

The growth and development of a fire depend to a great extent on the geometry and ventilation of the enclosure containing fire.

A fire usually starts because a material is ignited by a heat source. The development of a fire within an enclosure depends on the following factors:

(i) The item first ignited is sufficiently inflammable to allow a flame to spread over its surfaces.

(ii) The heat flux from the first ignited item is sufficient to irradiate adjacent materials which in turn begin to burn.

(iii) Sufficient fuel exists within the enclosure; otherwise, the fire may simply burn itself out.

(iv) The fire may burn very slowly because of a restricted supply of oxygen as in the case of a well sealed room and may eventually smoother itself.

(v) If there is sufficient fuel and oxygen available, the fire may totally involve the entire enclosure.

3.5 PATTERN OF FIRE

The pattern of every fire is different but the majority pass through the following stages:

Flashover is the rapid involvement of an enclosure's combustible contents as they ignite almost simultaneously. Thus, it is the time when the flames cease to be localised and flaming can be observed throughout the whole enclosure. **Flashover** is, in fact, the transition from the growth period to a steady state of combustion, or a fully developed stage in fire development.

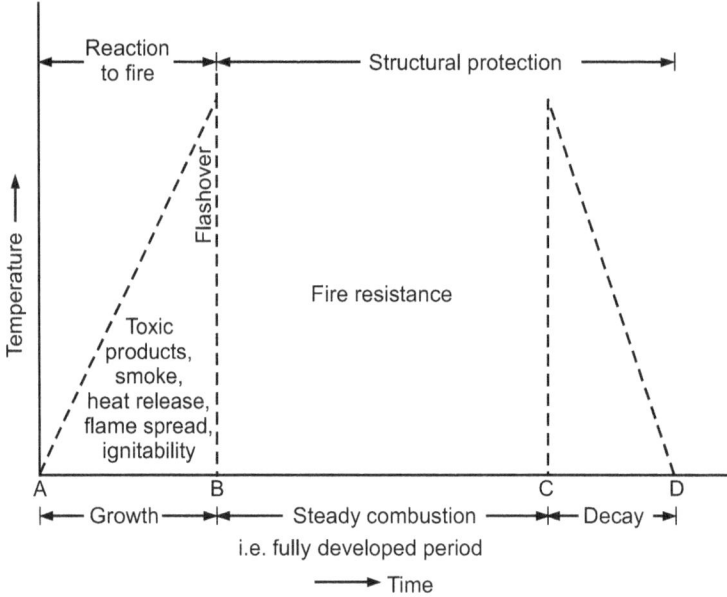

Fig. 3.1: Different phases of fire

The period A - B is known as the growth period. It is essentially the pre-flashover period during which the temperatures in the enclosure are relatively low and chances of escape are relatively high.

At B, the fire progresses rapidly through flashover to the fully developed stage upto C. During this period all the combustibles in the compartment are burning and the temperature within the enclosure is highest.

At C, the steady combustion period ends, the temperature begins to fall and C - D is the decay period.

Though the temperatures during the growth period are low, the duration of the growth period is very important as it determines the time available for escape and for the effective operation of the emergency fire fighting services.

3.6 FIRE SEVERITY

It may be defined as the destructive potential of a fire i.e. the potential impact that a fire in a given enclosure will have upon the structural and constructional components which form the enclosure and its components. Hence, fire severity has a direct relation to the structural performance in terms of a component's fire-resisting capabilities. Therefore, the fire resistance offered by a component during the fully developed stage of a fire is extremely important in evaluating the extent of fire severity.

3.7 FIRE RESISTANCE

If a fire burns unnoticed and uncontrolled in a building, the building elements can be subjected to very high temperatures. The temperature levels and the duration of heating are dependent upon a number of factors related to the design of the building and its contents. If the building elements can withstand this exposure without the building becoming unstable or suffering collapse and without the fire spreading unrestrictedly, they are considered to have adequate fire resistance.

Thus, **fire resistance** can be defined as the ability of an element of building construction to withstand the effects of fire for a specified period of time without loss of its fire separating and load bearing functions. Therefore, a structural component should be able to:
1. endure a fire without collapse,
2. prevent the penetration of flame,
3. resist the spread of fire by conduction through the component or by radiation from the face of the component not exposed to the fire.

The factors which determine the level of fire resistance of structural components are:
1. Type of occupancy,
2. Height of the building,
3. Floor area of the storey or compartment,
4. Cubic capacity of the building or compartment and
5. Location of the component
   i.e. (a) ground or upper storey
   (b) basement.

Unit: The fire resistance of a building or its structural elements is expressed in hours against a specified test load which is expressed in $kcal/m^2$ and against a certain intensity of fire.

The types of construction according to fire resistance are classified into four categories, namely, type 1, type 2, type 3 and type 4.

The following Table 3.1 gives the fire resistance ratings for various types of construction for structural elements.

Table 3.1: Fire resistance ratings of structural elements (in hours)

Structural Element		Type of Construction			
		Type 1	Type 2	Type 3	Type 4
1. Exterior walls					
Fire separation less than 3.7 m	Bearing	4	2	2	1
	Non-Bearing	2	$1\frac{1}{2}$	1	1
Fire separation of 3.7 m or more but less than 9 m	Bearing	4	2	2	1
	Non-Bearing	$1\frac{1}{2}$	1	1	1
Fire separation of 9 m or more	Bearing	4	2	2	1
	Non-Bearing	1	1	1	1
2. Fire walls and party walls		4	2	2	2
3. Fire separation assemblies		4	2	2	2
4. Fire enclosures of exit ways, hallways and stairways		2	2	2	2
5. Shaft other than exit ways, elevator hoist ways		2	2	2	2
6. Exit way access corridors		1	1	1	1
7. Vertical separation of tenant spaces		1	1	1	1
8. Dwelling unit separations		1	1	1	1
Non-bearing partitions		← At least half an hour →			
9. Interior bearing walls, bearing partitions, columns, girders, trusses (other than roof trusses) and framing	Supporting more than one floor	4	2	2	2
	Supporting one floor only	3	$1\frac{1}{2}$	1	1
	Supporting a roof only	3	$1\frac{1}{2}$	1	1
10. Structural members supporting walls		3	$1\frac{1}{2}$	1	1
11. Floor construction, including beams		3	$1\frac{1}{2}$	1	1
12. Roof construction, including beams, trusses and framing arches and roof deck	5 m or less in height to lowest member	2	$1\frac{1}{2}$	1	1
	More than 5 m but less than 6.7 m in height to lowest member	1	1	1	1
	6.7 m or more in height to lowest member	0	0	0	0

In relation to fire, the building materials can be classified into two categories - combustible and non-combustible. Combustible materials are those that catch fire themselves and contribute to the growth of fire. For example: wood, fibre board, straw board curtains, apparel etc.

Non-combustible materials are those that do not catch fire, but after being exposed to fire for some time, loose their inherent qualities. They may loose their shape and load carrying capacity and yield, thus resulting in the collapse of the structure For example: steel, stone.

3.8 SOME COMMON CONSTRUCTION MATERIALS

1. **Timber:** Though timber catches fire and is a combustible material, it has the ability to offer resistance to fire for a period of time. It gets charred, on exposure to fire and this coating of char on timber surface functions as an insulating material and slows down the process of combustion. However, on prolonged exposure to fire, it undergoes total combustion.
2. **Stone:** Stone is a non-combustible material but has very little fire resisting properties. Granite, when exposed to fire, breaks into pieces. Limestone and marble get calcined. Compact sandstone can withstand fire to some extent.
3. **Bricks:** Well burnt bricks have good fire resisting properties and may withstand temperatures upto $1200°C$.
4. **Iron and Steel:** Though iron and steel are non-combustible materials, they are very good conductors of heat. They expand, get wraped and loose their shape under exposure to prolonged fire. Thus, a steel structural component may yield under heat resulting in collapse of the structure.
5. **Concrete:** Concrete, in general, is a good fire-resistant material, but this resistance will depend to a large extent on the type of aggregates used. However, RCC structure with a good cover to reinforcement offers good resistance to fire.
6. **Glass:** Glass is a good fire resisting material because of its low thermal conductivity. However, it cannot tolerate sudden changes in temperature.

    For example: When it is exposed to extreme heat in the event of a fire, and the fire is doused with water, glass may crack. Reinforced glass has better fire resistance.
7. **Asbestos Cement:** Asbestos cement is an excellent fire resisting material. It is a combination of fibrous material and cement and is largely used in the construction of fireproof partition walls and roofs.

3.9 FIRE RESISTANT CONSTRUCTION

Walls and Columns: Fire ratings of some types of constructions for walls are given in the following tables. Specifications of materials should be so selected; as to give these ratings.

Table 3.2: Masonry walls: Solid (Required to resist fire from one side at a time)

Nature of Construction and Materials	Minimum Thickness (mm), Excluding any finish, for a fire resistance (Hours) of									
	Load Bearing					Non-load Bearing				
	1 hr.	1½ hrs.	2 hrs.	3 hrs.	4 hrs.	1 hr.	1½ hrs.	2 hrs.	3 hrs.	4 hrs.
1. Reinforced* cement concrete	120 (25)	140 (25)	160 (25)	200 (25)	240 (25)					
2. Unreinforced cement concrete	150	175	–	–	–					
3. No-fines concrete with:										
(a) 13 mm cement/sand or gypsum/sand						150	150	150	150	150
(b) 13 mm lightweight aggregate gypsum plaster						150	150	150	150	150
4. Bricks of clay:										
(a) Without finish	90	100	100	170	170	75	90	100	170	170
(b) With 13 mm lightweight aggregate gypsum plaster	90	90	90	100	100	75	90	90	90	100
5. Bricks of sand lime:										
(a) Without finish	90	100	100	190	190	75	90	100	170	170
(b) With 13 mm lightweight aggregate gypsum plaster	90	90	90	100	100	75	90	90	90	100
6. Blocks of concrete:										
(a) Without finish	90	100	100	–	–	75	90	100	140	150
(b) With 13 mm lightweight aggregate gypsum plaster	90	90	90	100	100	75	75	75	90	100
(c) With 13 mm cement/sand or gypsum/sand						75	90	90	100	140
7. Blocks of lightweight concrete:										
(a) Without finish	90	100	100	140	150	75	75	75	125	140
(b) With 13 mm lightweight aggregate gypsum plaster	90	90	90	100	100	50	63	75	75	75
(c) With 13 mm cement/sand or gypsum/sand						75	75	75	90	100
8. Blocks of aerated concrete:										
(a) Without finish	90	100	100	140	180	50	63	63	75	100
(b) With 13 mm lightweight aggregate gypsum plaster	90	90	100	100	150					

* Walls containing at least 1 percent of vertical reinforcement.   ( )   Minimum thickness of actual cover to reinforcement.

Table 3.3: Masonry walls, Hollows (Required to resist fire from one side at a time)

Nature of Construction and Materials	Minimum Thickness (mm), Excluding any finish, for a fire resistance (Hours) of:									
	Load Bearing					Non-load Bearing				
	1 hr.	1½ hrs.	2 hrs.	3 hrs.	4 hrs.	½ hr.	1 hr.	1½ hrs.	2 hrs.	3 hrs.	4 hrs.
1. Bricks of clay:											
(a) Without finish	170	170	170	200	200	75	100	100	170	170	200
(b) With 13 mm lightweight aggregate gypsum plaster	100	100	170	170	170	75	75	90	100	100	170
2. Blocks of concrete:											
(a) Without finish						90	125	125	140	140	150
(b) With 13 mm cement/sand or gypsum/sand						90	125	125	140	140	140
(c) With 13 mm light weight aggregate gypsum plaster	190	200	200	—	—	75	90	90	100	125	125
3. Blocks of light weight concrete:											
(a) Without finish	100	100	100	—	—	75	90	90	100	140	150
(b) With 13 mm cement/sand or gypsum/sand						75	75	75	100	140	140
(c) With 13 mm light weight aggregate gypsum plaster						63	63	75	75	90	100

Table 3.4: Framed construction, load bearing (Required to resist fire from one side at a time)

Nature of construction and materials / Timber studs at centres not exceeding 600 mm, faced on each side with	Minimum thickness (mm) of Protection for a fire resistance of 1 hr.
1. Plasterboard layers with joints staggered, joints in outer layer taped and filled – Total thickness for each face	25
2. One layer of 12.7 mm plasterboard with a finish of lightweight aggregate gypsum plaster.	13
3. Metal lath and plaster, thickness of plaster:	
(a) Sanded gypsum plaster (metal lathing grade)	22
(b) Lightweight aggregate gypsum plaster	13

Table 3.5: Framed construction, load bearing (Required to resist fire from one side at a time)

Nature of construction and materials/ Steel or Timber frame at centres not exceeding 600 mm, facing on both sides of	Stud Construction	Minimum thickness (mm) of Protection for a fire resistance of 1 h			
		$\frac{1}{2}$ hr.	1 hr.	$1\frac{1}{2}$ hrs.	2 hrs.
(A) Dry lining with materials fixed direct to studs (without plaster finish):					
1. One layer of plasterboard with taped and filled joints	Timber or steel	12.7			
2. Two layers of plasterboard with joints staggered, joints in outer layer taped and filled – Total thickness for each face	Timber or steel	19	25		
3. One layer of asbestos insulating board with transverse joints backed by fillers of asbestos insulating board not less than 9 mm thick or by timber	Timber	9			
	Steel	12			
4. One layer of wood wool slabs	Timber	25			
5. One layer of chipboard or of plywood	Timber or steel	18			
(B) Lining with materials fixed direct to studs, with plaster finish:					
1. Plasterboard of thickness:	Timber or steel				
(a) With not less than 5 mm gypsum plaster finish		9.5	12.7		
(b) With not less than 13 mm gypsum plaster finish					
(C) Wet finish:					
1. Metal lath and plaster, thickness of plaster:	Timber or steel				
(a) Sanded gypsum plaster	Timber	13	13	19	
(b) Lightweight aggregate gypsum plaster	Steel		13		15

Table 3.6 : Framed external walls load bearing (required to resist fire from one side at a time)

Nature of construction and materials	Minimum thickness (mm) of Protection for a fire resistance of 1 h
Timber studs at centres not exceeding 600 mm with internal linings of plaster board layers with joints in outer layer taped and filled, total thickness of plasterboard	31

Table 3.7 : Reinforced concrete columns

	Nature of construction and materials		Minimum dimensions (mm), excluding any finish for a fire resistance of					
			½ hr.	1 hr.	1½ hrs.	2 hrs.	3 hrs.	4 hrs.
1.	Fully exposed	Width	150	200	250	300	400	450
		Cover	20	25	30	35	35	35
2.	50 percent exposed	Width	125	160	200	200	300	350
		Cover	20	25	25	25	30	35
3.	One face exposed	Thickness	100	120	140	160	200	240
		Cover	20	25	25	25	25	25

Table 3.8 : Concrete beams

	Nature of construction and materials		Minimum dimensions (mm), excluding any finish for a fire resistance of					
			½ hr.	1 hr.	1½ hrs.	2 hrs.	3 hrs.	4 hrs.
1.	Reinforced concrete (simply supported)	Width	80	120	150	200	240	280
		Cover	20	30	40	60	70	80
2.	Reinforced concrete (continuous)	Width	80	80	120	150	200	240
		Cover	20	20	35	50	60	70
3.	Prestressed concrete (simply supported)	Width	100	120	150	200	240	280
		Cover	25	40	55	70	80	90
4.	Prestressed concrete (continuous)	Width	80	100	120	150	200	240
		Cover	20	30	40	55	70	80

Table 3.9: Encased steel columns, 203 mm × 203 mm (Protection applied on four sides)

Nature of construction and materials	Minimum thickness (mm) of protection for a fire resistance of				
	1 hr.	1½ hrs.	2 hrs.	3 hrs.	4 hrs.
(A) Hollow protection (without an air cavity over the flanges):					
1. *Metal lathing with trowelled lightweight aggregate gypsum plaster	13	15	20	32	—
2. Plasterboard with 1.6 mm wire binding at 100 mm pitch, finished with lightweight aggregate gypsum plaster not less than the thickness specified:					
(a) 9.5 mm plasterboard	10	15			
(b) 19 mm plasterboard	10	13	20		
3. Asbestos insulating boards, thickness of board:					
(a) Single thickness of board, with 6 mm cover fillets at transverse joints		19	25	38	50
(b) Two layers, of total thickness	50	50	50	75	100
4. Solid bricks of clay composition or sand lime, reinforced in every horizontal joint, unplastered	60	60	60		
5. Aerated concrete blocks	50	50	50	60	75
6. Solid blocks of lightweight concrete					
(B) Hollow protections (with an air cavity over the flanges)					
Asbestos insulating board screwed to 25 mm asbestos battens	12	19			
(C) Solid protections					
1. Concrete, not leaner than 1 : 2 : 4 mix (unplastered):					
(a) Concrete not assumed to be load bearing, reinforced †	25	25	25	50	75
(b) Concrete assumed to be load bearing	50	50	50	75	75
2. Lightweight concrete, not leaner than 1 : 2 : 4 mix (Unplastered) concrete not assumed to be load bearing, reinforced †	25	25	25	40	60

* So fixed or designed, as to allow full penetration for mechanical bond.

† Reinforcement shall consist of steel binding wire not less than 2.3 mm in thickness, or a steel mesh weighing not less than 0.5 kg/m³. In concrete protection, the spacing of that reinforcement shall not exceed 200 mm in any direction.

Table 3.10 : Encased steel beam, 406 mm × 176 mm (Protection applied on three sides)

Nature of construction and materials	Minimum thickness (mm) of Protection for a fire resistance of					
	½ hr.	1 hr.	1½ hrs.	2 hrs.	3 hrs.	4 hrs.
(A) Hollow protection (without an air cavity beneath the lower flange)						
1. *Metal lathing with trowelled lightweight aggregate gypsum plaster (metal lathing grade)	13	13	15	20	25	
2. Plasterboard with 1.6 mm wire binding at 100 mm pitch, finished with lightweight aggregate gypsum plaster not less than the thickness specified:						
(a) 9.5 mm plasterboard	10	10	15	20		
(b) 19 mm plasterboard	10	10	13			
3. Asbestos insulating board, thickness of board:						
(a) Single thickness of board, with 6 mm cover fillets at transverse joints			19	25		
(b) Two layers, of total thickness					38	50
(B) Hollow protection (with an air cavity below the lower flange):						
1. Asbestos insulating board screwed to 25 mm asbestos battens	9	12				
(C) Solid protection:						
1. Concrete not leaner than 1 : 2 : 4 mix (unplastered):						
(a) Concrete not a‡ssumed to be load bearing, reinforced ‡	25	25	25	25	50	75
(b) Concrete assumed to be load bearing	50	50	50	50	75	75
2. Lightweight concrete § not leaner than 1 : 2 : 4 (mix) unplastered	25	25	25	25	40	60

* So fixed, or designed, as to allow full penetration for mechanical bond.
† Where wire binding cannot be used, expert advice should be sought regarding alternative methods of support to enable the lower edges of the plasterboard to be fixed together and to the lower flange, and for the top edge of the plasterboard to be held in position.
‡ Reinforcement shall consist of steel binding wire not less than 2.3 mm in thickness or a steel mesh weighing not less than 0.5 kg/m³. In concrete protection, the spacing of that reinforcement shall not exceed 200 mm in any direction.
§ Concrete not assumed to be load bearing, reinforced.

Every opening in the wall should be protected by a fire resisting door having a fire rating of not less than 1 hour.

In load bearing structures, bricks are preferred to stones because of their fire resisting properties. In framed structures, RCC frames are better than structural steel frames.

In RCC frame work the reinforcement should have proper cover to prevent it from being exposed to fire.

Partition walls also should be of fire resisting material such as hollow concrete blocks, bricks, reinforced glass, asbestos cement board etc.

All walls should be plastered with fire resisting mortar.

The use of inflammable surface finishes on walls (including external facade of the building) and ceilings affects the safety of the occupants of a building. Such finishes tend to spread the fire and even though the structural elements may be adequately fire resistant, serious danger to life may result. Therefore, the finishing materials used for various surfaces and decor should not add to the spread of fire and in addition should not generate toxic fumes and smoke.

Floors and Roofs:

The fire ratings of some floors are given in the following tables. The specifications of materials should consider these ratings.

Table 3.11: Concrete floors

	Nature of construction and materials		Minimum Dimensions (mm), Excluding any finish for a fire resistance of:					
			$\frac{1}{2}$ hr.	1 hr.	$1\frac{1}{2}$ hrs.	2 hrs.	3 hrs.	4 hrs.
1.	Reinforced concrete (simply supported)	Thickness	75	95	110	125	150	170
		Cover	15	20	25	35	45	55
2.	Reinforced concrete (continuous)	Thickness	75	95	110	125	150	170
		Cover	15	20	20	25	35	45

Table 3.12: Concrete floors: Ribbed open soffit

	Nature of construction and materials		Minimum Dimensions (mm), Excluding any finish for a fire resistance of:					
			$\frac{1}{2}$ hr.	1 hr.	$1\frac{1}{2}$ hrs.	2 hrs.	3 hrs.	4 hrs.
1.	Reinforced concrete (simply supported)	Thickness	70	90	105	115	135	150
		Width	75	90	110	125	150	175
		Cover	15	25	35	45	55	65
2.	Reinforced concrete (continuous)	Thickness	70	90	105	115	135	150
		Width	75	80	90	110	125	150
		Cover	15	20	–	35	45	55

Table 3.13: Timber floors - Any structurally suitable flooring of timber or particle boards

Nature of construction and materials 37 mm (minimum) timber joists with a ceiling of	Minimum thickness (mm), of protection for a fire resistance of:	
	$\frac{1}{2}$ hr.	1 hr.
1. Timber lathing and plaster, plaster of thickness	15	
2. Metal lathing and plaster, thickness of plaster for:		
(a) Sanded gypsum plaster (metal lathing grade)	15	
(b) Light weight aggregate gypsum plaster	13	19
3. One layer of plaster board with joints taped and filled and backed by timber	12.7	
4. Two layers of plaster board, with joints staggered, joints in outer layer taped and filled total thickness.	25	
5. Two layers of plaster board, each not less than 9.5 mm thick, joints between boards staggered and outer layer finished with gypsum plaster	5	
6. One layer of plaster board not less than 9.5 mm thick, finished with:		
(a) Sanded gypsum plaster	13	
(b) Lightweight aggregate gypsum plaster	15	
7. One layer of plasterboard not less than 12.7 mm thick, finished with:		
(a) Sanded gypsum plaster	15	
(b) Lightweight aggregate gypsum plaster	13	
8. One layer of asbestos insulating board with any transverse joints backed by fillets of asbestos insulating board not less than 9 mm thick, or by timber	12	

RCC floors are most suitable for fire resistance. Flat roofs are preferred to sloping or pitched roofs. A surface covering, of non-combustible and non-toxic material, should be laid directly on the incombustible floor. Flooring materials like concrete tiles and ceramic files are quite suitable.

Linings or false ceilings should not be encouraged in buildings.

In some cases, requiring provision of skylights, monitor lights or north lights in the roofs; glazings should be of glass in metal frames with a fire rating of minimum half an hour.

Staircase: All internal staircases must be of fire resisting materials such as RCC stairs. It should be constructed as a self contained unit and should be completely enclosed.

3.10 MEANS OF ESCAPE

The present method of providing means of escape from buildings is by observing specifications and rules i.e. rules that have evolved through time and are deemed to provide a satisfactory escape route.

The main objective of the provision of a means of escape is that the occupants should be able to reach a place of safety unharmed, in the event of a fire occurring.

A place of safety is normally associated with an area outside the building away from the threatened space. It may also be a protected corridor, a protected staircase or a place of refuge within the buildings.

Places of refuge are necessary in very tall buildings because the evacuation of these buildings may take two hours or more. Refuge floors may be provided every six or eight floors up the building, depending on the nature of occupancy, so that occupants of the fire floor, floors below the fire and above the fire can be evacuated to a place of safety.

Evacuation Time:

This is the time taken for a person to go from any occupied part of the building to a place of safety. Ideally this should be 2 – 3 minutes, but evacuation time will vary according to a person's speed of travel depending upon his age and general physical condition.

In fact, 2 - 3 minutes evacuation criterion is derived from studies which conclude that such a time is reasonable for people in a stressful situation, before panic conditions develop. Thus, it is highly desirable to evacuate people before a state of irrational behaviour starts.

In multistoreyed buildings, where this evacuation time of 2 – 3 minutes cannot be achieved, places of safety must be provided within the building.

Travel Distance:

Travel distance is the distance to be traversed in order to reach a place of safety from which dispersal can take place. This place of safety can be a protected escape route, an external escape route or a final exit.

A range of travel distances is given in the following table; varying relative to purpose, grouping and particular situation.

Table 3.14: Travel distance for occupancy and type of construction

Sr. No.	Group of occupancy	Construction types	
		1 and 2 (m)	3 and 4 (m)
1.	Residential	22.5	22.5
2.	Educational	22.5	22.5
3.	Institutional	22.5	22.5
4.	Assembly	30.0	30.0
5.	Business	30.0	30.0
6.	Mercantile	30.0	30.0
7.	Industrial	45.0	30.0
8.	Storage	30.0	30.0
9.	Hazardous	22.5	22.5

The travel distance to an exit from the dead end of a corridor should not exceed half the distance specified in the above table, except in educational, assembly and institutional occupancies, in which case it should not exceed 6 m.

These distances have been established by experience over many years and give guidance for particular applications. However, the distance to be travelled must be related to the risk involved i.e. the rapidity of flame and smoke spread. When a fire is in the growth stage, a great deal of smoke can be produced and this smoke can move, on occasions, more quickly than normal walking pace. It is, therefore, essential that travel distances can be such that persons can reach a place of safety before smoke-logging of the means of escape occurs.

Exit Requirements:

Entrances, exits and circulation areas are provided in all buildings for normal use. Means of escape considerations should utilize existing arrangements wherever possible.

An exit may be a doorway, corridor, passageway to an internal staircase, external staircase, verandah or terrace which has access to the street or to the roof of a building or a refuge area. An exit may also include a horizontal exit leading to an adjoining building at the same level. Lifts and escalators are not considered as exits.

The primary consideration should be with regard to the sufficiency of existing exits in terms of:

(i) disposition,

(ii) width and

(iii) number.

(i) Disposition: The position of exits as a means of escape in the case of a fire is absolutely critical. Exits should be clearly visible and the routes to reach the exit should be clearly marked and signs should be posted to guide the population of the floor concerned.

Exits should be so arranged, that they may be reached without passing through another occupied unit. They should also be located in such a way that the prescribed travel distances are not exceeded.

(ii) Width: It is essential while designing that bottlenecks i.e. areas where congestion will occur, are avoided. Thus, corridors should not become narrower as they approach a storey exit or staircase. No obstructions should be kept in the corridors which will reduce the effective width of the corridors.

Building codes have specified a unit of exit width of 50 cm to measure the capacity of any exit. A clear width of 25 cm is counted as an additional half unit. Clear widths less than 25 cm should not be counted for exit widths.

The following table gives the number of occupants discharged per minute in a single file through different exits.

Table 3.15: Occupants per unit exit width

Sr. No.	Group of occupancy	Number of occupants		
		Stairways	Ramps	Doors
1.	Residential	25	50	75
2.	Educational	25	50	75
3.	Institutional	25	50	75
4.	Assembly	40	50	60
5.	Business	50	60	75
6.	Mercantile	50	60	75
7.	Industrial	50	60	75
8.	Storage	50	60	75
9.	Hazardous	25	30	40

A width of 50 cm is not acceptable in practice. Hence, the national building code has specified that:

(a) Every exit doorway must have a minimum width of 100 cm and a minimum height of 200 cm.

(b) No door, when opened, should reduce the required width of a stairway or landing to less than 90 cm.

(c) Landing width of the stairway must be equal to at least the width of the door.

(d) Width of exit-corridor and passageways should not be less than the required aggregate width of exit doorways leading from them in the direction of travel to the exterior.

(e) Minimum width of stairs in residential buildings should be 1.0 m and in public buildings 1.5 m, as per NBC.

(f) Width of a straight flight in a fire escape stair should not be less than 75 cm and in case of a spiral fire escape, its diameter should not be less than 150 cm.

(iii) Number: Every building meant for human occupancy must be provided with exits sufficient to permit safe escape of occupants, in case of fire or other emergency.

All buildings which are 15 m or more in height and all buildings used as educational, assembly, institutional, industrial, storage and hazardous occupancies, having area more than 500 m^2 on each floor must have a minimum of two staircases.

3.11 FIRE DETECTING SYSTEMS

One method of increasing escape potential and reducing fire casualties would be the introduction of fire-detection systems as a component of escape route design, linked to a warning alarm system which would alert the occupants of a building to the presence of fire.

Various types of fire detectors are available for installation in buildings intended for different occupancies. Fire detectors may respond to the generation of heat, smoke and flames and accordingly there are heat detectors, smoke detectors and flame detectors.

3.12 FIRE EXTINGUISHING SYSTEMS

The method of extinguishing fire will depend on the building type, building occupancy and the nature of hazard. The following are some of the fixed fire extinguishing systems:

(a) Automatic water sprinkler system,

(b) Automatic high velocity water spray or emulsifying system,

(c) Fixed foam installation, and

(d) Carbon dioxide fire extinguishing system.

An automatic sprinkler system consists of an arrangement of pipes at a regular spacing under the ceiling or the most hazardous part of the building. This network of pipes is supplied with water from the fire tank pumps at regular intervals, depending upon the hazards. These sprinkler heads contain a fusible plug which is designed to open at a predetermined temperature. Thus, the heat of the flame raises the temperature of the nearest sprinkler to its operating point and it opens up, releasing a flow of water under pressure and dousing the fire beneath. To avoid unnecessary damage due to water, the sprinkler system can be provided with a water flow alarm to sound at some fire alarm headquarters.

IMPORTANT POINTS

- Introduction to fire, its consequences and purpose of fire safety legislation.
- Classification of buildings based on occupancy, its types – Hazard classification for buildings.
- Fire load, its limits, certain rules and regulations for buildings.
- Phases of fire resistance of structural components.
- Fire resistant construction: Masonry walls solid, masonry walls hallow, encased steel columns etc.
- Means of escape: Evacuation time, travel distance and exit requirements.
- Fire extinguishing systems and its types.

QUESTIONS

1. How does fire occur in buildings? What is the purpose of fire safety legislation?
2. How are buildings classified? How does the classification become a factor in risk determination?
3. What is fire load? What are the general requirements which contribute to safety from fire?
4. What factors influence fire development in a building?
5. What is the pattern generally followed by a fire in a building?
6. What is fire resistance of a building element? What factors determine the level of fire resistance?
7. How would you plan means of escape in the event of a fire in a building?
8. Discuss different types of fire-detecting systems.
9. Explain the methods of extinguishing an accidental fire in a building.
10. Explain fire grade.
11. Explain the term fire load. How do you determine it?
12. Compare fire resisting properties of timber and concrete.
13. Explain the terms:
    (a) Fire load (b) Evacuation time (c) Travel distance
14. What are different fire extinguishing systems? Explain any one in detail.
15. Write a note on fire escape elements.
16. Compare fire resisting properties of:
    (a) Concrete (b) Store
17. What exit requirements are to be provided in a public building to escape from fire.
18. State commonly adopted fire extinguishing services. Describe any one in detail.
19. What is fire hazard. How will you carry on fire resisting construction.
20. Explain points to be observed for making walls and columns fire resistant.
21. What is fire load and how fire safety is achieved?
22. How would you plan means of escape in the event of fire in a building?
23. Discuss important considerations in fire protection.
24. State the various fire resistant materials that can be used for walls and floors.

Chapter 4

BUILDING SERVICES

4.1 CONSTRUCTIONAL REQUIREMENTS FOR DIFFERENT BUILDING SERVICES

While designing building (residential, commercial, institutional etc.), factors which should be considered are: (1) Elegance, (2) Safety, (3) Economy, (4) Comfort. i.e. a building should be beautiful to look at, should be safe, the owner should get maximum returns and the user should find the stay in the building comfortable. Elegance can be achieved by various architectural forms, building materials, colour schemes, etc. Safety includes structural safety, durability, health safety and fire safety. Economy can be achieved through proper use of building materials, economic design of building components etc. Necessary building services play a very important role in providing comfort to the user if environment is not suitable. These services include electrical, air handling, air conditioning, heating, ventilation, lighting and plumbing services. Other services include vertical circulation, telecommunication, entertainment services etc.

4.1.1 Electrical Services

An electrical service is very essential for any type of building to provide required power for operating various types of electrical appliances, providing artificial lighting, artificial ventilation for pumping water, etc. The installation should be carried out in a building in conformity with the requirements of Indian Electricity Act, 1910; Indian Electricity Rules, 1956 and also the relevant regulations of the electric supply authority for the area in which the building is located. For a proposed electrical work or extension of existing work or major modifications, permission of the concerned electrical local authority should be taken. The work of electrical installations shall be carried out by a licensed electrical contractor and under the direct supervision of a competent person.

The design and planning of an electrical wiring installation involves a thorough understanding of all prevailing conditions. It should consider the type of building (residential, commercial, industrial etc.) and requirements of consumers. Therefore, an architect should consult an electrical engineer during the building planning stage to provide electrical installations adequate for their intended purpose and safe and efficient in their use. While designing and planning electrical services, an architect should consider the following points:

1. The type of supply, occupancy, proposed electrical load and available earthing arrangement.
2. The atmospheric conditions which are likely to affect the installation adversely.
3. The degree of mechanical and electrical protection necessary.

4. The importance of continuity of electric supply and the possible need for stand-by supply.
5. The probable operation maintenance cost and electrical supply tariffs.
6. The relative costs of various alternative methods.
7. Ease of maintenance and safety aspects.
8. Energy conservation.
9. Space required for accommodation of substation, transformer, switch rooms, service cable ducts, rising mains, distribution cables, subdistribution boards openings and chasel in floors and walls for all required electrical installations.
10. Immediate requirements and requirement of services during the intended life of the building.

While planning a building site, provision should be made for space for installation of substation. As far as possible, it should be at the ground level for direct access from the street for installation or removal of the equipment. The level of the substation should be above the highest flood level. It is preferable to provide electrical substation adjacent to the air conditioning plant room, if provided.

4.1.2 Switch Room

In large installations, a separate switch room is provided. It should be located very close to the electrical load centre and suitable ducts are laid with a minimum number of bends from the point of entry of the main supply cable to the position of main switch gear. While placing the switch room, care is taken to provide rising ducts from upper floors of the building in one straight vertical line. If more than one rising duct is required, horizontal ducts are provided for running cables from the switch room to the foot of each rising main.

4.1.3 Energy Meters

Energy meters are installed in residential buildings at such a place which is accessible to the owner of the building and authority. These meters are installed at a suitable height from where meter reading can be noted. These meters are protected with a protective covering like a glass window or they are mounted inside a completely enclosed box having hinged or sliding doors with locking arrangement.

4.1.4 Layout and Installation of Wiring

An electrical layout for wiring is drawn by considering proper locations of all outlets for lamps, fans, appliances, both fixed and transportable motors etc. The exact positions of wiring and all points are marked on the plan. In the layout, wiring should be designed keeping in view disposition of the lighting system to meet the illumination levels. Power and heating subcircuits are kept separate and distinct from lighting and fan subcircuit.

Electrical installation in a new building is generally commenced immediately on the completion of the main structural building work and before finishing work such as plastering except in case of surface wiring which is carried out after the plastering work. If electrical wiring is to be concealed within the structure, the necessary conduits and ducts are positioned firmly by tying the conduit to the reinforcement before concreting.

In the building, 15 A socket outlets are provided for the use of domestic appliances such as air conditioners, water coolers, emulsion heaters, refrigerators, etc. with individual fuse or miniature circuit breaker. 5 A socket outlets are provided for lighting fittings and fans. The schedule of socket outlets depends upon the requirements of the buildings. In residential buildings normally the following schedule of socket outlet is provided.

Table 4.1: Requirements of number of socket outlets in residential buildings

Location	Number of 5 A socket outlets	Number of 15 A socket outlets
Bed room	2 – 3	1
Living room	2 – 3	2
Kitchen	1	2
Dining room	2	1
Garage	1	1
For refrigerator	–	1
For air conditioner	–	(one for each)
Verandah	1 per 10 m^2	1
Bathroom	1	1

4.1.5 Telecommunication Services

The requirements of telecommunication facilities like telephone connections, private branch exchange, intercommunication facilities, telex and telegraph lines are to be planned well in advance so that suitable provisions are made in the building plan in such a way that the demand for telecommunication services in any part of the building at any floor are met at any time during the life of the building. Once a building is completed, it is almost impossible, even with the greatest care, to carry out telephone wiring on a large scale without causing unsightliness, some damage to decoration and inconvenience to residents. Wiring for telecommunication in small buildings is undertaken by the telephone department on the surface of the walls. But in large multi-storeyed buildings intended for commercial, business and office use as well as for residential purposes, wiring for telephone connections is generally done in a concealed manner through conduits.

The following are essential requirements:
(a) Feed in ducts for the main cables from the public telephone distribution system, the number of intake points will depend on the design and internal arrangement of the building.
(b) A main distribution case or main distribution frame for connecting the lead in cables with internal wiring system.
(c) One or more vertical riser ducts, continuous throughout the height of the building.
(d) Horizontal ducts or chases for cables from the vertical duct to the telephone position in each dwelling.

It is important to discuss the above requirements with the local telephone authorities and provide for the same at the construction stage itself.

4.1.6 Entertainment Services

In multi-storeyed apartment houses and hotels where many TV receivers are located, a common master antenna system may preferably be used to avoid mushrooming of individual antennae. During the design of the building itself, local conditions should be studied to see which type of an external aerial is necessary for reception of sound and television signals. Individual installations may damage walls and also do not give satisfactory reception. Cable TV network can be integrated with the aerial system.

The master antenna is generally provided at the topmost convenient point in any building and a suitable room of the topmost floor or terrace for housing the amplifier unit etc. may also be provided in consultation with the architect or engineer. From the amplifier room conduits are laid in a recess to facilitate drawing coaxial cables to individual flats. Tap off boxes are also provided in every flat of the building or room in hotels.

4.1.7 Air Handling, Conditioning and Air Heating

Central Air Conditioning System: In this system, various units like filters, heaters, coolers, humidifiers or dehumidifiers etc. are installed at a central place. The conditioned air is supplied to various parts of the building through a duct system provided in the walls or ceiling. A duct system is a continuous passage way for the transmission of air which in addition to ducts, may include duct fittings, dampers, plenums, fans and accessories of air handling equipment.

The equipment for air conditioning consists of air filters, air heaters, refrigeration units, humidifiers, dehumidifiers, air distribution system (ducts, outlets, pumps etc.)

In a central air conditioning system, selection of location for the equipment room and provisions for duct system play an important role in the design of buildings. In selecting the location for plant room, the aspects of efficiency, economy and good practice should be considered. This room is located as centrally as possible with respect to the area to be air conditioned and should be free from obstructing columns. Wherever possible, a separate isolated equipment room should be provided. The clear headroom below soffit of beam should be between 3 – 3.6 m from the finished floor level. The floors of the equipment rooms should be light coloured and finished smooth. While designing the building, structural provisions are made for supporting water pipes on the slabs. Adequate floor-drain for disposal of waste water from the equipment room should be provided. To prevent noise transmission, no windows are generally provided in the equipment room and ventilation is provided by mechanical means. The plant machinery is founded on anti-vibratory supports.

Equipment room for air handling unit is located as centrally as possible of the area air conditioned contiguous to the corridors or other spaces for carrying air ducts. In large and multi-storeyed buildings, depending upon the design of buildings, separate air handling unit rooms are provided. Depending upon the prevailing wind directions, provision is made for the entry of fresh air.

Openings provided in external walls for inlets and outlets of air are shielded properly from weather and insects. They are fitted with corrosion resistant screens of mesh of suitable gauge. All air handling rooms should have proper arrangement for water on the floors. The floor should be light coloured, smooth and finished with terrazo tiles. If possible in the structural design, obstruction to the passage of supply and return air ducts due to beams should be avoided. Acoustical treatment to air handling equipment should be given.

When air is supplied to a number of floors by a centralised air handling unit, air risers for supply ducts and return air are provided. These risers are provided from the roof of the air handling room to the slab of the last floor. The walls of risers in passages or other spaces are constructed initially upto 1 m height and extended upto the ceiling after installation of ducts.

To supply conditioned air, supply ducts and return air ducts are provided on each floor. Provision for sufficient space should be made to accommodate these ducts. The supports which are provided for the ducts are cast with ceiling slabs. A false ceiling should be provided after the installation of the ducts. Independent supports should be provided for false ceilings and ducts. When a duct passes through a masonry wall, it should be lined from outside with felt to isolate the duct from the masonry. Openings in the walls and ceilings are provided for entry and return of air. While constructing a building, provision should be made for a shaft for condenser chilled water and refrigeration pipes from the main equipment room to the air handling unit rooms and cooling towers (if provided).

Sometimes, it is necessary to install a cooling tower on the roof of the building, as it is a source of noise. While designing the structure, load of the cooling tower should be considered. A make up water tank separate from overhead water tank is provided for the cooling tower.

To minimise the heating load and reduce energy cost, necessary precaution should be taken in glazing work. The building should be oriented suitably and minimum glazing is provided in walls subjected to heavy sun exposure. Double glazing or heat resistant glass also helps in reducing the flow of heat. Necessary sun breakers are provided to shade glazed area. Sometimes reflecting surfaces are provided on the exterior walls to reduce the heat load. The exposed roof surfaces, ceilings and floors which are not air conditioned are suitably insulated to reduce thermal transmittance.

A central air conditioning system can be used for the central heating system by providing hot water or steam boilers, heating coils, thermostat etc.

4.1.8 Vertical Circulation: Lifts and Escalators

A lift is an appliance designed to transport persons or materials between two or more levels in a vertical or substantially vertical direction by means of a guided car or platform. An escalator is a power driven inclined continuous stair way used for raising or lowering passengers. The inclination of the stair with the horizontal should not be more than 30° and speed of movement is 45 cm/s. Escalators are arranged in pairs one for upward movement and the other for downward movement. While designing a building, the architect should consider the following points:

1. Number of lifts and size of position of lift well.
2. Particulars of lift well enclosure.
3. Size, position, number and type of landing doors.
4. Number of floors served by the lift.
5. Height between floor levels.
6. Number of entrances.
7. Total headroom.
8. Provision of access to machine room.
9. Provision of ventilation and if possible natural lighting of machine room.
10. Height of machine room.
11. Depth of lift pit.
12. Position of lift machine above or below lift well.
13. Electrical supply requirements of lifts or escalators.

The outline dimensions of machine room, pit depth, total headroom, overhead distance are shown in Tables (4.2) to (4.5).

Table 4.2: Dimensions of Passenger Lifts
(All dimensions in millimetres)

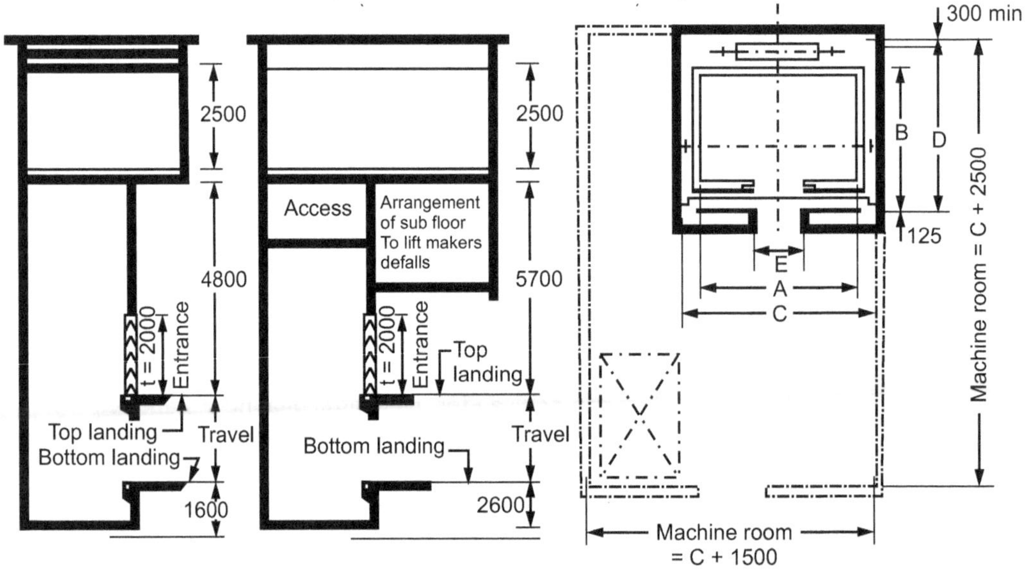

Fig. 4.1

Load		Car Inside		Lift Well		Entrance
Persons	kg	A	B	C	D	E
(1)	(2)	(3)	(4)	(5)	(6)	(7)
4	272	1100	700	1900	1300	800
6	408	1100	1000	1900	1600	800
8	544	1300	1100	1900	1900	800
10	680	1350	1300	1900	2100	800
13	884	2000	1100	2500	1900	900
16	1088	2000	1300	2500	2100	1000
20	1360	2000	1550	2500	2400	1000

Notes:
1. The total headroom has been calculated on the basis of car height of 2.2 m.
2. In the case of manually operated doors, clear entrance will be reduced by the amount of projection of handle on the landing door.
3. Four and six passenger lifts are generally limited to a speed of 1 m/s.

Table 4.3: Dimensions of Goods Lifts (For speeds upto 0.5 m/s)

(All dimensions in millimeters)

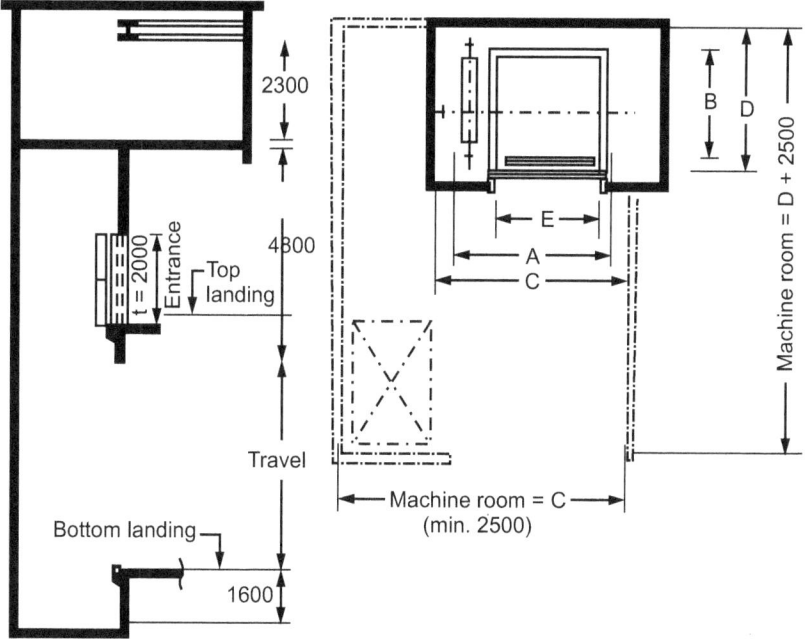

Fig. 4.2

Load	Car Inside		Lift Well		Entrance
kg	A	B	C	D	E
(1)	(2)	(3)	(4)	(5)	(6)
500	1100	1200	1900	1500	1100
1000	1400	1800	2300	2100	1400
1500	1700	2000	2600	2300	1700
2000	1700	2500	2600	2800	1700
2500	2000	2500	2900	2800	2000
3000	2000	3000	2900	3300	2000
4000	2500	3000	3400	3300	2500
5000	2500	3600	3400	3900	2500

Notes:
1. The width of the machine room shall be equal to the lift well width 'C' subject to a minimum of 2500 mm.
2. The total headroom has been calculated on the basis of a car height of 2.2 m.
3. Clear entrance width 'E' is based on vertical lifting car-door and vertical bi-parting doors. For collapsible mid-bar doors, the clear entrance width will get reduced by 200 mm or over, depending on the lift design.

Table 4.4: Dimensions of Hospital Lifts (For speeds upto 1.5 m/s)
(All dimensions in millimeters)

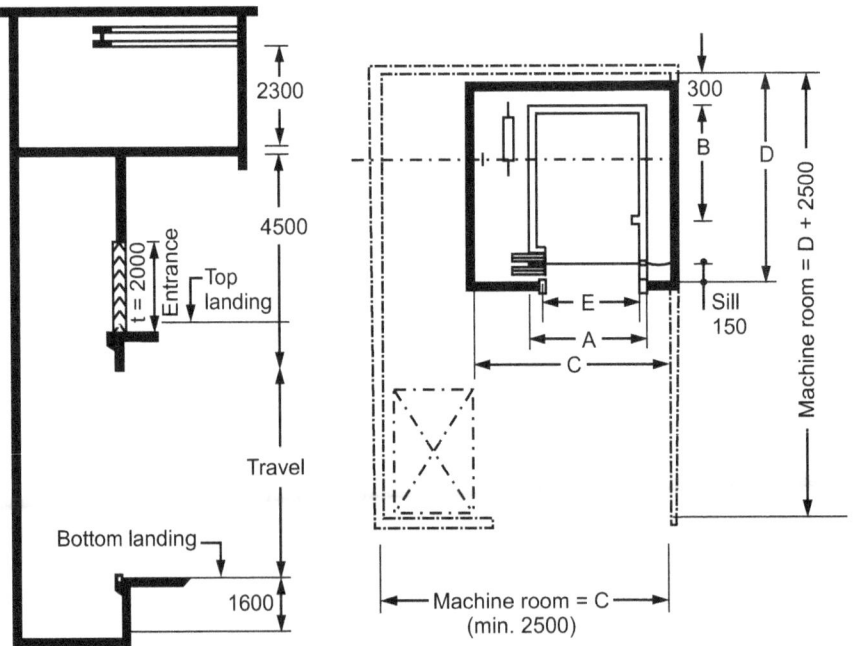

Fig. 4.3

Load		Car Inside		Lift Well		Entrance
Persons	kg	A	B	C	D	E
(1)	(2)	(3)	(4)	(5)	(6)	(7)
15	1020	950	2400	1700	3000	800
20	1360	1300	2400	2200	3000	1200
26	1768	1600	2400	2350	3000	1200

Notes:
1. The total headroom has been calculated on the basis of a car height of 2.2 m.
2. In case of manually operated doors, clear entrance will be reduced by the amount of projection of handle on the landing door.

Table 4.5: Dimensions of Service Lifts (For speeds upto 0.5 m/s)
(All dimensions in millimeters)

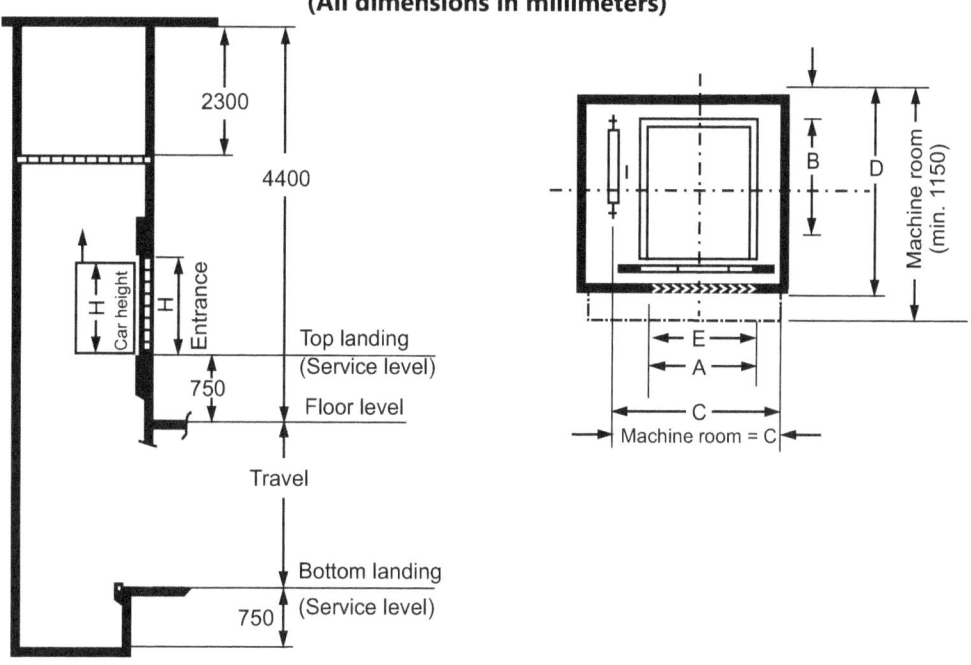

Fig. 4.4

Load	Car Inside			Lift Well		Entrance
kg	A	B	H	C	D	E
(1)	(2)	(3)	(4)	(5)	(6)	(7)
100	700	700	800	1200	900	700
150	800	800	900	1300	1000	800
200	900	900	1000	1400	1100	900
250	1000	1000	1200	1500	1200	1000

Note: Entrance width 'E' is based on assumption of provision of vertical bi-parting doors (no car door is normally provided).

While designing a building, number of lifts and capacity of lifts is determined by considering quantity of service required and the quality of service designed. The other factors which are to be considered are number of floors to be served, number of passengers to be handled, floor area and floor to floor heights. A thorough investigation should be made for assessing the most suitable location for the lifts; the architect should consider the immediate and future requirements. The lifts should be easily accessible from all entrances to the buildings. For better efficiency, lifts are grouped near the centre of the building. The passage provided to the lift should be wide enough for providing space for waiting passengers and for through passengers. The passenger lifts in small residential buildings are placed adjoining a stair case with the lift entrances serving direct on to the landings. In commercial buildings, preferably two or more number of lifts are provided at convenient locations. Sometimes, two lifts serve alternate floors. One lift serves floor numbers 1, 3, 5, 7 etc. and the other 2, 4, 6, 8 etc. While deciding the position of goods lift, the requirements of the industrial units should be considered. The machine room is placed immediately above the lift. A lift pit is provided at the bottom of every lift. This pit should be soundly constructed and maintained in a dry condition by providing necessary drainage.

In the designing of escalators, the factors which are to be considered are:

1. Floor to floor level.
2. Maximum capacity required.
3. The speed of the escalator.
4. Available space.

The escalators should not have angle of inclination more than $30°$. The width of the step (tread) should not be less than 40 cm and the riser between treads should not be less than 20 cm. The tread surface of each step is slotted in a direction parallel to the travel of the steps. A combprate at the entrance and exit of every escalator. The combprate teeth shall be meshed with and set into the slots in the tread surface so that the points of the teeth are always below the upper surface of the treads. Combprate shall be adjustable variety.

4.2 SOLAR WATER HEATING SYSTEM

Solar water heaters, they are also sometimes called solar domestic hot water systems, may be a good investment for you and your family. Solar water heaters are cost competitive in many applications when you account for the total energy costs over the life of the system. Although the initial cost of solar water heaters is higher than that of conventional water heaters, the fuel (sunshine) is free. They are environmentally friendly. To take advantage of these heaters, you must have an unshaded, south-facing location (a roof, for example) on your property.

These systems use the sun to heat either water or a heat-transfer fluid, such as a water-glycol antifreeze mixture, in collectors generally mounted on a roof. The heated water is then stored in a tank similar to a conventional gas or electric water tank. Some systems use an electric pump to circulate the fluid through the collectors.

Solar water heaters can operate in any climate. Performance varies depending, in part, on how much solar energy is available at the site, but also on how cold the water coming into the system is. The colder the water, the more efficiently the system operates.

Solar Water Heater Basics:

Solar water heaters are made up of collectors, storage tanks, and depending on the system, electric pumps.

There are basically three types of collectors: flat-plate, evacuated-tube and concentrating. A flat-plate collector, the most common type, is an insulated, weather-proofed box containing a dark absorber plate under one or more transparent or translucent covers.

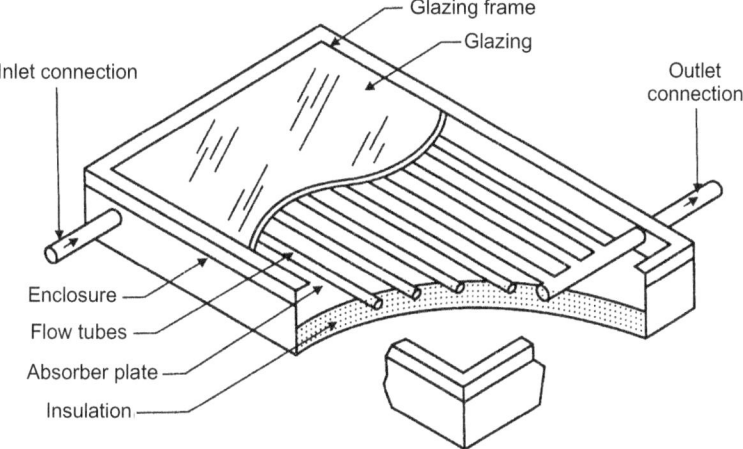

Fig. 4.5: Flat-plate collector

Evacuated-tube collectors are made up of rows of parallel, transparent glass tubes. Each tube consists of a glass outer tube and an inner tube, or absorber, covered with a selective coating that absorbs solar energy well but inhibits radiative heat loss. The air is withdrawn ("evacuated") from the space between the tubes to form a vacuum, which eliminates conductive and convective heat loss.

Concentrating collectors for residential applications are usually parabolic troughs that use mirrored surfaces to concentrate the sun's energy on an absorber tube (called a receiver) containing a heat transfer fluid.

Most commercially available solar water heaters require a well-insulated storage tank. Many systems use converted electric water heater tanks or plumb the solar storage tank in series with the conventional water heater.

Some solar water heaters use pumps to recirculate warm water from storage tanks through collectors and exposed piping. This is generally to protect the pipes from freezing when outside temperatures drop to freezing or below.

Types of Solar Water Heaters:

Solar water heaters can be either active or passive. An active system uses an electric pump to circulate the heat-transfer fluid; a passive system has no pump. The amount of hot water a solar water heater produces depends on the type and size of the system, the amount of sun available at the site, proper installation, and the tilt angle and orientation of the collectors. Solar water heaters are also characterized as open loop (also called "direct") or closed loop (also called "indirect"). An open-loop system circulates household (potable) water through the collector. A closed-loop system uses a heat-transfer fluid (water or diluted antifreeze, for example) to collect heat and a heat exchanger to transfer the heat to household water.

Active Systems:

Active systems use electric pumps, valves, and controllers to circulate water or other heat-transfer fluids through the collectors. They are usually more expensive than passive systems but are also more efficient. Active systems are usually easier to retrofit than passive systems because their storage tanks do not need to be installed above or close to the collectors.

Open-Loop Active Systems:

Open-loop active systems use pumps to circulate household water through the collectors. This design is efficient and lowers operating costs but is not appropriate if your water is hard or acidic because scale and corrosion quickly disable the system.

These open-loop systems are popular in non-freezing climates such as Hawaii. They should never be installed in climates that experience freezing temperatures for sustained periods. You can install them in mild but occasionally freezing climates, but you must consider freeze protection.

Recirculation systems are a specific type of open-loop system that provide freeze protection. They use the system pump to circulate warm water from storage tanks through collectors and exposed piping when temperatures approach freezing. Consider recirculation systems only where mild freezes occur once or twice a year at most. Activating the freeze protection more frequently wastes electricity and stored heat.

Ofcourse, when the power is out, the pump will not work and the system will freeze. To guard against this, a freeze valve can be installed to provide additional protection in the event the pump doesn't operate. In freezing weather, the valve dribbles warmer water through the collector to prevent freezing.

Closed-Loop Active Systems:

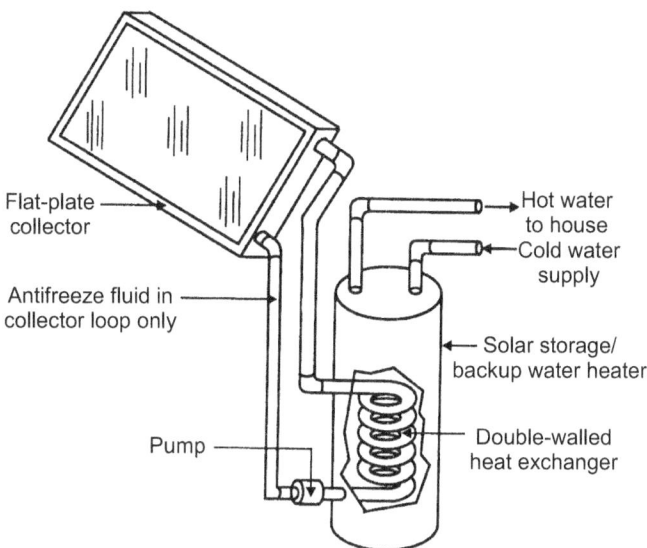

Fig. 4.6: Closed-loop Active System

These systems pump heat-transfer fluids (usually a glycol-water antifreeze mixture) through collectors. Heat exchangers transfer the heat from the fluid to the household water stored in the tanks.

Double-walled heat exchangers prevent contamination of household water. Some codes require double walls when the heat transfer fluid is anything other than household water.

Closed-loop glycol systems are popular in areas subject to extended freezing temperatures because they offer good freeze protection. However, glycol antifreeze systems are a bit more expensive to buy and install, and the glycol must be checked each year and changed every 3 to 10 years, depending on glycol quality and system temperatures.

Drainback systems use water as the heat transfer fluid in the collector loop. A pump circulates the water through the collectors. The water drains by gravity to the storage tank and heat exchanger; there are no valves to fail. When the pumps are off, the collectors are empty, which assures freeze protection and also allows the system to turn off if the water in the storage tank becomes too hot.

Pumps in Active Systems:

The pumps in solar water heaters have low power requirements, and some companies now include direct current (D.C.) pumps powered by small solar-electric (photovoltaic, or PV) panels. PV panels convert sunlight into D.C. electricity. Such systems cost nothing to operate and continue to function during power outages.

Passive Systems:

Passive systems move household water or a heat-transfer fluid through the system without pumps. Passive systems have no electric components to break. This makes them generally more reliable, easier to maintain, and possibly longer lasting than active systems.

Passive systems can be less expensive than active systems, but they can also be less efficient.

Batch Heaters:

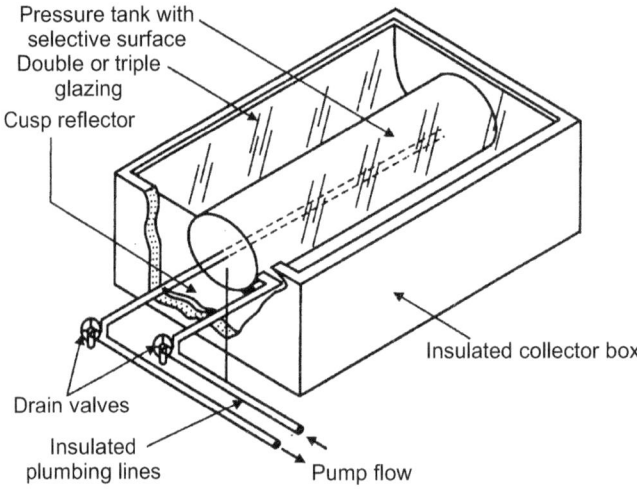

Fig. 4.7: Batch solar collector

Batch heaters (also known as "bread box" or integral collector storage systems) are simple passive systems consisting of one or more storage tanks placed in an insulated box that has a glazed side facing the sun. Batch heaters are inexpensive and have few components, in other words, less maintenance and fewer failures. A batch heater is mounted on the ground or on the roof (make sure your roof structure is strong enough to support it). Some batch heaters use "selective" surfaces on the tank(s). These surfaces absorb sun well but inhibit radiative loss. In climates where freezing occurs, batch heaters must either be protected from freezing or drained for the winter. In well designed systems, the most vulnerable components for freezing are the pipes, if located in uninsulated areas, that lead to the solar water heater. If these pipes are well insulated, the warmth from the tank will prevent freezing. Certified systems clearly state the temperature level that can cause damage. In addition, you can install heat tape (electrical plug-in tape to wrap around the pipes to keep them from freezing), insulate exposed pipes, or both. Remember, heat tape requires electricity, so the combination of freezing weather and a power outage can lead to burst pipes.

Thermosiphon Systems:

A thermosiphon system relies on warm water rising, a phenomenon known as natural convection, to circulate water through the collectors and to the tank. In this type of installation, the tank must be above the collector. As water in the collector heats, it becomes lighter and rises naturally into the tank above. Meanwhile, cooler water in the tank flows down pipes to the bottom of the collector, causing circulation throughout the system. The storage tank is attached to the top of the collector so that thermosiphoning can occur. These systems are reliable and relatively inexpensive but require careful planning in new construction because the water tanks are heavy. They can be freeze-proofed by circulating an antifreeze solution through a heat exchanger in a closed loop to heat the household water.

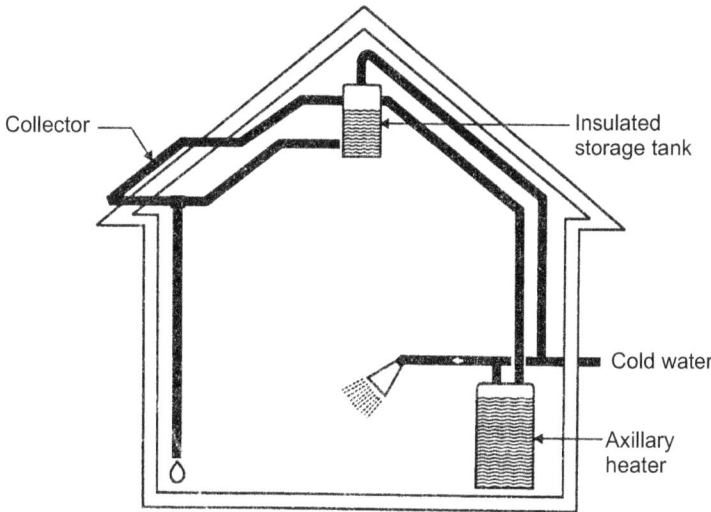

Fig. 4.8: Thermosiphon solar water heater

Benefits of Solar Water Heaters:

There are many benefits to owning a solar water heater, and number one is economics. Solar water heater economics compare quite favorably with those of electric water heaters, while the economics are not quite so attractive when compared with those of gas water heaters. Heating water with the sun also means long-term benefits, such as being cushioned from future fuel shortages and price increases, and environmental benefits.

Fig. 4.9: Evacuated Tube Collector (ETC) based on solar water heater

4.3 PLUMBING SERVICES

A plumbing system includes the water supply and distribution pipes, plumbing fittings and traps, soil, pipes, vent pipes and antisiphonage pipes, building drains and building sewers including their respective connections, devices and appurtenances within the property lines of the premises and water treating or water using equipment.

4.4 WATER SUPPLY REQUIREMENTS FOR BUILDINGS

The requirements regarding water supply, drainage and sanitation for residences shall assume, that a minimum water supply of 200 litres per head per day is assured together with a full flushing system. In case of Lower Income Group (LIG) and Economically Weaker

Sections of society (EWS), the minimum value of water supply may be reduced to 135 litres per head per day. Requirements of water supply for buildings other than residences are given in Table 4.6.

Table 4.6: Water Requirements for Buildings other than Residences

Sr. No.	Type of Building	Consumption per head per day (litres)
(1)	(2)	(3)
(i)	Factories where bathrooms are required to be provided.	45
(ii)	Factories where no bathrooms are required to be provided.	30
(iii)	Hospitals (including laundry) per bed:	
	(a) Number of beds not exceeding 100	340
	(b) Number of beds exceeding 100	450
(iv)	Nurses homes and medical quarters	135
(v)	Hostels	135
(vi)	Hotels (per bed)	180
(vii)	Offices	45
(viii)	Restaurants (per seat)	70
(ix)	Cinema halls, concert halls and theatres (per seat)	15
(x)	Schools:	
	(a) Day schools	45
	(b) Boarding schools	135

General Requirements of Plumbing System:

1. The plumbing work which is required to be carried out in a building should be executed only by a licensed plumber under the control of the authority and should be responsible to carry out all lawful directions given by the authority.
2. All premises intended for human habitation, occupancy or use should be provided with the supply of pure and wholesome water.

3. Plumbing fixtures, devices and appurtenances should be supplied with water in sufficient volume and at pressures adequate to enable them to function satisfactorily without undue noise under all normal conditions of use. There should be atleast a residual head of 0.018 N/mm² at the consumer's tap.
4. Plumbing system should be designed and adjusted to use the minimum quantity of water required for proper performance and cleaning.
5. Plumbing fixtures, installed in a building should be connected to a public sewer. If such a sewer does not exist near the building, suitable arrangements like septic tanks and soak pits should be made.

4.5 STORAGE OF WATER

In a building, provision is required to be made for storage of water for the following reasons:
1. To provide against interruptions in supply caused by repairs to mains,
2. To reduce the maximum rate of demand on the mains,
3. To tide over periods of non-supply in an intermittent supply system.
4. To maintain a storage for fire fighting requirement of the building (optional) minimum 10,000 litres.

As per I.S. 2065 – latest the storage capacity required, for premises occupied by tenements with common conveniences is calculated at the rate of 500 litres per tenement on each floor. For premises occupied as flats or blocks, the storage requirement is calculated as 8000 litres per tenement.

Reservoirs and tanks for reception and storage of water can be constructed of reinforced concrete, cast iron, galvanised mild steel plates. These tanks should be covered with a close fitting, dust tight, insect and fly-proof lid. These tanks are constructed either underground, above ground or above the building (overhead tanks). If the storage capacity required is more than 5000 litres, it is advantageous to arrange it in a series of tanks, so interconnected that each tank can be isolated for cleaning and inspection without interfering with the supply of water. The design of an underground storage tank is carried out with a provision for the draining of the tank when necessary.

The quantity of water to be stored is calculated by considering the following factors:
1. Supply rate, pressure and water supply hours to fill up the overhead storage tanks.
2. Frequency of replenishment of overhead tanks during 24 hours.
3. Regularity in water supply.
4. Types of building like public buildings, school buildings, hospitals etc.

The water supply system consists of municipal water supply mains, distributing pipes, consumers pipes, stopcocks, various types of taps, underground storage tanks, overhead reservoirs etc. Water is supplied to kitchen, bathrooms, W.C. etc. by service pipes and valves. The water supply arrangement in a multi-storeyed building is shown in Fig. 4.10.

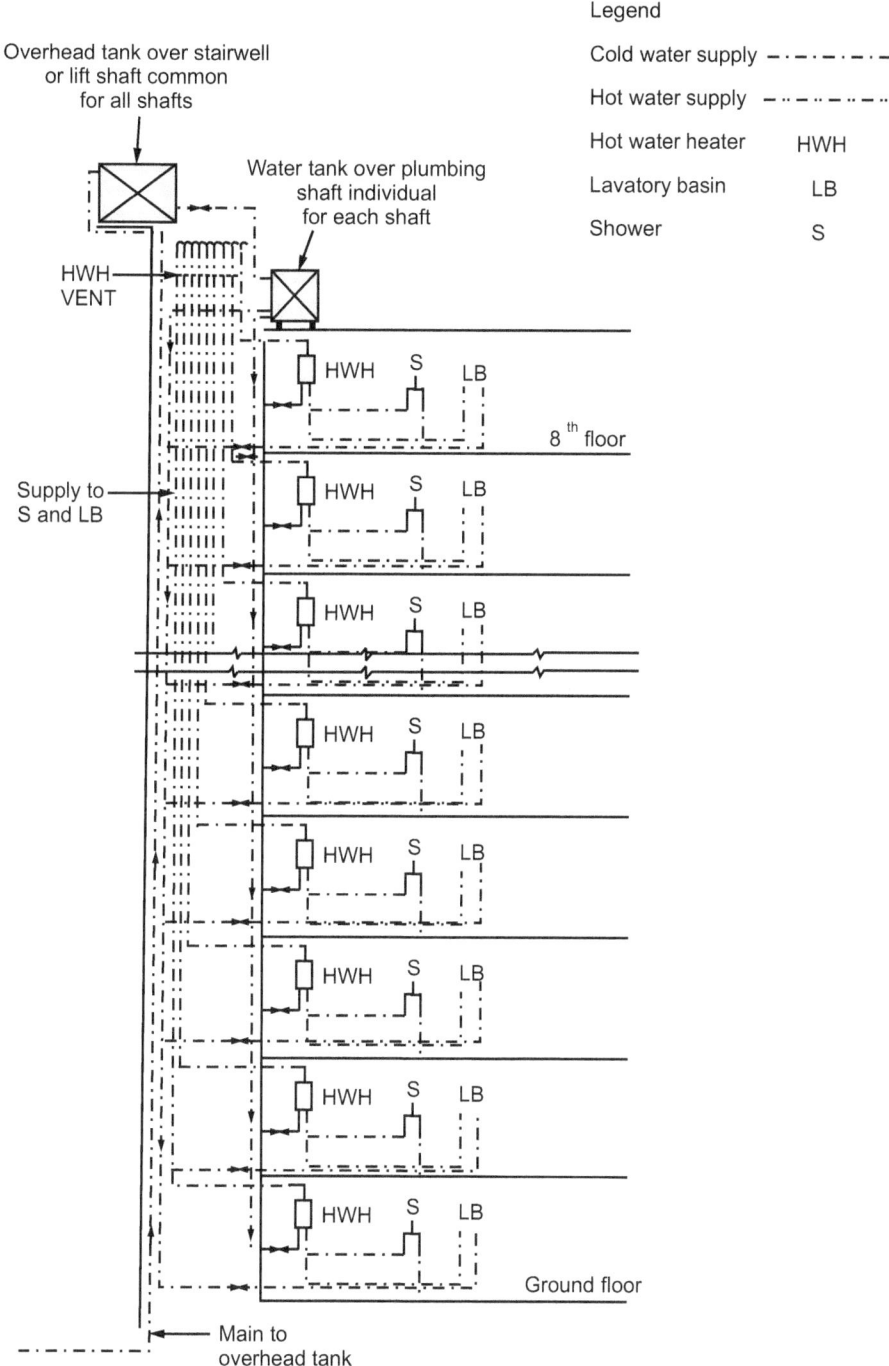

Fig. 4.10: Installation of water supply connections for 8-storeyed building

4.6 LAYOUT OF WATER SUPPLY AND DRAINAGE SYSTEM

Before commencing the plumbing work, a detailed layout showing the arrangements for water supply and drainage is prepared. The layout plan should contain location of service main water supply line, position of underground and overhead tanks, position of service connection depending upon various units of the building. It should also contain details regarding the drainage system which includes street sewer line, positions of manholes, inspection chambers, gully traps, drainage lines for sewage and sullage and rain water. The direction of flow should also be marked on this layout. A layout for water supply and drainage system for a multi-storeyed structure is shown in Fig. 4.11 on last page.

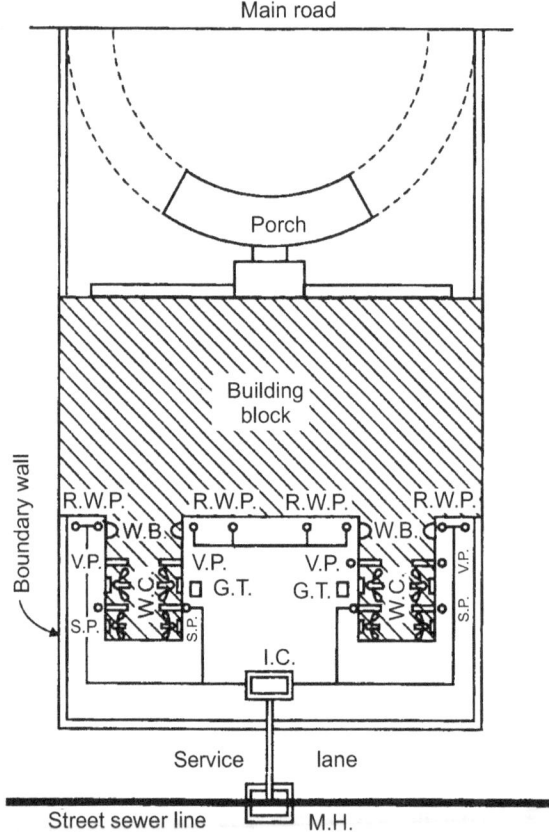

Fig. 4.11: Typical drainage layout plant of a terrace house drained at back

House Drainage Plans:

Before starting the plumbing work, it is most essential first to prepare the drainage plans. In the same way detailed drawings are prepared before the starting of the construction of buildings, the detailed drainage plans should be also be prepared.

The following points should be kept in mind while preparing the drainage plans:

(i) The drains should be laid in such a way so as to remove the sewage quickly from the building. The quick removal is governed by the fall of the pipes. The drains should be laid at such a slope that self-cleaning velocity is developed in them. The following slopes are usually sufficient:

1 in 40 for	10 cm pipe
1 in 60 for	15 cm pipe
1 in 90 for	23 cm pipe

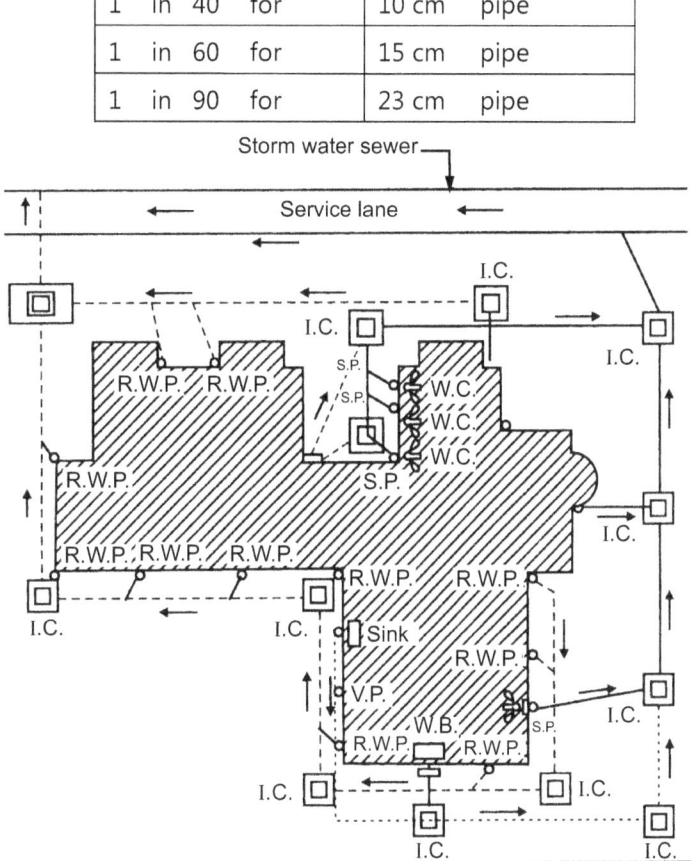

Fig. 4.12: Typical drainage layout of a large building

4.7 PLUMBING SYSTEM FOR WASTE WATER

The removal of any liquid by a system constructed for the purpose is called as drainage system. In designing a drainage system for an individual building, the aim is to provide a system of self cleaning conduits for conveyance of foul, a surface or subsurface waters.

And for the removal of such waste speedily and efficiently to a sewer or other outlet without risk of nuisance and hazard to people. The different types of wastes, which are required to be removed through the drainage system, include night soil (waste from W.C.), sullage from bath and kitchen and rain water collected over the building or on the premises. In the drainage system, generally, rain water is dealt with separately from sewage and sullage.

Following are the main systems of plumbing for the building drainage:

(a) Two-pipe System:
   (i) This is the most common system used in India. This method provides an ideal solution, where it is not possible to fix the fixture closely.
   (ii) All the drainage system should be properly ventilated on the house side. The ventilation pipe should be carried sufficiently high above the buildings. All the inspection chambers should provided with fresh air inlets.
   (iii) All the drains should be laid in such a way so as to ensure their safety in future.
   (iv) The drain should be laid in such a way that in future extension can be done easily if desired.
   (v) If the quantity of sewage flowing in a pipe is small, an automatic flushing tank may be provided on its top for flushing it.
   (vi) All the rain water pipes, sweeping from house and bath water should discharge over gully traps and should be disconnected from the drain.
   (vii) All soil pipes should be carried direct to the manholes without gully traps.

In this system, two pipes are provided. One pipe collects the foul soil and lavatory wastes, whereas the second pipe collects the unfoul water from kitchen, bathrooms, house washings, rain water etc. The soil pipes (pipes carrying the soil waste) are directly connected to the drain whereas the waste pipes (pipes carrying unfoul waste water) are connected through the gully trap. All the traps used in this system are fully ventilated.

(b) One-pipe System:

In this system, only one main pipe is provided which collects both the foul soil waste as well as unfoul waste from the buildings. The main pipe is directly connected to the drainage system. If this system is provided in multi-storeyed buildings the lavatory blocks of various floors are so placed one over the other, so that the waste water discharged from the different units can be carried through short branch drains.

All the traps of the W.C., basins, sinks etc. are fully ventilated and connected to the ventilation pipe.

(c) Single-stack System:

This is similar to single pipe system, the only difference being that no ventilation is provided even in the traps too.

(d) Single-stack Partially Ventilated System:

This system is in between the one pipe and single-stack system. In this system, only one pipe is provided to collect all types of waste water foul as well as unfoul. A relief vent pipe is provided for ventilating only the water closet-traps.

Now-a-days in modern multi-storeyed buildings one pipe system is becoming popular due to its low cost. C.B.R.I. Roorkee, after doing extensive research on this system, has recommended it in modern buildings. An analysis of this system showed that the flow from the appliance to the stack through branch is momentarily halted at the sharp change of flow of direction. Sometimes a plug of water is formed immediately at the junction, which depends upon the rate of change of discharge and the size of branch. This gives rise to unequal pressures at the seals for the lower floors of the building and sometimes this breaks the water seals of the sanitary appliances. C.B.R.I. has recommended the use of aerator and deaerator in the stack to increase its capacity.

The function of the **aerator** is to prevent the formation of the plugs of water in the vertical stack and to make a mixture of water and air of low specific gravity. The aerators are provided at every floor.

  (a) For supply of water to various sanitary fittings.
  (b) For collection of waste water from the sanitary fittings.
  (c) For collection of rain water from the roofs, house and courtyard washings.

The fixing of sanitary appliances in the walls, floor and other places and their connected pipe works are to be done carefully for their proper functioning.

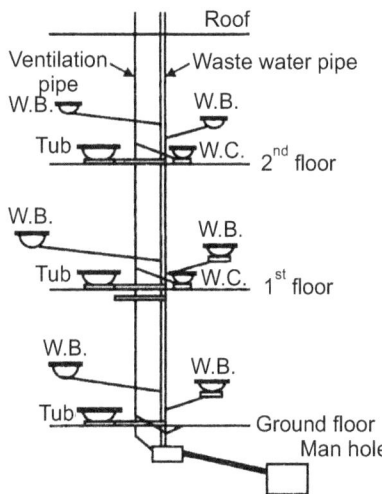

Fig. 4.13: Single stack partially ventilated system

Deaerators are provided at the foot of the stack to separate air and water to avoid excessive back pressure. Studies carried out by C.B.R.I. revealed that 100 mm diameter stack with these fittings can be safely used upto 15 storeys, whereas a single stack system without these fittings can be used only upto 5 storeys.

The two pipe system is costly as it requires much labour and material with antisyphonage pipe, as compared with single stack system of plumbing. No antisyphonage pipe is required. The single stack system is becoming popular in the modern building construction. The tests done by C.B.R.I. on 5 storeyed building shows that there was no break of water seals. As it is the common practice in India to discharge the waste water from the sinks and wash basin to the floor trap, therefore, sanitary appliance carrying, unfoul waste water do not require deeper seals. 100 mm diameter stack with two appliances at each floor can be safely used upto 5 storeyed building.

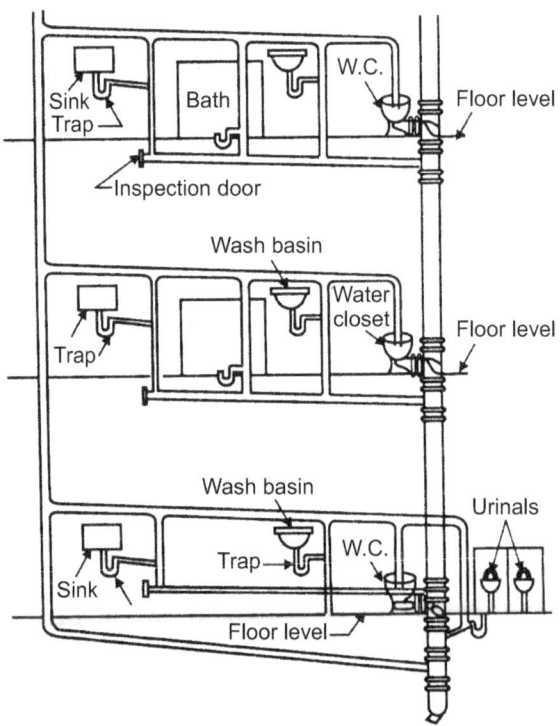

Fig. 4.14: Plumbing work of one-pipe system

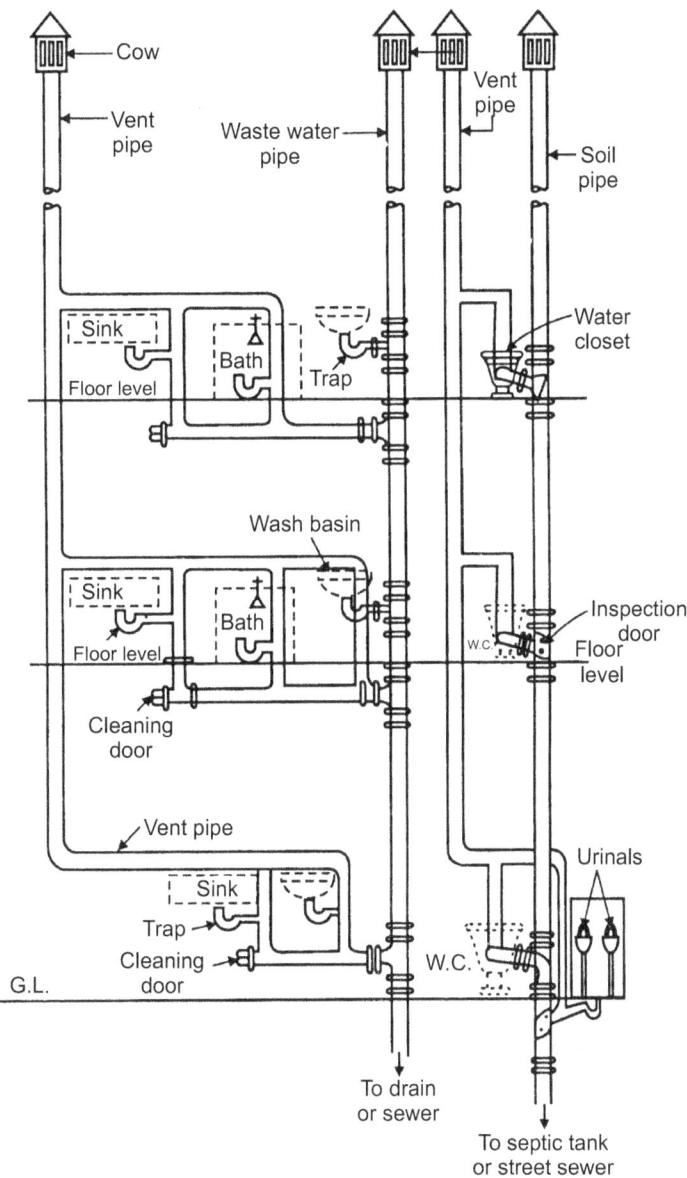

Fig. 4.15: Plumbing work of two-pipe system

Septic Tank: In the rural areas and the fringe areas of suburban towns and also in case of isolated buildings and institutions, hostels, hotel, hospital, school, small residential colonies, underground sewage system with complete treatment of sewage may be neither feasible nor economical. Under such cases septic tanks followed by subsurface disposal of effluent are provided. In the areas having porous soil, this method gives satisfactory results. The location of the septic tanks should be as far as possible away from the buildings, and should not be located in swampy areas or areas prone to flooding. In case of clayey, non-porous soils or where houses are closely spaced, suitably designed leading pits may have to be used, if septic tank cannot be avoided. The septic tank effluent should not be allowed into open drainage system, because it may cause health hazards, nuisance and mosquit, breeking. If the facilities for connection to a sewer are available, the effluent from the septic tank should be connected to sewers.

Also it should be located at the lowest contour.

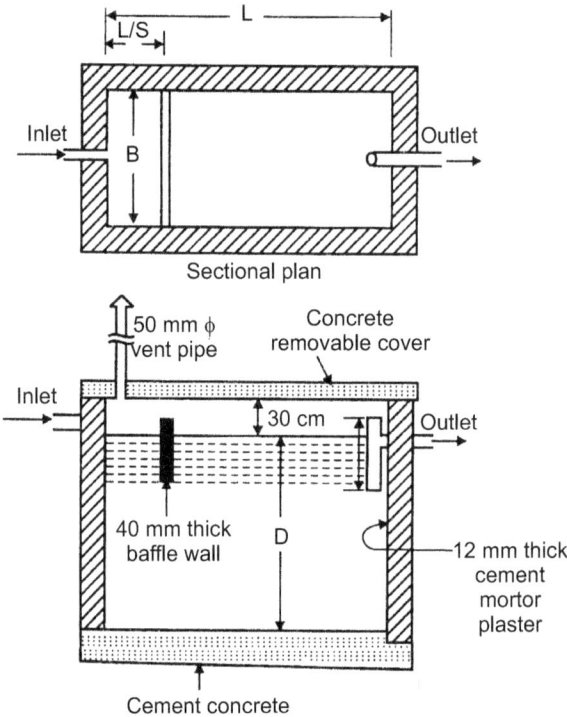

Fig. 4.16: Septic tank

Sewage Flow:

The maximum flow of sewage to the tank is based on the number of plumbing fixtures discharging simultaneously rather than the number of users and per capita waste water flow expected to reach the septic tank. For this purpose various sanitation appliances such as water closets, wash basins, bath etc. are equated in terms of fixture units as given in Table 4.2. A fixture unit is a standard receptacle which gives a discharge of 10 lpm when flushed.

Table 4.7: Fixture equivalents

Sanitary fixture	Equivalent fixture unit
1. Water closet	1.0
2. Bath	0.5
3. Wash basin/kitchen sink	0.5
4. Urinal with automatic flush	1.0
5. Urinal without automatic flush	0.5
6. Slope sink	1.0
7. Ablution tap	0.5
8. Dish washer	0.5
9. Combination fixture	1.0
10. Laboratory sink	2.0
11. Shower bath	1.0
12. Bath tub	2.0
13. Drinking fountain	0.5

Tables 4.8, 4.9 and 4.10 gives the estimated number of fixture units and the number of fixture units that contribute to the peak discharge in small installations-residential colonies and hostels etc.

Table 4.8: Estimated peak discharge for small establishments

Number of users	Number of fixture units	Probable no. of fixture units discharging simultaneously	Probable peak discharge lmp
5	1	1	10
10	2	2	20
15	3	2	20
20	4	3	30
25	5	4	40
30	6	4	40
35	7	5	50
40	8	6	60
45	9	6	60
50	10	7	70

Table 4.9: Estimated peak discharge for residential housing colonies

No. of users	No. of house holds	No. of fixture units	Probable peak discharge based on 60% fixture units discharging simultaneously in lpm
100	20	40	240
150	30	60	360
200	40	80	480
300	60	120	720

Table 4.10: Estimated peak discharge for casting establishments boarding schools and similar establishments

No. of Users	W.C.	Bath	Wash basin kitchen sink	No. of fixture units	Probable peak discharge based on 70% fixture units discharging simultaneously in lpm
50	6	6	6	12	84
100	12	12	12	24	168
150	19	19	19	38	266
200	25	25	25	50	350
300	37	37	37	74	518

Construction Details:

Following are the construction details of septic tanks:

(a) It is rectangular in plan, the length is usually 2 to 4 times the breadth.

(b) For smaller tanks liquid depth of 100 cm is provided, for larger tanks it may be upto 180 cm. Free board of 30-45 cm is provided above the level of liquid for fixing of pipes, scum, gases etc.

(c) An elbow pipe, usually T-pipe submerged to a depth of 15-25 cm below the liquid level is provided as inlet pipe. More number of inlet pipes may be provided for larger tanks.

(d) Single elbow or T-shaped outlet pipe is provided. It should also be submerged at least 15 cm below the liquid level. For very large tanks, weir type outlet similar to settling tanks are provided.

(e) In smaller tanks one baffle of hanging type is enough, the bafflet is usually placed 20 to 30 cm from the inlet pipe and remains 15 cm above and 30 cm below the liquid level. Outlet baffle is provided only in large tanks, when weir type outlet is provided.

(f) Usually R.C.C. slab with C.I., manhole covers are provided.

(g) Ventilation pipe of usually 7.5 to 10 cm diameter of A.C. or C.I. is used for taking out the foul smells. Their tops are provided with cowls.

Table 4.11: The sizes of septic tanks as per I.S. 2470 (Part I) 1963

No. of users	Length L	Breadth B	Liquid depth D min.	Liquid capacity to be provided	Free board min.	Sludge to be removed	Recommended interval of cleaning
	metre	metre	metre	m³	cm	m³	
1	2	3	4	5	6	7	8
5	1.5	0.75	1.0	1.12	30	0.18	6 months
			1.0	1.12	30	0.36	1 year
			1.05	1.18	30	0.72	2 years
10	2	0.9	1.0	1.8	30	0.36	6 months
			1.0	1.8	30	0.72	1 year
			1.4	2.52	30	1.44	2 years
15	2	0.9	1.0	1.8	30	0.54	6 months
			1.3	2.34	30	1.08	1 year
			2.0	3.6	30	2.16	2 years
20	2.3	1.1	1.0	2.53	30	0.72	6 months
			1.3	3.3	30	1.44	1 year
			1.8	4.55	30	2.88	2 years
50	4	1.4	1.0	5.6	30	1.8	6 months
			1.3	7.28	30	3.6	1 year
			2.0	11.2	30	7.2	2 years

Design of Septic Tanks:

As septic tank is a settling-cum-digestion tank, it requires space for:
(i) Settling of incoming sewage.
(ii) Degestion of the settled sludge.
(iii) Storage of digested sludge till it is taken out.

Design for space for settling: This is calculated for the average flow and detention period. Smaller tanks are designed on the basis of average flow and 24 hours detention period, while larger tanks are designed for 12 hours detention period.

Both surface area and detention of depth are important factors in the settling of flocculant particles such as sewage solids. For average Indian conditions at a temperature of 25°C, the surface area required will be 0.92 m² for every 10 lpm peak rate flow. This is based on 75% removal of sewage particles of 0.05 mm size and above with a specific gravity of 1.2. A minimum depth of sedimentation of 25-30 cm is necessary. The length of the septic tank is kept 2-4 times the breadth.

If only the discharge from the latrines flow is in the septic tank, the average flow per capita per day may be taken as 45 litres. On the other hand if all the waste water of the houses is to be treated in septic tank the average flow should be taken per capita per day depending on the water supply.

Design for digestion space: In the septic tank, the operation goes in natural way and there is no control over all it such as mixing, heating, etc. a provision of 0.0425 m^3 per capita should be done for it.

The fresh sludge stay in the tank should be long enough to undergo satisfactory anaerobic digestion so that as much of the organic matter as possible may be destroyed and the sludge may become innocuous and suitable for dewatering or drying. The time required for digestion depends on the temperature. The per capita suspended solids entering the septic tank may be taken as 70 gm/day. Assuming that 60% of the solids are removed along with fresh sludge, of which 70% is volatile, with a solid content of 5% or moisture 95%, the volume of fresh sludge works out to 0.00083 m^3/cap./day. Now considering that 2/4 of the volatile matter is destroyed of which 1/4 is mineralised during digestion and solid content of 13% in the digested sludge, the volume of the digested sludge works out to 0.0002 m^3/cap./day. The digestion zone contains both fresh and digesting sludge. Therefore, the digestion space should provide for the average volume of the mixture of fresh and digested sludge which works out to 0.000515 m^3/cap./day. Now based on the period of digestion, the capacity required for the digestion zone can be worked out. At 25°C, the capacity for sludge digestion works out to 0.032 m^3/capita.

Design of space for storage of digested sludge: The digested sludge produced per capita in different periods is as follows:

Table 4.12

Period of Cleaning	Storage capacity
6 months	0.0283 m^3
1 year	0.049 m^3
2 years	0.0708 m^3
3 years	0.085 m^3

The design of space for storage of digested sludge is done on the basis of period of cleaning and the number of persons using the tank.

Adequate space should be provided in the septic tank for the storage of digested sludge and scum, otherwise their accumulation interferes with the efficiency of the tank by encroaching upon the space provided for sedimentation and digestion. A sludge storage capacity of 7.3 m^3/100 persons for an interval of cleaning of one year is provided below the sedimentation zone.

Total Capacity: The tank should also provide for a free board of atleast 30 cm, which should be sufficient to include the scum depth above the liquid surface. Addition capacity for seed sludge is not required. Care should be taken to leave 25-50 mm depth digested sludge for seed purpose. When the cleaning is yearly, at 25°C for 10 persons the tank capacity shall be 2.15 m as per details below:

(i) Sedimentation = Probable Peak flow 320 lpm

Area required = $\dfrac{0.92 \, (m^2)}{10 \, (lpm)}$ = 1.84 m^2

Provided a depth of 30, volume = 1.84 × 3 = 0.55 m^3
(ii) Digestion space = 0.32 m^3
(iii) Space for sludge storage = 0.73 m^3
(iv) Space for free board including 0.25 m^3
for seed sludge (1.84 × 0.3) = 0.055 m^3

Total = 2.15 m^3

A septic tank designed on the criteria given above normally provides a detention period of 24-48 hours, based on an average daily flow of sewage. But as the average daily flow varies so widely from one installation to another, detention period should not be considered as an important criteria for the design of septic tanks.

Example 4.1: Design a septic tank for 50 users, assuming the rate of water supply as 60 litres/head/day.

Solution: Assuming the detention period as 24 hours and the time of cleaning the sludge as 3 years.

Space required for setting = $\dfrac{50 \times 60}{1000}$

= 3.0 m^3

Space required for design = 50 × 0.0425

= 2.125 m^3

Space required for storage of sludge

= 50 × 0.085

= 4.25 m^3

Total space required = 3.0 + 2.125 + 4.25

= 9.375 m^3

= (9.5 m^3) say

Providing free board of 30 cm.

Provide the septic tank of 4 × 1.4 × 2.0 metres.

Garbage Disposal Arrangement:

Refuse is all the solid and semisolid waste matter of a community except night soil. It can be broadly divided into two parts:

(1) Organic matter, (2) Inorganic matter.

The organic matter of the refuse is very offensive and creates health problems. The quantity and quality of refuse depends on various factors such as season, climatic condition, geographic location, habits of people, standards of living, etc. Garbage includes all sorts of putrescible waste obtained from hotels, restaurants, kitchens etc. Garbage should be handled carefully as flies, insects, rats etc. breed in it. Garbage decomposes very quickly and produces unpleasant odours. Garbage can be used after proper processing as fertilizer.

The garbage is stored in the houses, industries and business centres, temporarily in containers and it is dumped periodically in the refuse collection boxes or chambers provided along the streets for this purpose. In multi-storeyed buildings, refuse chute system is provided for collecting and transporting in a sanitary way.

This system has three components:
1. The chutes
2. Inlet hopper
3. Collection chamber.

Occupants of the building from successive floors drop their refuse into the inlets and the refuse is collected in the collecting chamber from where the refuse is cleared at suitable intervals. The inlet hopper is located in the passage near the kitchen or at the end of a common passage. Sufficient ventilation and lighting should be provided near the inlets. The collection chamber is provided at ground level for easy clearance.

IMPORTANT POINTS

- Solar water heating system its need and location.
- Accessories for making solar water heaters.
- Types of solar water heaters :
  (I) Active Systems
      (a) Open-loop active systems (b) Closed-loop active systems.
  (II) Passive system of solar water heater
- Plumbing system for waste water and its types:
  (a) Two pipe system
  (b) One pipe-system
  (c) Single-stack
  (d) Single-stack partially ventilated system
- Septic tank, its need and location. Construction details of septic tank along with its three design parameters.
- Utility of septic tank.
- Garbage disposal system with components.

QUESTIONS

1. What are the requirements of plumbing system?
2. Explain one-pipe and two-pipe plumbing system.
3. Explain two pipe plumbing system.

UNIT 2

Chapter 5

PLANNING OF RESIDENTIAL BUILDINGS

5.1 INTRODUCTION

As per National Building Code of India (SP : 7-1970) Residential Buildings (Group A) are those buildings in which sleeping accommodation is provided for normal residential purposes, with or without cooking or dining or both facilities. It is a building, where one dwells or resides permanently or for a considerable time can be called as a residential building; it may be a bunglow, a block of flats, a hill side cottage or a hotel. Every type of residential building serves the purpose of dwelling in one way or the other, only there is difference of type. Buildings of group A are further sub-divided as follows:

(i) **Sub-division A-1: Lodging or Rooming Houses:** These include any building or group of buildings under the same management, in which separate sleeping accommodation for a total of not more than 15 persons, on either transient or permanent basis with or without dining facilities, but without cooking facilities for individuals, is provided.

A lodging or rooming house is classified as a dwelling in sub-division A-2 if no room in any of its private dwelling units is rented to more than three persons.

(ii) **Sub-division A-2: One or two Family Private Dwellings:** These include any private dwelling which is occupied by members of a single family and has a total sleeping accommodation for not more than 20 persons.

If rooms in a private dwelling are rented to outsiders, these should be for accommodating not more than 3 persons.

If sleeping accommodation for more than 20 persons is provided in any one residential building, it should be classified as a building sub-division A-3 or A-4 as the case may be.

(iii) **Sub-division A-3: Dormitories:** These include any building in which group sleeping accommodation is provided, with or without dining facilities, for persons who are not members of the same family, in any one room or a management, for example, school and college dormitories, students and other hostels and military barracks.

(iv) Sub-division A-4: Apartment Houses (Flats): These include any building or structure in which living quarters are provided for three or more families living independently of each other and with independent cooking facilities, for example, apartment houses, mansions and chawls.

(v) Sub-division A-5: Hotels: These include any building or group of buildings under single management in which sleeping accommodation, with or without dining facilities, is provided for hire to more than 15 persons who are primarily transient, for example, hotels, inns, clubs and motels.

5.2 SITE SELECTION

In case of buildings, particularly residential, selection of a site and designs of a building before its construction, are two important aspects. Every individual has a desire to live in an ecofriendly atmosphere with a good aspect for all the natural benefits like light, air etc.

Therefore, before starting planning of any residential building, following main points should be considered by planner.

(a) Climate of site and its effects.
(b) Living habits of the owner and his requirements.
(c) Budget of owner.
(d) Bye-laws and regulations for sanctioning.
(e) Materials of construction and method of construction.

5.3 TYPES OF STRUCTURE

1. Load bearing structure.
2. Framed structure.
3. Composite structure.

1. Load Bearing Structure:

In this method, the entire load of the structure is transmitted through the brick or stone masonry walls of a structure. The walls are supported on continuous foundations, which are resting on firm soil at shallow depth. Load bearing structure can be constructed maximum upto four storeys, but usually two storeys are constructed. In this type of structure, beam and trusses etc. rest on a load bearing walls.

2. Framed Structures:

Framed structures consist of frames. These frames are formed by columns, slabs, footings and beams. The columns are created usually on independent foundations and braced together by beams at floor levels and roof levels. In some cases, instead of providing independent foundations, combined or raft foundations are provided depending on the underlying soil and load conditions.

3. **Composite Structure:**

   This is a combination of load bearing and framed structure. The outer walls can be of load bearing type, whereas column and structure can be provided internally. Thus, floors and roof are supported by walls as well as by frame. This type of construction is generally adopted for industrial buildings or ware houses where span are very large.

5.3.1 Comparison Between Different Types of Structures

The three types of structures described above can be compared with respect to the following aspects: (Refer Table 5.1)

Table 5.1

Aspect	Load bearing	Frame structure	Composite structure
Soil/Foundation strata	Soil of good S.B.C. available at shallow depth.	Can be suitable for any type of soil at any depth.	Soil of good S.B.C. available at shallow depth.
Floor space	Thick walls cause reduction in floor space.	More floor area due to thinner walls.	Intermediate floor space available.
Height (No. of storeys)	Allowed upto 4 storeys.	Multistoreyed construction possible.	Allowed upto 2 to 3 storeys.
Time of construction	Slow and time consuming construction.	Fast and speedy construction.	Intermediate time required.
Economy	Economical upto 2 storeys.	Economical for multistoreyed buildings.	Less cost than framed structure upto 2 to 3 floors.
Flexibility in planning.	Less flexible due to load bearing walls.	Flexible due to walls serving as partition only.	Internal arrangement can be modified.
Resistance to vibration	Susceptible to vibration due to machines and earthquake.	Withstand machine vibration and earthquake forces if provision is made in design.	Better than load bearing.

5.4 ARRANGEMENT OF ROOMS FOR RESIDENTIAL BUILDINGS

1. **Drawing Room or Living Room:**

   It is the main room and living area where friends are entertained and family members relax. It can also be used as a combined drawing and dining room. It should be situated on the front entrance of a building and should not provide direct access to the bedrooms and toilet block. It should be spacious to accommodate furniture for sitting, well lighted, ventilated and adjacent to dining room.

   An important factor in arranging the living room is due consideration to seating accommodation of different groups. The size and shape of the furniture depends upon the living standard of the family and allied purposes it is going to serve. The living room may be used as bed room, it may be combined kitchen-cum-living room or it may accommodate the dining space or have attached dining recess. There would be many variety of the shape and size of the living rooms to suit all types of activities which may be accommodated in them. (Refer Table 5.2). Rooms are generally more satisfactory if rectangular than square, but irregular shapes with long and narrow rooms should be avoided.

   Doors and windows should be planned in view of the 'aspect', 'prospect' light and ventilation, as well as to leave good wall-spaces against which furniture can be placed. Doors should be as few as possible and not less than 0.9 m in width 1.1 m is preferable.

   Table 5.2: Approximate sizes of various furniture pieces

	Name	Size
(1)	Large couch or settee	0.9 m × 2.1 m or 0.75 m × 2.05 m
(2)	Reclining or club chair	0.75 m × 0.9 m or 0.65 m × 0.75 m
(3)	Twin chair or sofa	0.75 m × 1.35 m
(4)	Office chair or small chair	0.45 m × 0.45 m
(5)	Chair without arms for dining	0.45 m × 0.45 m
(6)	Writing table	1.35 m × 0.75 m
(7)	Small desk	1.20 m × 0.60 m
(8)	Bridge or card table	0.90 m × 0.90 m
(9)	Coffee or card table	1.0 m diameter
(10)	End table or end piece	0.60 m × 0.30 m or 0.60 m diameter

2. **Dining Room:**

   Dining room should be adjacent or attached to kitchen. For attached dining room, the activities of kitchen should be screened by a screen wall or partition. Location of drawing, dining and kitchen should be side by side. A wash basin should be provided attached or inside the dining room. It is preferred, that the dining and drawing room remain connected through connecting door. Also according to the recent trends, these two rooms are combined into one big size room.

   The floor area of the separate dining room depends on the type of furniture and the minimum number of persons to be served at a time. The dining room may also serve alternative purposes such as children's study room, occasional sitting room for ladies etc. It should be well lighted and ventilated. There should be as few doors as possible, one joining either to living room or connecting passage and another for providing access to kitchen. Provision of one or two cupboards for keeping plates, crockery, glasses etc. and a wash-basin is essential for convenience.

3. **Kitchen:**

   In every house kitchen is one of the important rooms. The primary function in the kitchen is food preparation and service and may accommodate in addition to these dining, cleaning space etc.

   Kitchen should be located in a corner of the house such that smoke of the kitchen does not spread in all the rooms of the house. There should be no connection with toilet block provision of cooking shelves, cupboards, storage shelves and washing utensils should be made in the kitchen. The sequence of operations needs to be taken into account while planning the kitchen. The operation in connection with meals start with collection of goods, grains, flour, vegetables, dairy and poultry products, and storing them. The food is to be prepared and cooked. The next step is to keep food in readiness to be served and then service or distribution of food. Rest of the food to be stored and preserved. The used plates and dishes need to be washed and put away.

   It is essential to have good lighting in kitchens both by day and night. Windows should be planned preferably with north and east aspect to give even and adequate lighting for all working areas. A flooring of non-absorbent and smooth nature should be provided. The equipment of the working kitchen comprises of sink of size (60 cm × 45 cm × 25 cm) and at least 0.75 cm to 0.9 m height from floor level. Cooking range (chulla), working table, water storage, storage cabinets, larder and refrigerator.

4. **Bed Room:**

    This room should be located on one side of the building. It is should have at least one of its walls as an external wall so as to maintain good natural ventilation and light in the room. This room should be directly in front of the prevailing direction of wind. Attached bath and W.C. is preferable for modern planning. There should be no connection with the kitchen. The bed room should be located so as to maintain privacy. The probable bed room furniture comprises of the following pieces.
    1. Double bed – size 1.35 to 1.45 m × 2 to 2.10 m.
    2. Single bed – size 0.9 × 2.0 m.
    3. Single cot – size 0.75 × 1.80 m.
    4. Small chair – size 0.45 m × 0.45 m.
    5. Small arm chair – size 0.65 m × 0.45 m.
    6. Divan, port or settee – size 0.75 × 1.65 m.
    7. Dressing stool – size 0.45 × 0.38 m.
    8. Chest of drawers (small) – size 0.45 × 0.90 m.
    9. Chest of drawers (large) – size 0.60 × 0.30 m.
    10. Bed side table – size 0.60 × 0.30 m.
    11. Small dressing table – size 0.45 × 0.90 m.

    Above sizes are indicative of plan dimensions.

5. **Store Room:**

    For storing food grains and other articles it is preferable to place them in a store room. Ventilation and natural lightning is less important for this room. The left out space after fulfilling the requirements for all other rooms may be used as a store room.

6. **Pantry:**

    This is a small room which is attached to a dining room cooked food is kept in this room. This room should have cupboards and shelves.

7. **Guest Room:**

    This room should be located on one side of the front verandah. It may not have connection with other rooms except with the dining room. Separate toilets should be provided to the guest room to maintain privacy.

8. **Dressing Room:**

    This room should remain attached with bed room and bath and W.C. This room should have provisions of a dressing table, cupboard etc.

9. **Bath and W.C.:**

   Bath and W.C. may be separate or they combined in one room. If bath and W.C. are to be attached with a bed room, then they are generally combined. Both W.C. and bath should be well ventilated. There should be at least one separate bath and W.C. in the house, other than combined with the bed rooms. All the W.C. and bath rooms should have at least one of their wall as external walls so as to facilitate proper ventilation. Dado or glazed tiles should be provided or otherwise walls should be finished with smooth water-proof cement coat. They should also be provided with the necessary fixtures. Size and type of W.C. pans, wash basins, electrical installations for hot water, plumbing fixtures, washing machine etc. control the size of bathrooms and WC.

10. **Verandah:**

    For economic use of space the provision of verandah is becoming minimum in modern planning. But a certain amount of free space area for corridor and verandah (covered) is required to provide independent access to different rooms, seating space and for drying cloths etc. A minimum width of 1.2 m and having a length equal to that of a front room may be provided.

11. **Puja or Prayer Room:**

    A small room or space at least 1.2 m × 2.5 m should be provided for prayer by the side of bed room. This room should be lighted and ventilated.

12. **Stair:**

    Provision of a stair even for a single storyed building is necessary for the purpose of inspection, cleaning of the roof and also as outdoor sleeping area during peak summer nights. For storied building the location of a staircase should be such that each floor or flat is separated from general movement of stair. For family use it should be located centrally and most of the rooms should have easy approach for the stair provided that their privacy of any room does not suffer.

13. **Lobby:**

    It is a hall at the entrance of which remains connected to the other parts of the building through corridors.

14. **Porches:**

    It is constructed in the front of the building. This adds to the elevation of the building. Car can be parked in it temporarily.

15. **Garage and Servant's Room:**

    These rooms are connected in the back open space of the plot. They are always made in separate blocks.

16. **Corridor:**

    It is a covered common passage in the building for independent entrance to various rooms.

5.5 SIZE OF ROOMS FOR RESIDENTIAL BUILDINGS

This depends upon the standard of living and income of the individual family. Big size rooms are generally preferred. A bed room should not be over-congested by placing too-many furnitures. For luxurious planning, the size of a drawing or living room can be made as big as possible. But considering all the points as indicated above some average dimensions for High Income Group (H.I.G.), Middle Income Group (M.I.G.); Low Income Group (L.I.G.) and maximum size as per code of practice for building bye-laws are given below for general guidance. (Refer Plate No. 1 to 16 for).

Name of the room	H.I.G. All dimension	M.I.G.	L.I.G.	Minimum (as per I.S.)
		Length × Breadth are in metres		
Drawing room	5.0 × 4.2 to 7.2 × 5.5	4.2 × 3.6 to 4.5 × 4.0	3.5 × 3.0	9.5 sq.m.
Dining room	4.0 × 3.5 to 5.0 × 4.0	3.5 × 3.1 to 7.0 × 3.1 (drawing + dining)	3.0 × 2.8	7.5 sq.m.
Bed room	4.8 × 4.2	4.6 × 3.6	3.5 × 3.0	9.5 sq.m.
Office room	4.0 × 3.6	3.5 × 3.0	–	–
Guest room	4.0 × 3.6	3.5 × 3.0	–	–
Store	3.0 × 3.0	3.0 × 2.8	2.25 × 1.5	3.0 sq.m.
Kitchen	3.5 × 3	2.0 × 2.5	2.5 × 2.2 (Breadth min.)	4.5 sq.m. (Kitchen and dinning combined 5.0 sq.m.)
Pantry	3.0 × 2.5	–	–	–
Dressing	3.5 × 3.0	3.0 × 2.5	–	–
Bath and W.C. (combined)	3.5 × 2.5	3.0 × 1.6	2.10 × 1.5	1.0 × 1.8
Bath (separate)	3.0 × 2.0	2.0 × 1.5	1.50 × 1.20	1.0 × 1.2
W.C. (separate)	2.5 × 2.0	1.8 × 1.2	1.1 × 1.0	0.9 × 1.0
Box room	1.8 × 1.8	–	–	–
Servant's room	3.0 × 3.0	3.0 × 2.5	–	–
Garage (min. height 2.4 m)	5.8 × 5.5	5.0 × 2.80	–	5.0 × 2.5
Porch	6.0 × 3.0 to 4.8 × 3.0	–	–	–

5.6 PLANNING OF A RESIDENTIAL COMPLEX

To describe various types of drawings, which are required to be drawn by the architecture, a set of different drawings is furnished here. **(For additional set of drawings refer end pages of this chapter)**

1. Plate No. 1 – Shows layout of a residential complex which includes arrangement of different buildings, internal roads, garden etc.
2. Plate No. 2 – Shows typical floor plans for first, third and fifth floors.
3. Plate No. 3 – Shows typical floor plans for second, fourth and sixth floors.
4. Plate No. 4 – Shows parking floor plan.
5. Plate No. 5 – Shows front elevation.
6. Plate No. 6 – Shows terrace floor plan.
7. Plate No. 7 – Shows floor plan for lift, machine room, and R.C.C. water storage tank.
8. Plate No. 8 – Shows section and side elevation.
9. Plate No. 9 – Shows perspective of a building.
10. Plate No. 10 – Shows perspective view of the complex.
11. Plate No. 11, 12, 13, 14 – Show typical floor plans of other buildings in the same residential complex.
12. Plate No. 15 – Shows centre line plan of a building.
13. Plate No. 16 – Shows structural drawing showing R.C.C. design details, schedule of R.C.C. footing and columns.

SOLVED EXAMPLES

Planning of Typical R.C.C. Stairs:

Example 5.1: Plan a dog legged stair for a building with the following data:

(i) Vertical distance between the floors = 3.6 m.

(ii) Size of stair hall 2.5 m × 5 m.

(iii) Thickness of the floor slab = 140 mm.

(iv) Thickness of the waist slab and landing slab = 100 mm.

Solution: Assume, Rise = 150 mm
and Tread = 250 mm

$$\text{Width of the flight} = \frac{2.5}{2}$$
$$= 1.25 \text{ m}$$

∴ $\text{Height of each flight} = \dfrac{3.6}{2}$
$$= 1.8 \text{ m}$$

∴ $\text{Number of risers required} = \dfrac{1.8 \times 1000}{150}$
$$= 12 \text{ in each flight}$$

Number of treads in each flight = 12 − 1
$$= 11$$

∴ Space required for treads = 11 × 250 = 2750 mm
∴ Space left for passage = 5 − 1.25 − 2.75 = 1.00 m

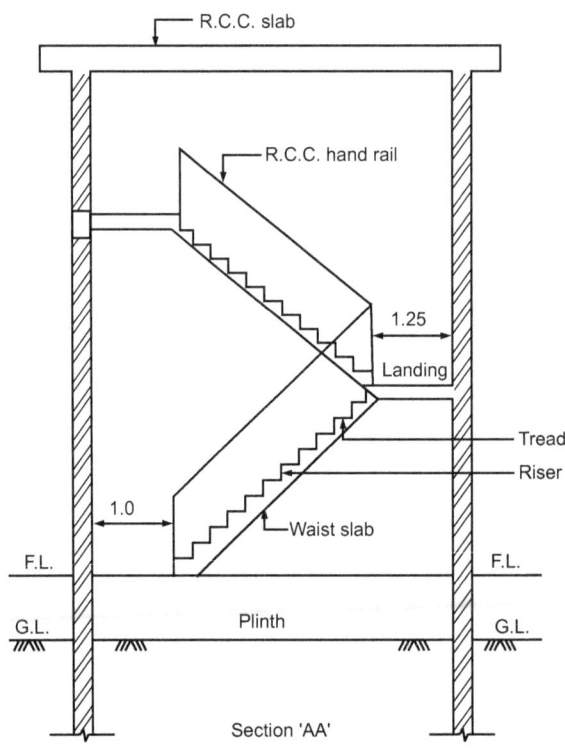

Fig. 5.1 (a)

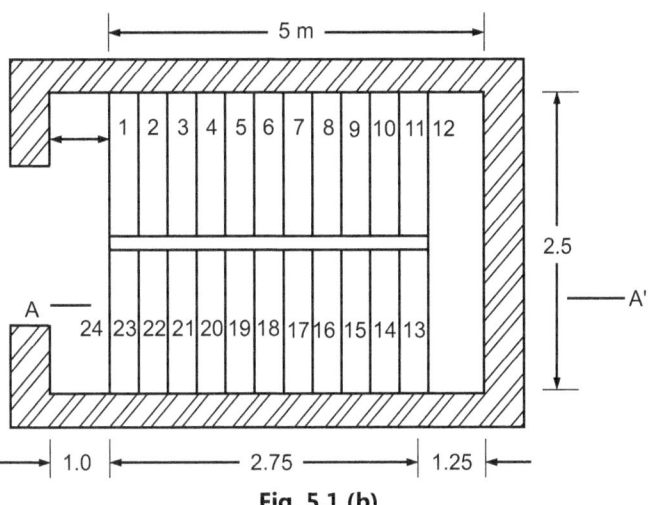

Fig. 5.1 (b)

Example 5.2: Calculate number of risers and treads in each flight for dog legged stair, floor to floor height is 3.3 m and riser is 150 mm.

Solution: Given data:

$$\text{Floor to floor height} = 3.3 \text{ m}$$
$$\text{Riser} = 150 \text{ mm}$$
$$\therefore \text{Total number of risers} = \frac{3300}{150}$$
$$= .22$$

Assuming two flights, number of risers in each flight = 11 number and number of treads in each flight = 11 – 1 = 10 number.

Example 5.3: Plan a staircase for a residential building in which the vertical distance between each floor is 3.36 m. The size of the stair hall is limited to 4.5 × 3 m.

Solution: Given data:

(i) Floor to floor height = 3.36 m
   Let, Width of landing = 1.5 m
              =..Width of stairs
   Assume, Rise = 16 cm
$$\therefore \text{Total number of risers} = \frac{3.36 \times 100}{16}$$
$$= ..21 \text{ risers} \Rightarrow \begin{array}{l} 11 \text{ in first flight} \\ 10 \text{ in second height} \end{array}$$

Provide 11 risers in each flight
∴ Number of treads in first flight = 11 – 1 = 0
          in second flight = 10 – 9 = 9

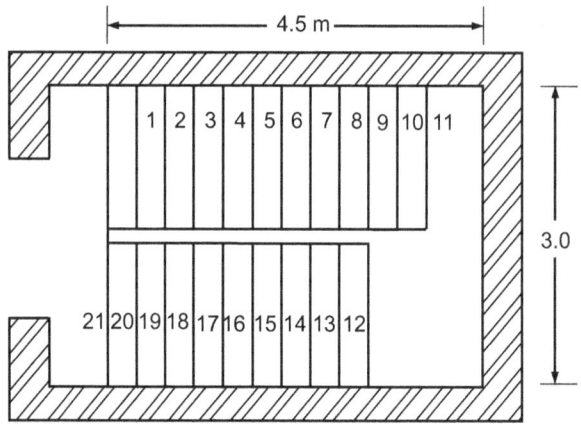

Fig. 5.2

IMPORTANT POINTS

- Types of Group-A buildings i.e.
  (a) Lodging (b) One or two family private dwellings
  (c) Dormitories (d) Flats (e) Hotels
- Arrangement of rooms for residential buildings.
- Planning and drawing as per data given.
- Planning and drawing if a line plan is given.

QUESTIONS

1. A line plan for a Residential Building is shown in Fig. 5.3.

   Data:

   (a) All walls are 230 mm thick.
   (b) Walls indicated by ⊗ are 100 mm thick.
   (c) RCC framed structure.
   (d) Beam sizes 0.23 m × 0.38 m.
   (e) Column sizes 0.23 m × 0.30 m.
   (f) Floor to floor height 3.30 m.
   (g) Plinth height 0.60 m.

   Based on the data and Fig. 5.3:

   (i) Draw to a scale 1 : 50 detailed plan.
   (ii) Draw to a scale 1 : 50 detailed section A-A.
   (iii) Prepare schedule of openings and also show design for staircase.
   (iv) Assuming cost of construction ₹ 4000/- per sq.m., find cost of construction.

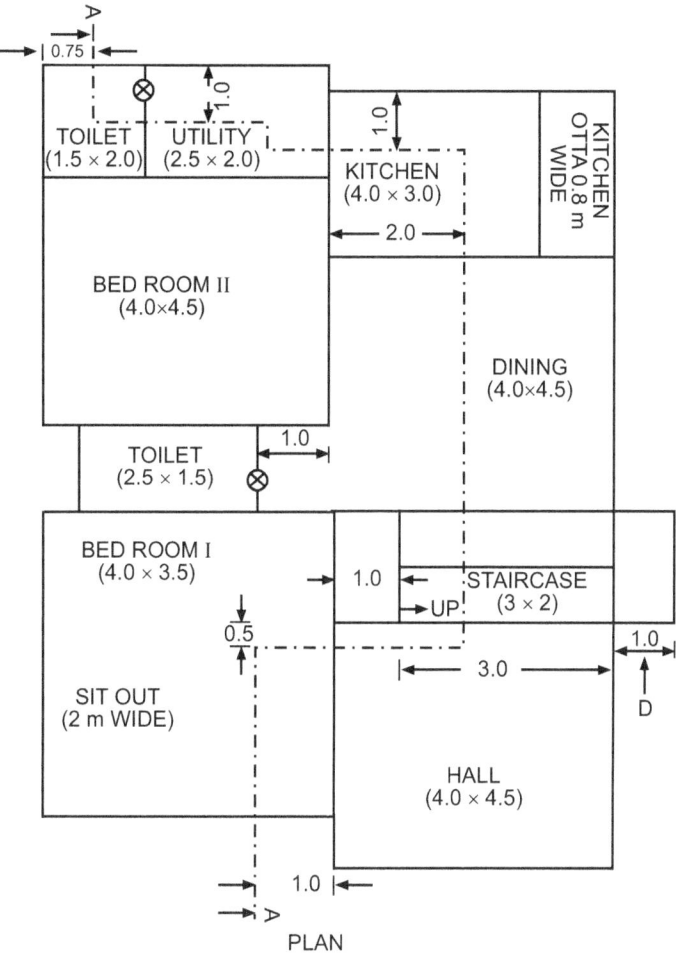

Fig. 5.3

2. A line plan for a residential building is given in Fig. 5.4. Draw to a scale of 1 : 50 or suitable:

   (a) Detailed plan for RCC framed structure.

   – All external walls and those marked ⊗ are 230 mm thick.

   – All internal walls are 115 mm thick.

   (b) Detailed section A-A assuming depth of foundation 1200 mm below G.L. Floor to floor height is 3150 mm. Riser – 175 mm, Tread – 250 mm.

   (c) Calculate X and Y dimensions.

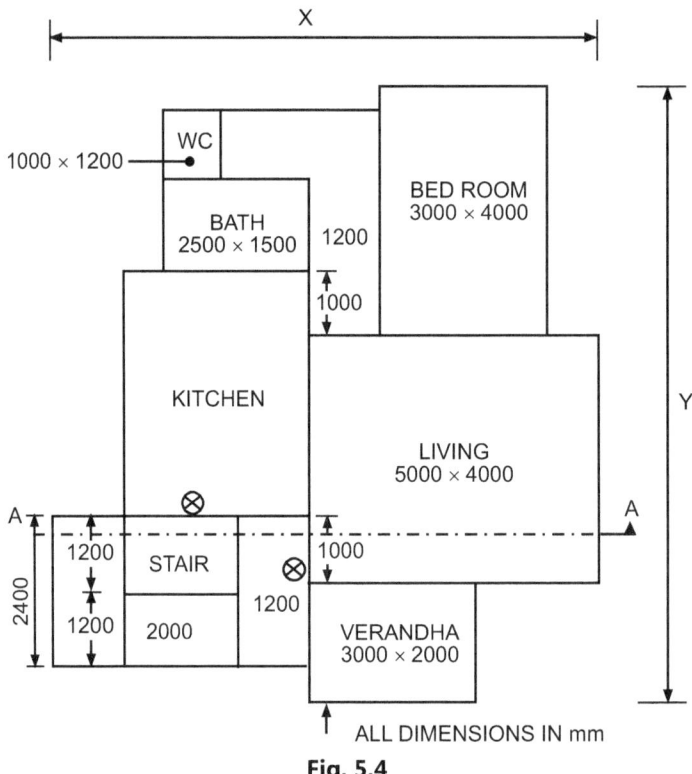

Fig. 5.4

3. Develop the line plan shown in Fig. 5.5. Scale 1 : 50.

   (i) Draw detailed plan.

   Wall thickness: external 230 thick.

   internal 150 thick.

   Doors standard size as per IS code.

   Window opening 15% of room area.

   Proof pitched to 30 degrees, hipped end, RCC.

   Assume other relevant details.

   (ii) Draw detailed section showing

   (a) Stair details

   (b) W.C. details

   (c) Foundation details.

   (iii) Prepare budget. Assume cost ₹ 5,000/- per sq.m. Calculate cost of building.

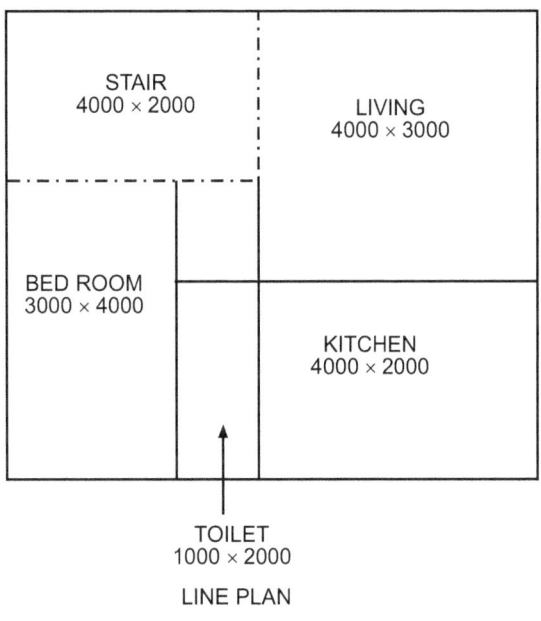

Fig. 5.5

4. A plan for a residential building is shown in Fig. 5.6.

   Draw to scale of 1 : 50

   (1) Detailed plan for R.C.C. framed structure.

   Take: External walls 230 thick

   Internal walls 115 thick

   Column size 230 × 450

   (2) Detailed section S.S.

   The different levels are:
   - Foundation level — – 1200
   - Ground level — – 450
   - Plinth level — ± 000
   - Sill level — – 900
   - Lintel level — – 2100
   - Slab level — – 3000
   - Slab above stair — – 3900

   (3) Write schedule for doors and windows.

   (4) Show North direction.

   (5) Calculate X and Y dimensions.

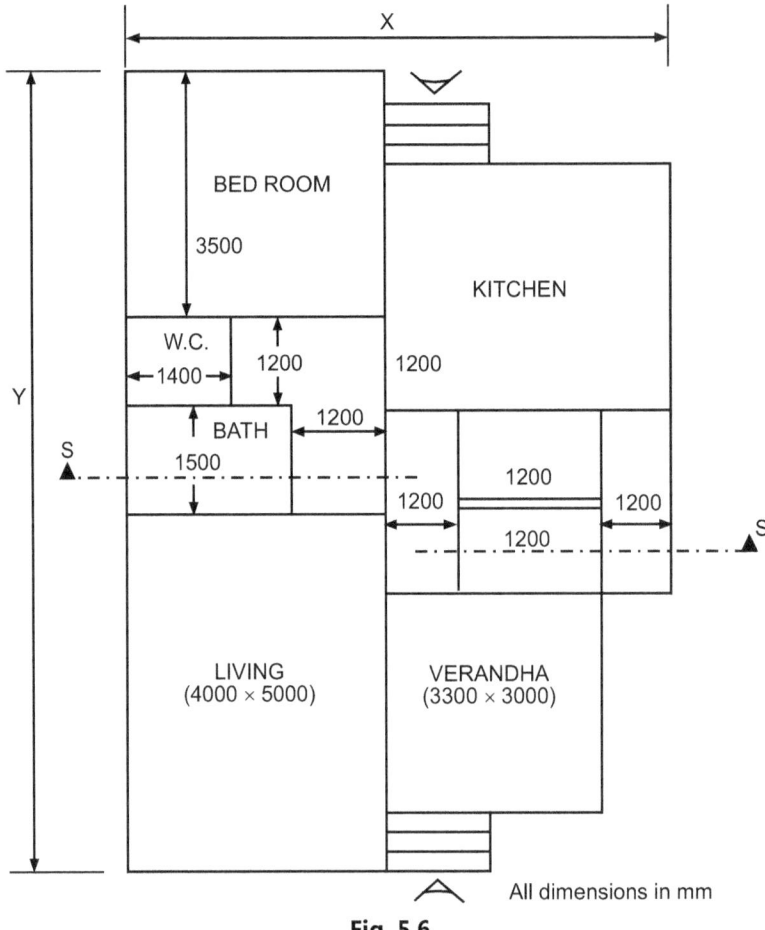

Fig. 5.6

5. (a) Draw a detailed floor plan to a scale 1 : 50 or suitable of a residential building for a given line plan as shown in Fig. 5.7.

Data:
1. The structure is load bearing
2. All dimensions are in mm
3. Thicknesses of all walls are 230 mm and those marked by encircled X are 115 mm thick.
4. The building is single storey.
5. Assume proper sizes of doors and windows.
6. Consider plinth height as 900 mm (0.9 m)
7. Give the detailed dimensions.

(b) For the line plan shown in Fig. 5.7 draw the detailed sectional elevation along line XY assume suitable dimensions for the footing:

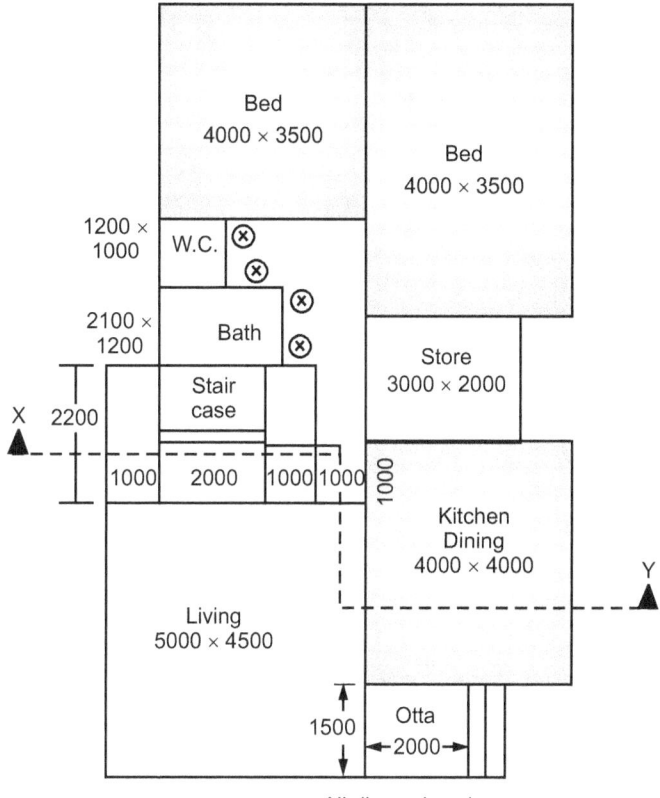

All dimensions in mm
Fig. 5.7

6. (a) Draw detailed plan to a scale a 1 : 50 of a residential building for the line plan shown in Fig. 5.8.
    Fig. 5.8 is not to scale.
    Refer the following guidelines:
    (1) The structure is load bearing.
    (2) All the walls are 230 mm thick.
    (3) The building has got ground floor only.
    (4) Access to the terrace is provided through staircase.
    (5) All dimensions are in mm.
    (6) Assume suitable sizes of doors and windows.
    (7) Locate doors and windows at suitable positions.
    (8) Provide sufficient number of doors and windows.
    (9) Take plinth height = 600 mm.
    (10) R.C.C. slab is provided on all rooms.

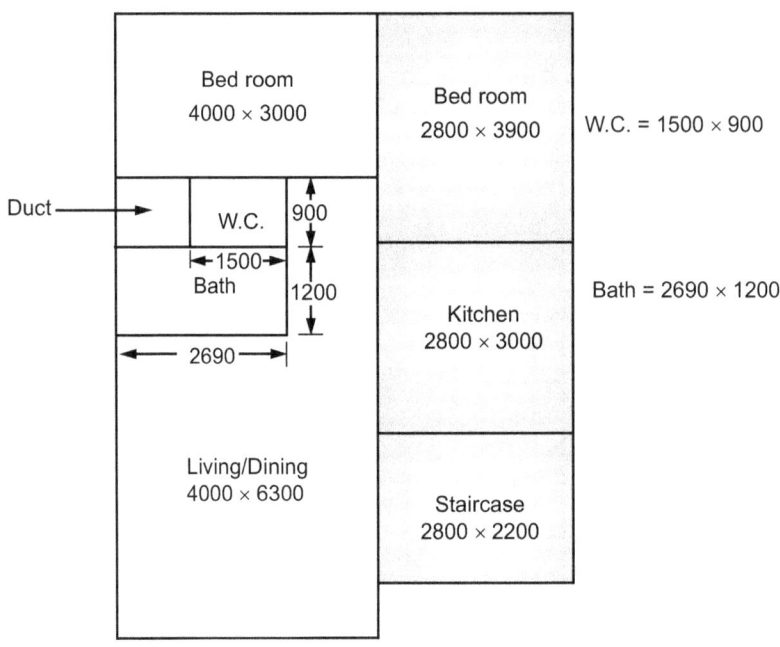

Fig. 5.8

(b) Write detailed schedule for doors and windows as per the format given:

Sr. No.	Type of door/window	No. of doors/windows	Size of opening in mm

7. Plan a residential building having G + 1 framed structure with the following requirements:

Sr. No.	Type of unit	No. of Units	Internal Area of Unit in sq. m.
1.	Living room	01	18
2.	Bed room	02	12
3.	Additional bed room with attached toilet	01	16
4.	Kitchen	01	12
5.	W.C.	01	1.5
6.	Bath	01	2.8
7.	Staircase	01	Use suitable dimensions

8. A line plan for a residential building is given in Fig. 5.9. Draw to a scale of 1 : 50 or suitable:
   (a) Detailed plan for R.C.C. framed structure:
       All external walls and those marked ⊗ are 230 mm thick:
       8. All internal walls are 115 mm thick;
       9. Locate doors and windows.
   (b) Detailed section A-A assuming depth of foundation 1500 mm below GL and floor to floor height 3150 mm.
   (c) Calculate X and Y dimensions and built-up area.

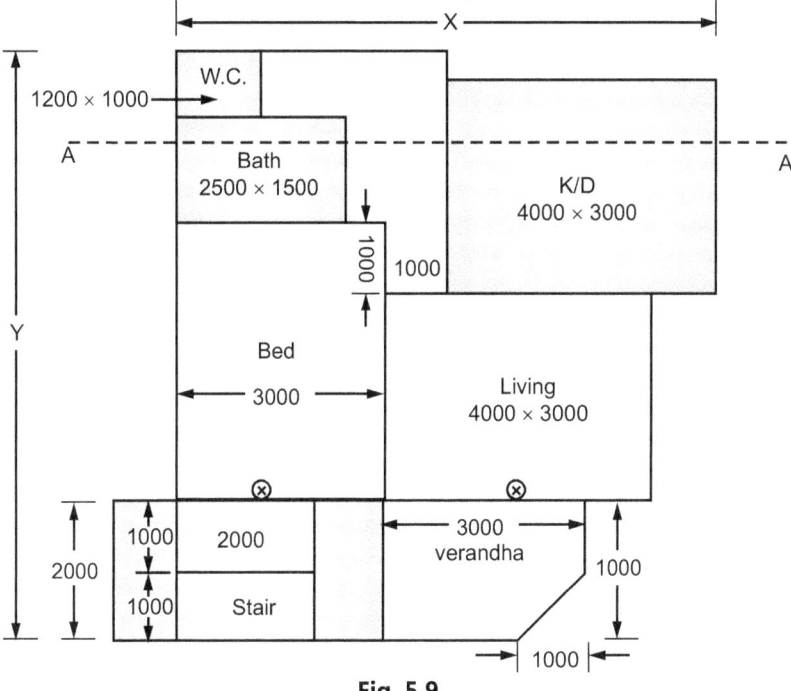

Fig. 5.9

All dimensions in mm
All external walls and those marked ⊗ are 230 thick
All internal walls are 115 thick.

9. A line plan for a residential building is given in Fig. 5.10. Draw to a scale of 1 : 50 or suitable:
   (a) Detailed sectional plan for R.C.C. framed structure.
       • All external walls and those of the staircase room are 230 mm thick.
       • All internal walls are 115 m thick. Locate doors and windows.
   (b) Locate columns of size 230 mm × 400 mm.
   (c) Show northline to orient the building.

(d) Detailed Section A-A, assuming depth of foundation 1000 mm below ground level. Floor to floor height is 3150 mm.

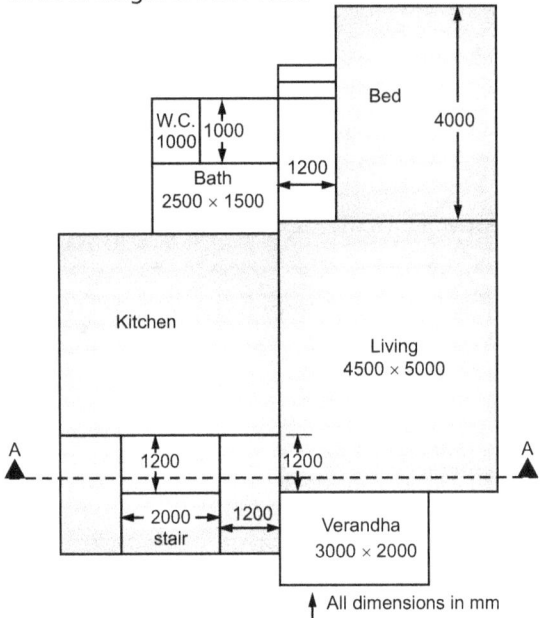

Fig. 5.10

10. Develop the line plan shown in Fig. 5.11.
    Data: Wall external BBM 230 tk.
    - Wall internal BBM 150 tk.
    - Door – As per IS code.
    - Windows – Opening 10% of floor area.
    - RCC framed structure.
    - Assume other details and state them clearly.

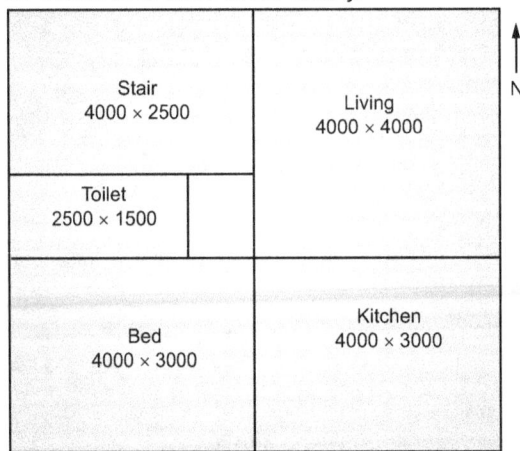

All dimensions in mm

Fig. 5.11

11. A line for a Residential Building shown in Fig. 5.12.

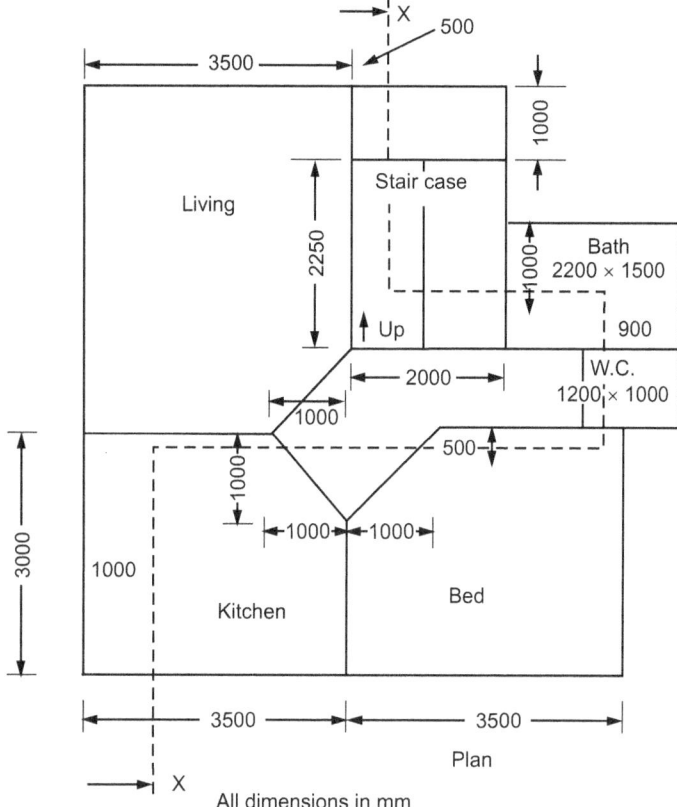

Fig. 5.12

Data:
(a) All walls are 230 mm thick.
(b) Partition wall of W.C. and Bath – 100 mm thick.
(c) Size of W.C. room – 1200 mm × 1000 mm.
(d) Size of Bath room – 2200 mm × 1500 mm.
(e) R.C.C. framed structure.
(f) Beam sizes 230 mm × 380 mm.
(g) Column sizes 230 mm × 300 mm.
(h) Floor to floor height – 3000 mm.
(i) Plinth height – 450 mm.
   (i) Draw to a scale 1 : 50 detailed plan.
   (ii) Draw to scale 1 : 50 detailed section XX.
   (iii) Calculate Built-up area.
   (iv) Show design calculations for a staircase.
   (v) Show entrance steps at proper location in plan.

12. A line plan for a residential building is given in Fig. 5.13. Draw to scale of 1 : 50 or suitable:

    (a) Detailed plan for R.C.C. framed structure:
    - All external walls and those marked are 230 mm thick.
    - All internal walls are 115 mm thick
    - Locate doors, windows and columns of size 230 mm × 400 mm.

    (b) Detailed section AA assuming depth of foundation 1500 mm below ground level. Floor to floor height 3150 mm. Floor to ceiling height 3000 mm. Rise 175 mm, tread – 250 mm for R.C.C. stair.

    (c) Write schedule for doors and windows.

    (d) Calculate X and Y.

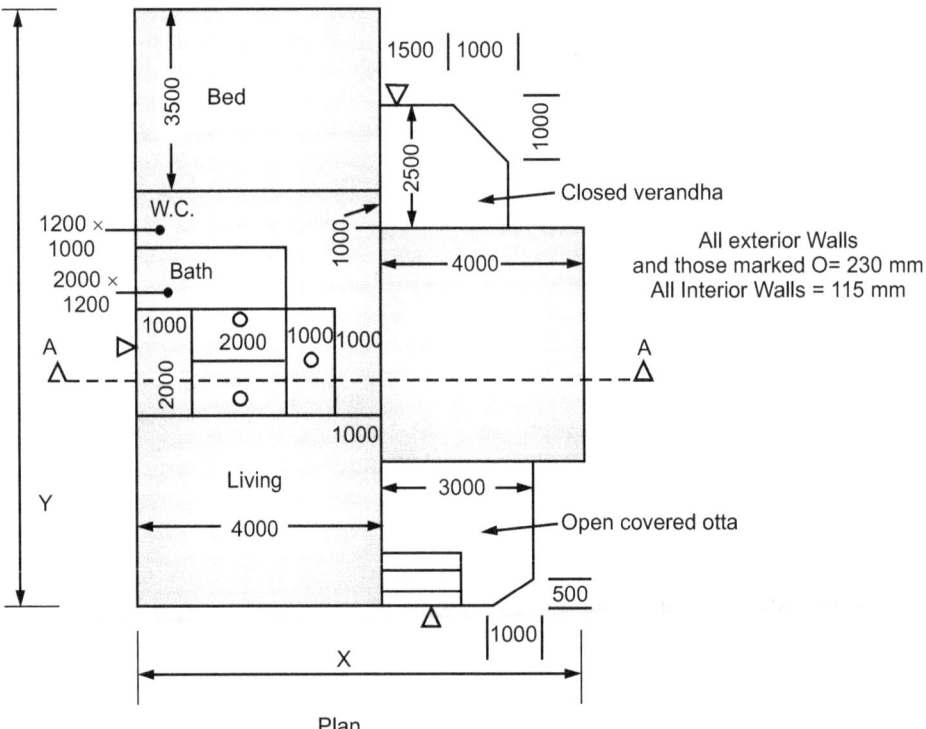

Fig. 5.13

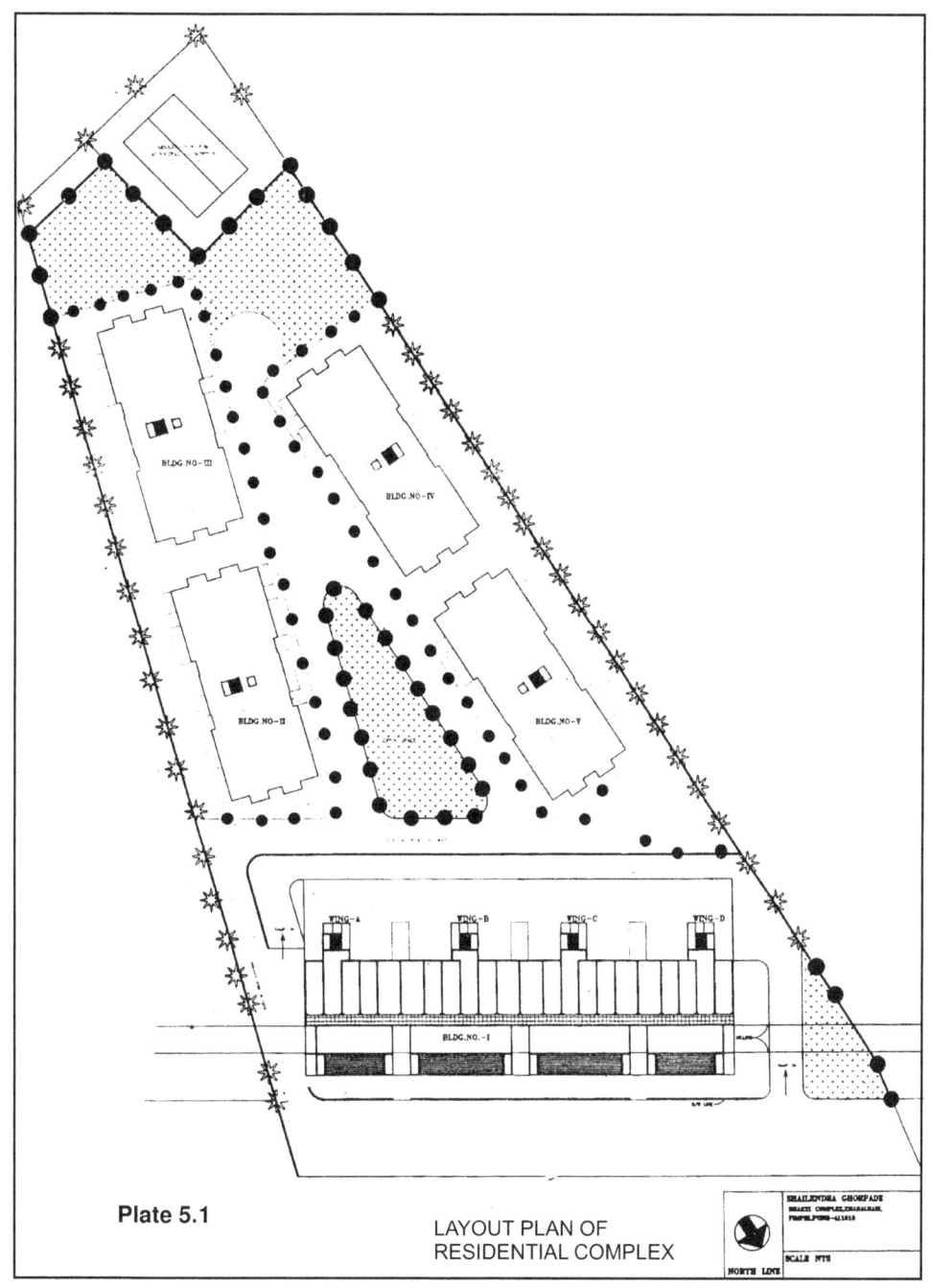

Plate 5.1 LAYOUT PLAN OF RESIDENTIAL COMPLEX

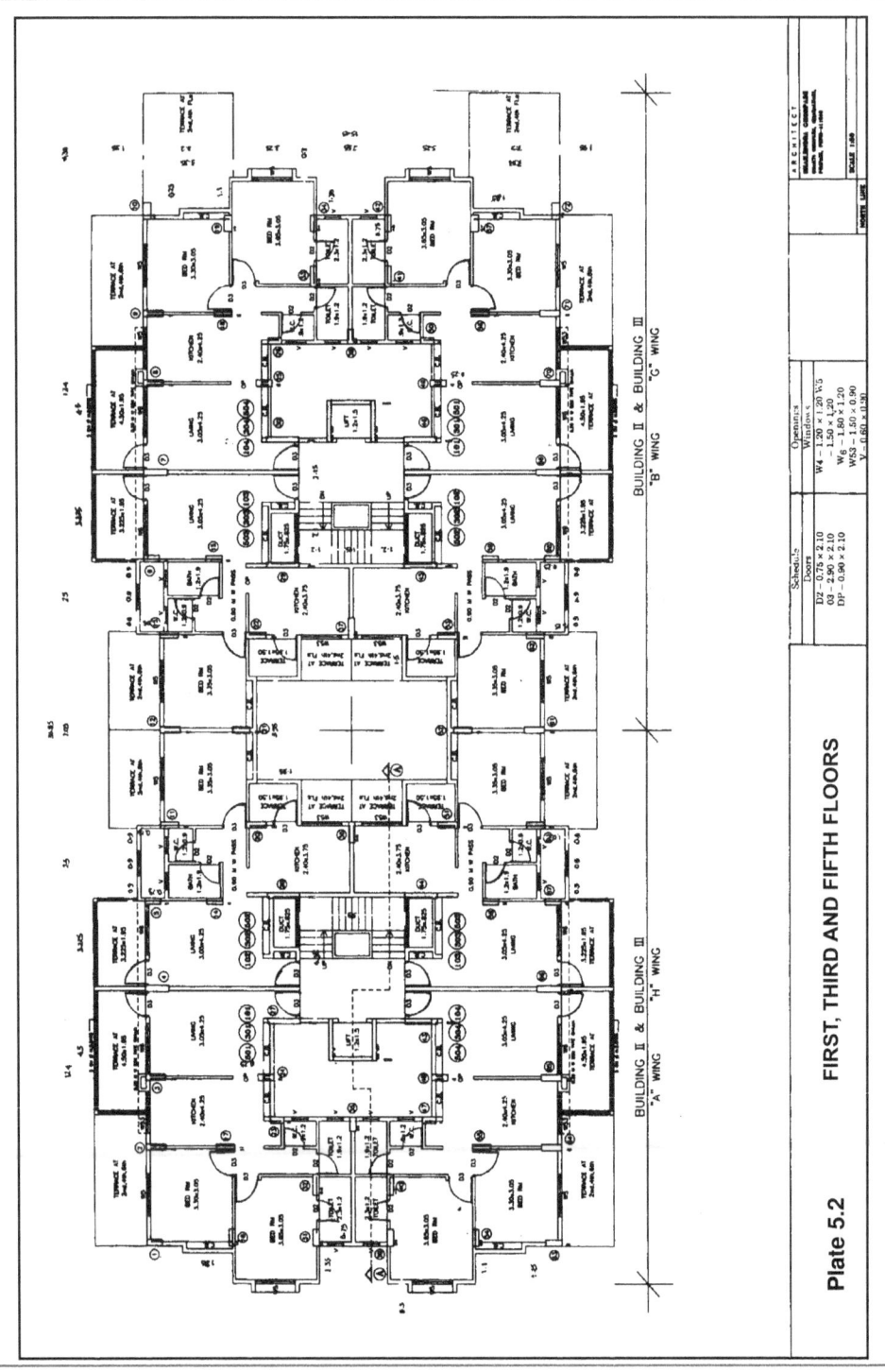

Plate 5.2 FIRST, THIRD AND FIFTH FLOORS

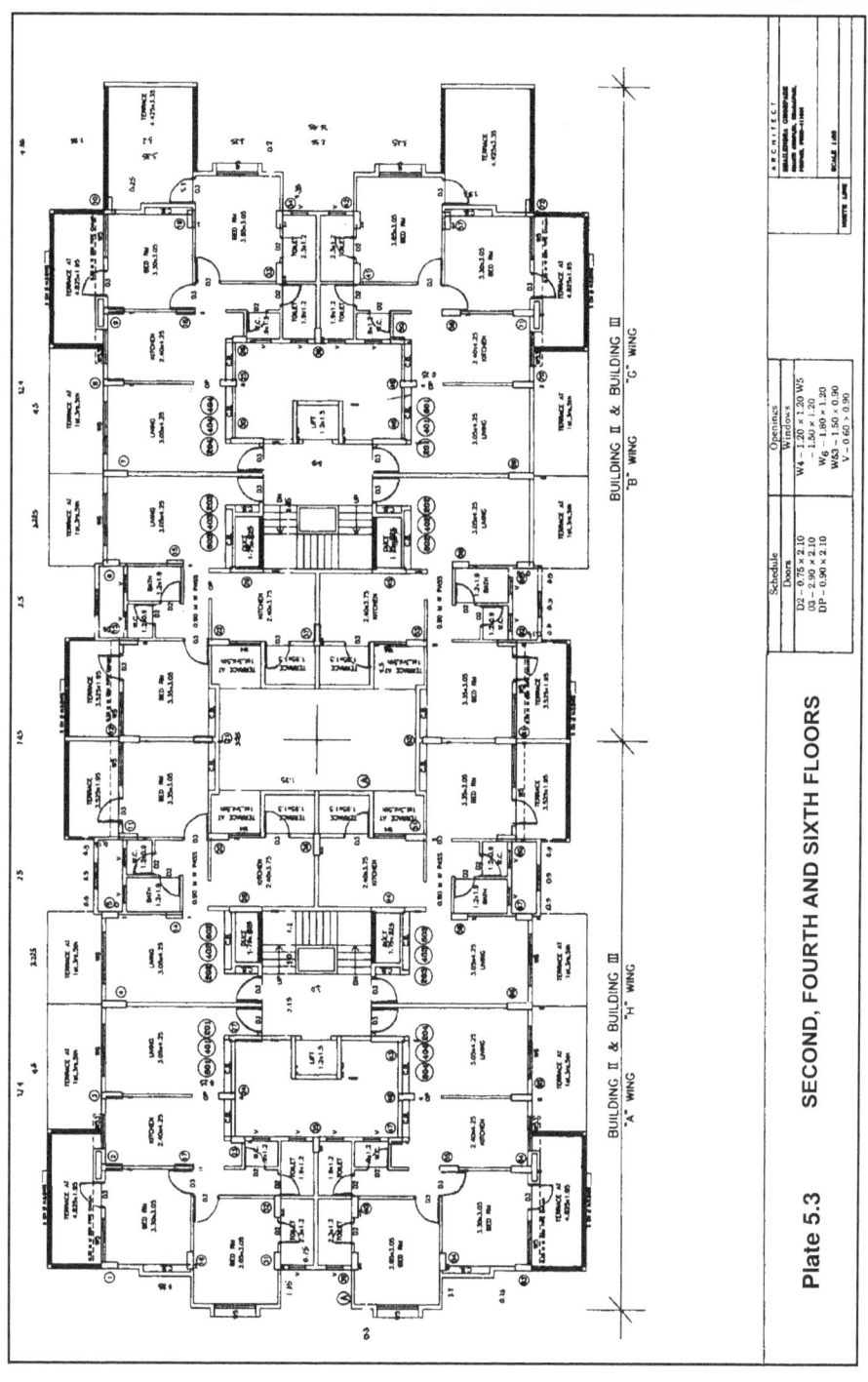

Plate 5.3 SECOND, FOURTH AND SIXTH FLOORS

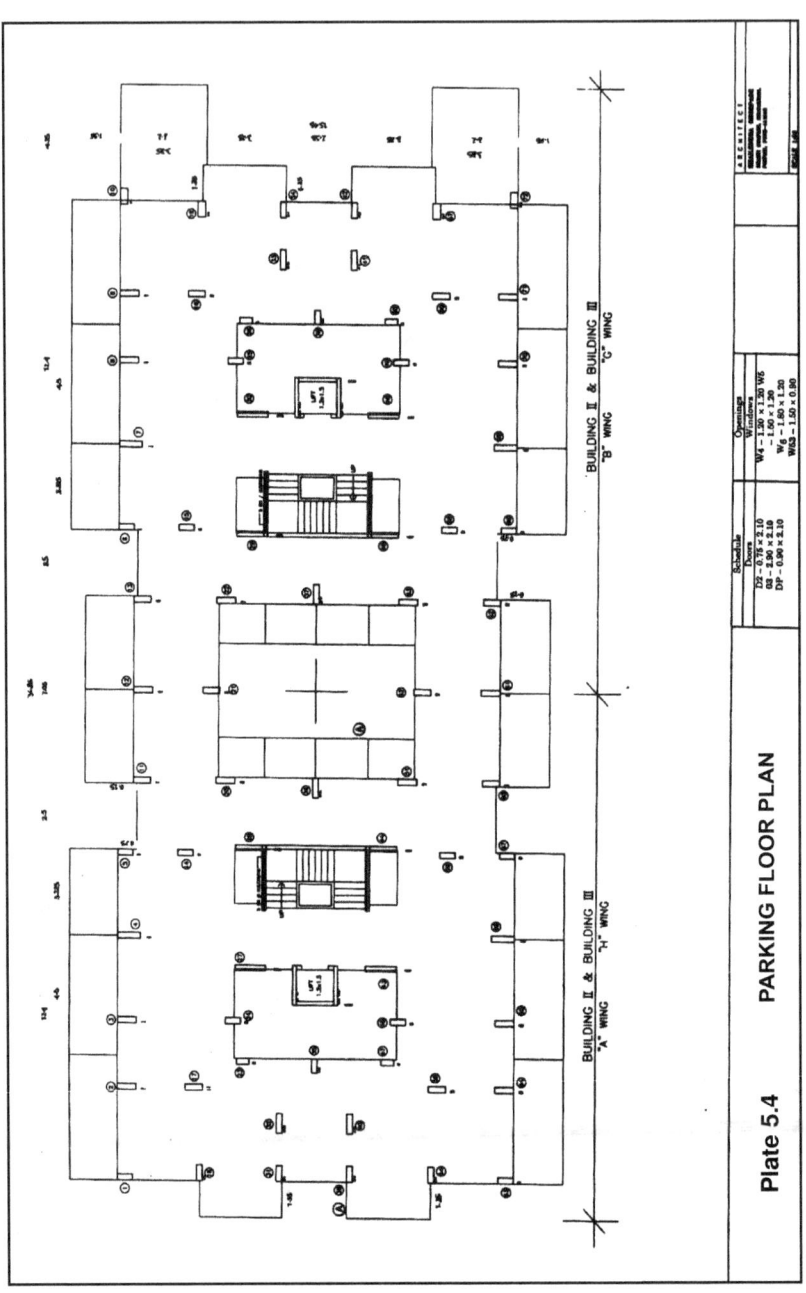

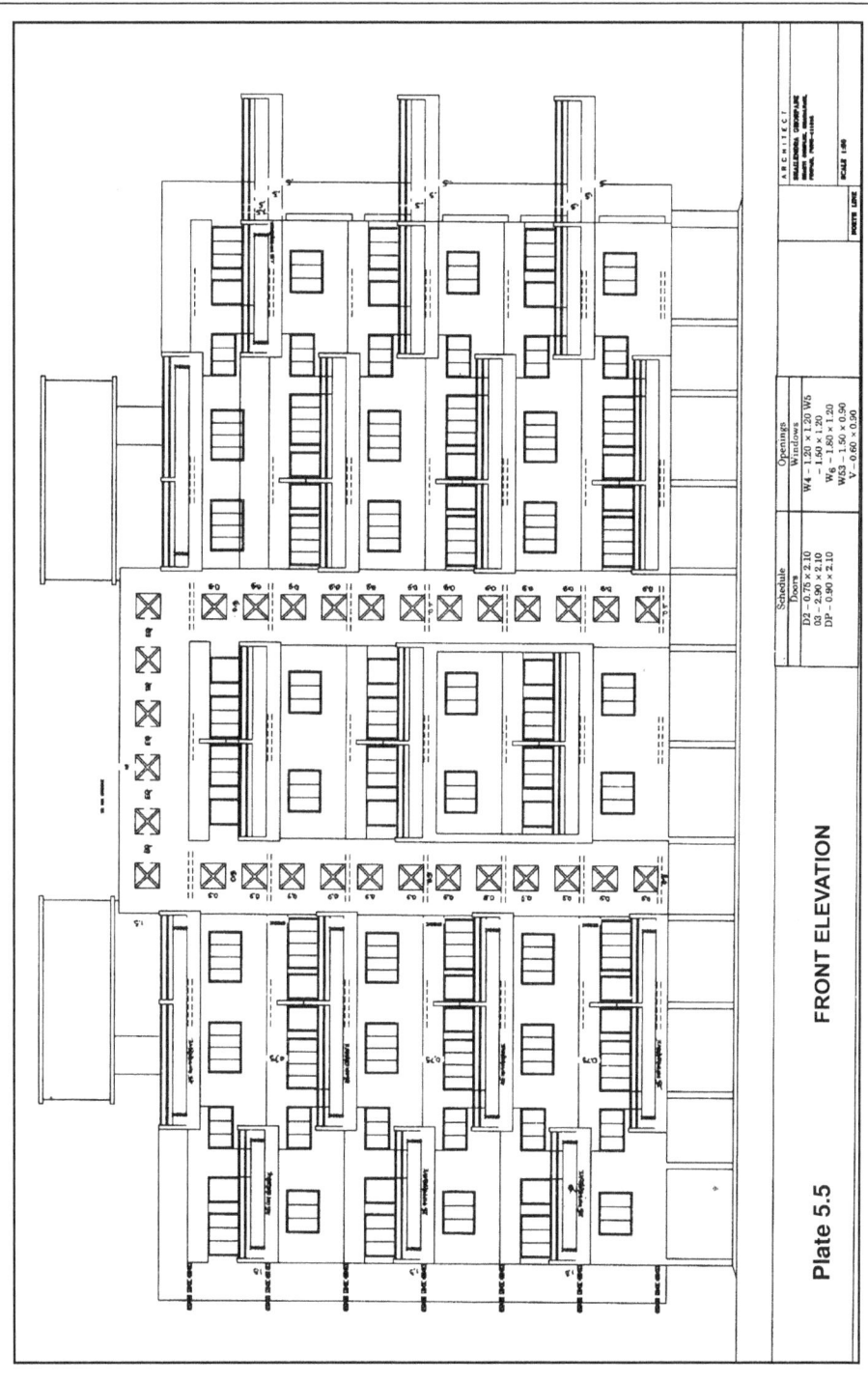

Plate 5.5 FRONT ELEVATION

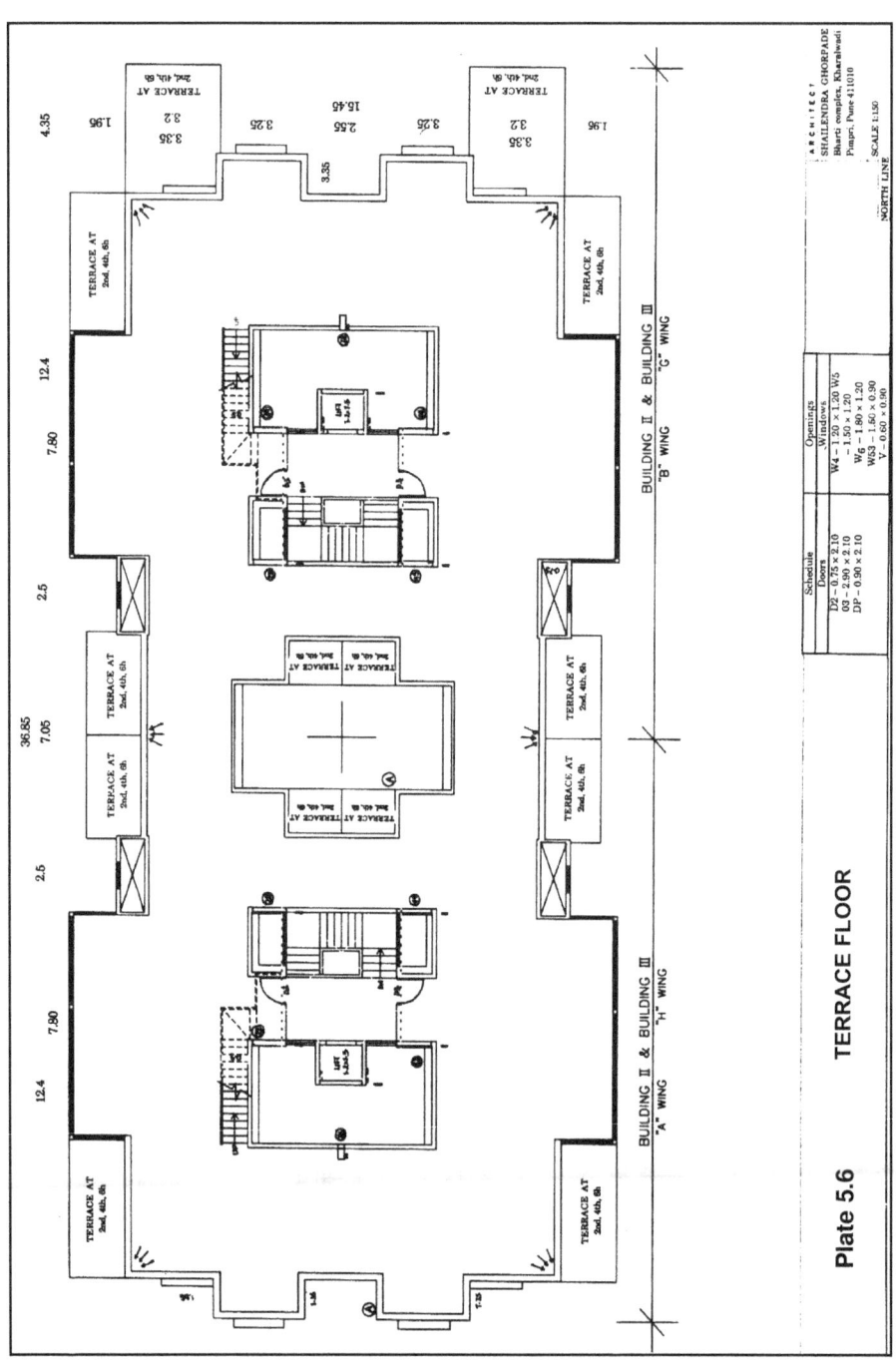

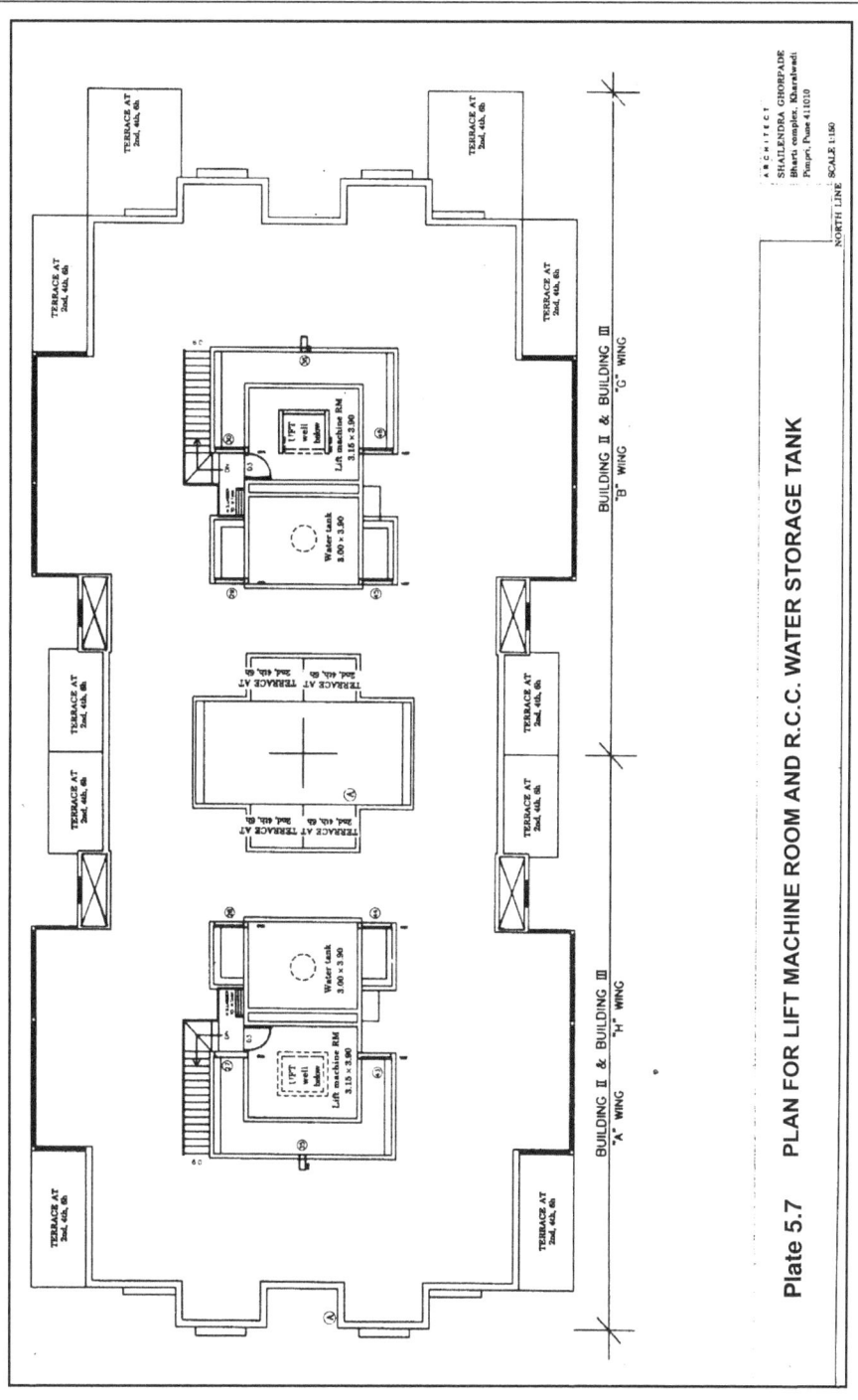

Plate 5.7   PLAN FOR LIFT MACHINE ROOM AND R.C.C. WATER STORAGE TANK

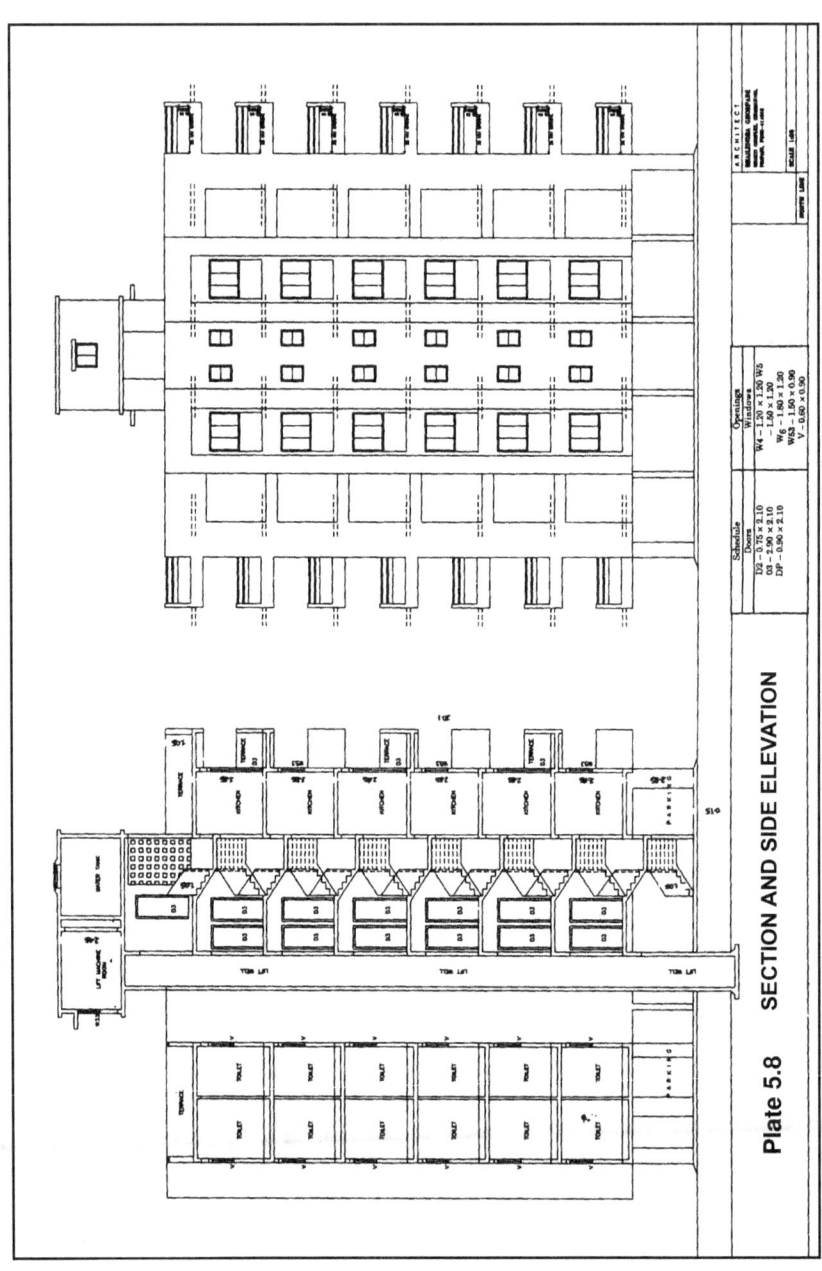

Plate 5.8 SECTION AND SIDE ELEVATION

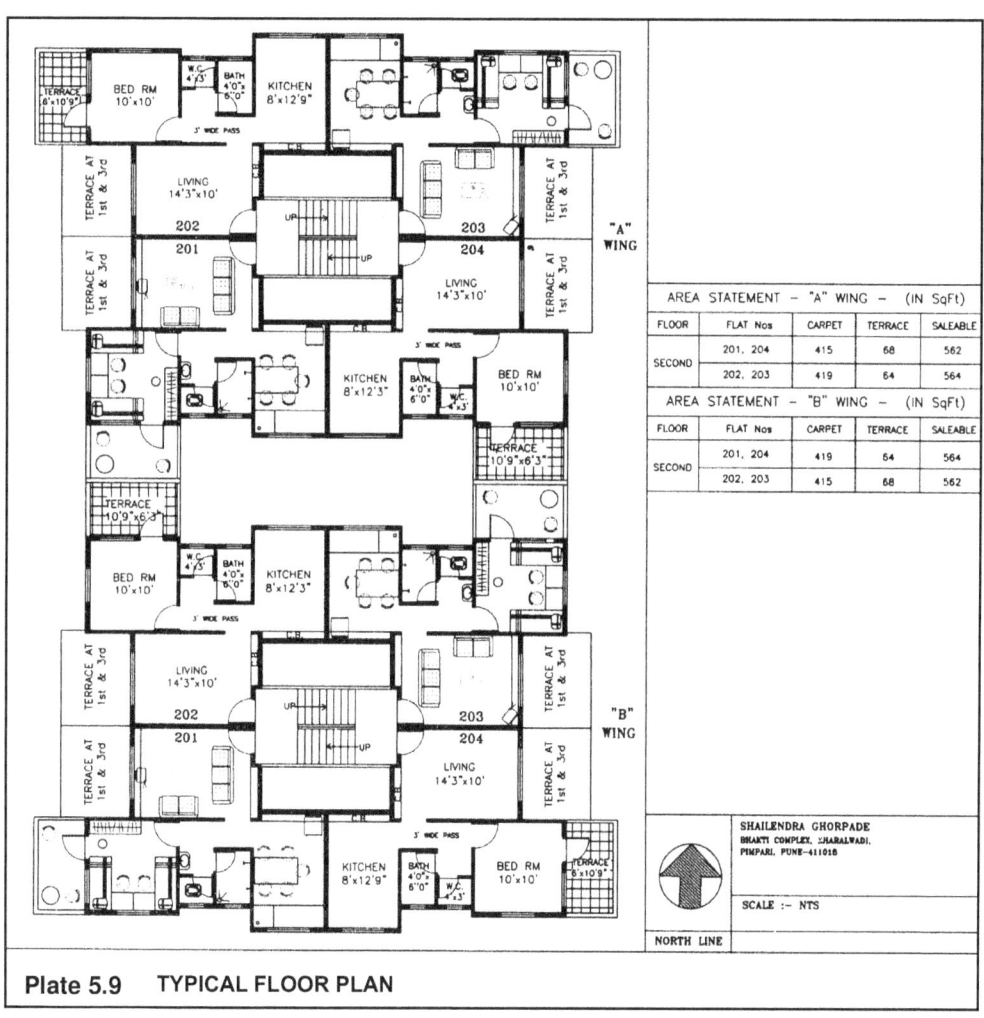

Plate 5.9   TYPICAL FLOOR PLAN

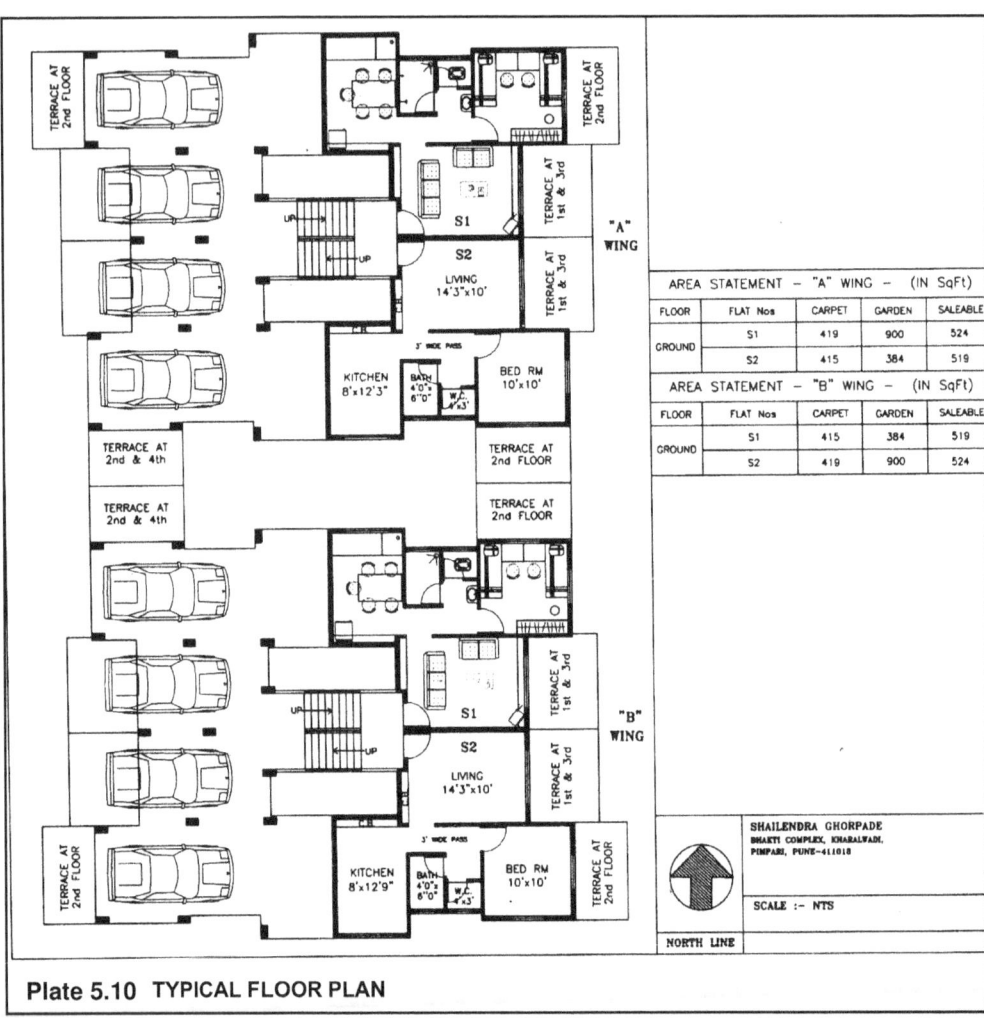

Plate 5.10 TYPICAL FLOOR PLAN

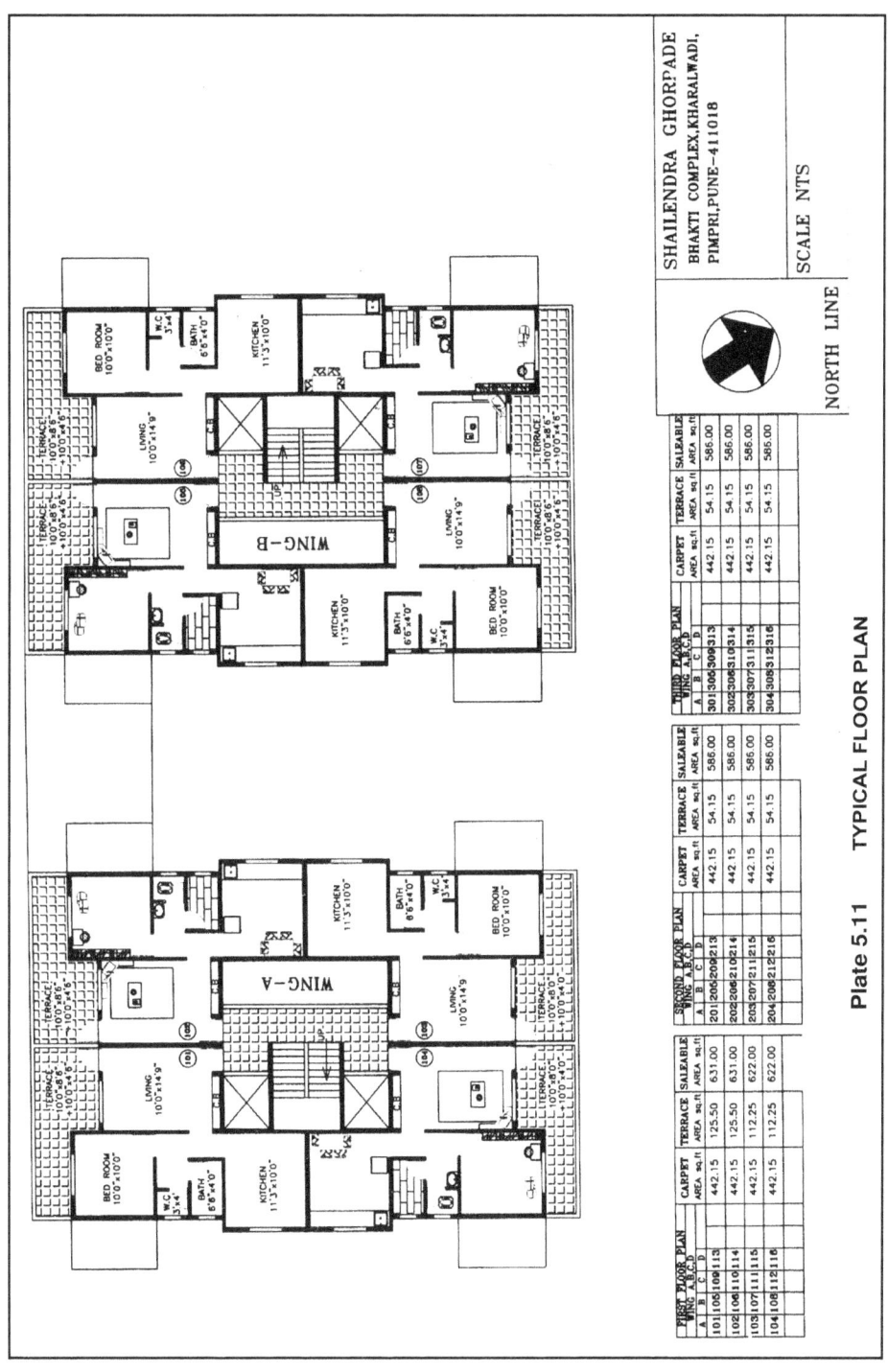

Plate 5.11   TYPICAL FLOOR PLAN

Plate 5.12 TYPICAL FIRST AND THIRD FLOOR PLAN

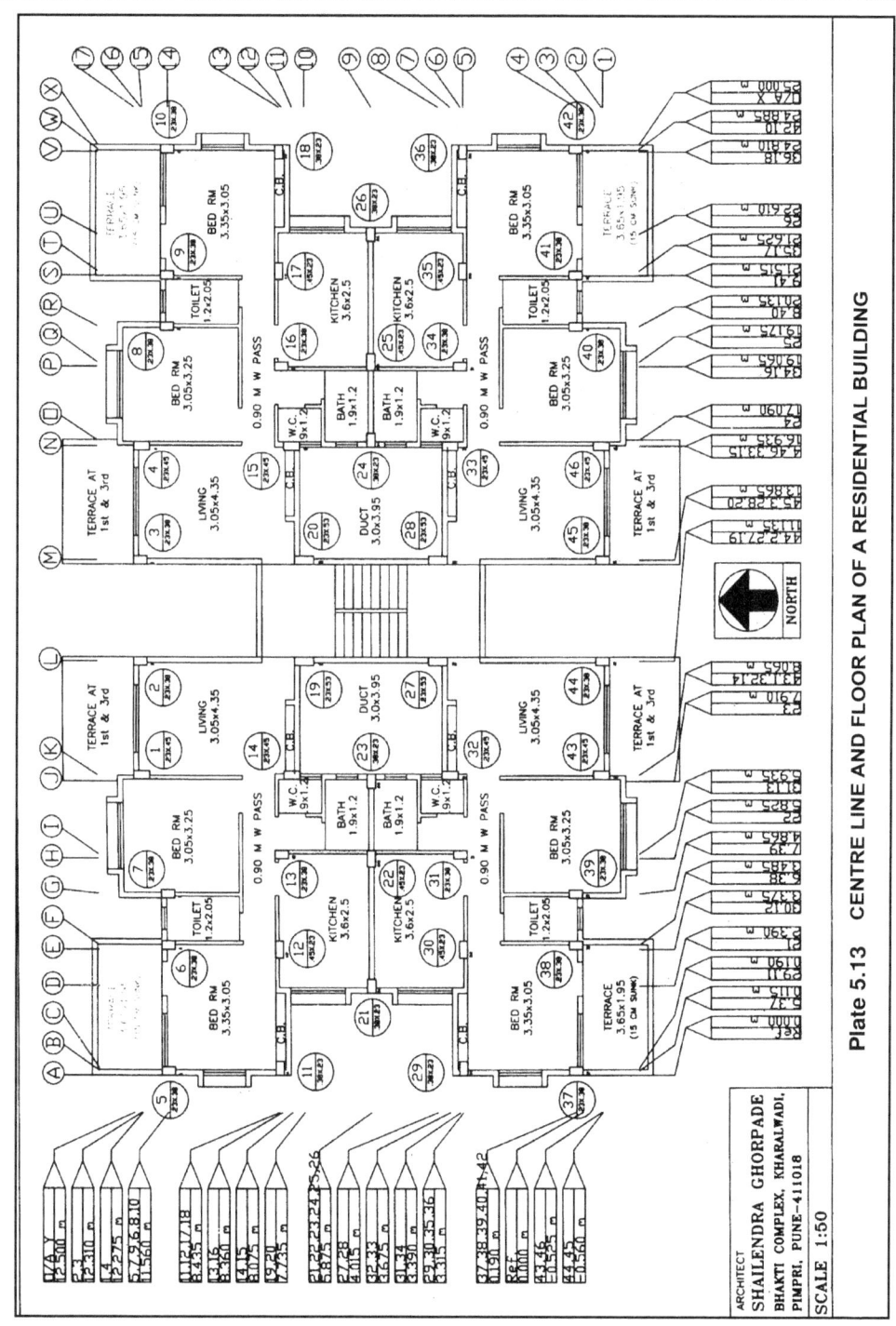

Plate 5.13 CENTRE LINE AND FLOOR PLAN OF A RESIDENTIAL BUILDING

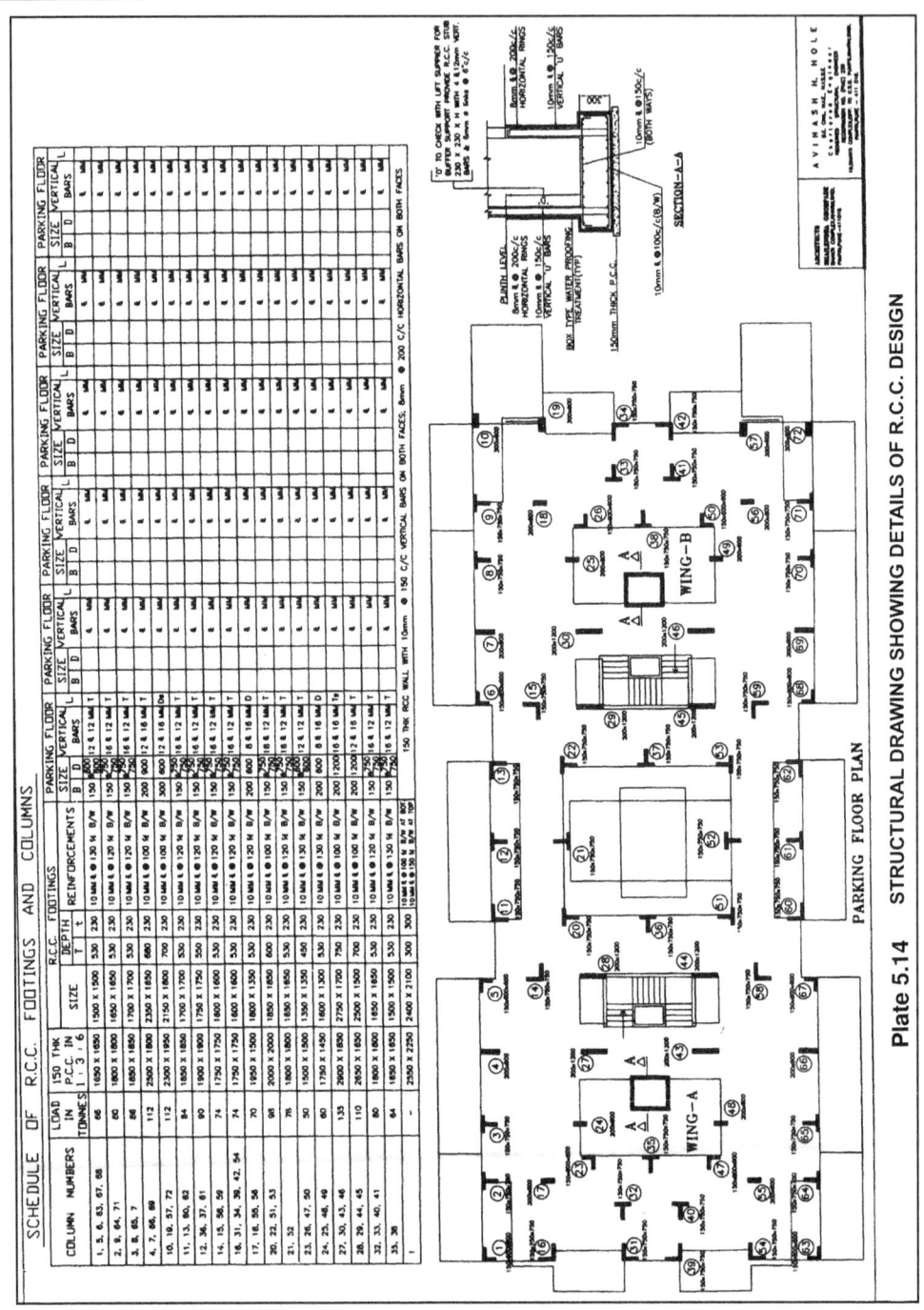

Plate 5.14 STRUCTURAL DRAWING SHOWING DETAILS OF R.C.C. DESIGN

Chapter 6
WORKING DRAWING

6.1 INTRODUCTION

Drawing is a Language of Engineers. For Civil Engineers, drawing is most important part of subjects to understand the different activities for execution of work. Building Drawing is a language of communication between an Architect and Engineer, Engineer and Surveyors, supervisors and skilled labours etc.

For execution of Civil Engineering projects, at various stages, different types of drawings are required necessarily.

Various types of drawings are required in fields of work for civil engineers, architects, contractors, draftsmen, structure engineers, supervisors etc.

Building drawings are required to be prepared for approval of owner, for approval of sanctioning authority, for preparing estimates, for executing work at site etc.

In Building Drawings:
1. Layout drawings and presentation drawings are prepared for owners.
2. Submission plans for approval of sanctioning authority like Munciple corporation, collector, grampanchayat, development authorities etc.
3. Working and detailed drawings for estimates and construction of buildings at site.

By means of graphical symbols, like lines, projections, drawings are prepared.

6.2 TYPES OF DRAWINGS

1. Plan (Top view)
2. Elevations (Front view)
3. Side elevations (Side view)
4. Sections
5. Working and detailed drawings like, details of doors, windows, stairs, foundation plan, roof plan, site plan, area statement, construction notes etc.
6. Isometric views
7. Oblique views
8. Perspective views.

According to method of preparing drawings they can be classified as:
1. Data drawings.
2. Measured drawings.
3. Structural drawings.
4. Working drawings or Detailed drawings.
5. Presentation drawings.

6.3 USE OF I.S. SPECIFICATIONS

For clear meaning of drawings and their purpose, it is a must to prepare a drawings with clear dimensions and notes. Any wrong dimension or wrong notes can misinterprete and waste of time may be there.

Uniformity is achieved in drawing by adopting specification I.S. - 962 - 1967.

This codes gives sizes of drawings (scales), sizes of lettering; dimensioning methods, symbols and abbreviations, methods of projections; units of measurement in drawing, etc.

Various Standard Specifications from I.S. Code of Practice:

Lines: Various types of lines required to be drawn are:

1. **Visible line or construction line:**

   _____

   (0.60 mm to 1.30 mm thick)

2. **Centre line:**

   — — — — — — — — — —

   (4 : 1), (Thin), (0.20 mm to 0.30 mm thick)

3. **Hidden line:** These lines shows the hidden portion of the object.

   - - - - - - - - - - - - - - - - - -

   (Medium), (0.40 mm to 0.50 mm thick)

4. **Section line:**

   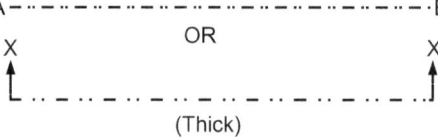

   (Thick)

5. **Short break lines:**

    (Free hand)

6. **Long break lines:**

BUILDING DESIGN AND DRAWING (N.M.U.)   WORKING DRAWING

7. **Dimension lines and extension lines:**

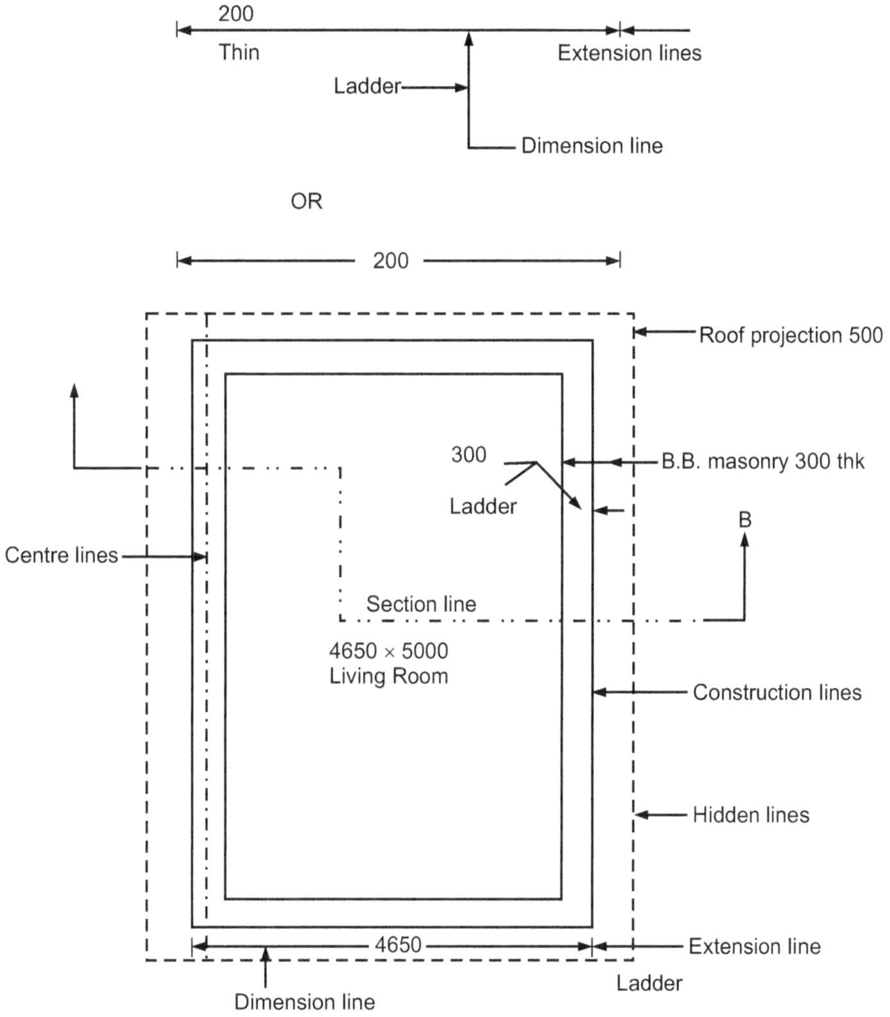

Fig. 6.1: Types of lines

- While writing dimension of units i.e. internally, in fashion 4650 × 5000, 4650 indicates (horizontal on paper) or length and 5000 indicates (Vertical on paper) or width of the unit.
- In dimension arrows should not be greater than 4 mm in length.

Fig. 6.2: Arrow head

- Dimensions of an object is not at all related with scale. It should give actual size of structure.
- All dimensions should be easily readable from the bottom or right hand edge of drawing.
- At places where it is not possible to write the note or dimension of part of object; then in such cases it is written slightly away from this, with the help of leaders.
- To show the continuity of the object, long break lines and short break lines are used as shown in Fig. 6.3.

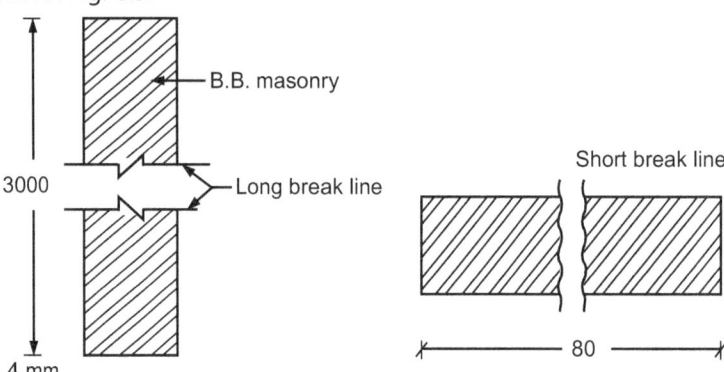

Fig. 6.3: Section of masonry with long break and short break lines

6.4 GRAPHICAL SYMBOLS

Sketches below, shows the graphical symbols for every materials of construction followed by abbreviations.

Sr. No.	Materials of Construction	Graphic Symbol
1.	Timber	
2.	Glass	
3.	Brick Masonry	
4.	UCR Masonry	

5.	Concrete	
6.	Rubble	
7.	Murum	
8.	Mortar	
9.	Wash Basin	
10.	W.C. (water closet)	
11.	Urinals	
12.	Steel Bars	
13.	Stirrups	
14.	Celling Fan	
15.	Ground Level	

16.	Door: (i) Single shutter	
	(ii) Double shutter	
	(iii) Gate	
17.	Stair Case	Plan, Section, Elevation
18.	Window	Lintel, Chajja, Section, Plan
19.	Single Leaf Double Swing Door	
20.	Double Leaf Double Swing Door	

No.	Name	Symbol
21.	Side Hinge	
22.	Centre Hinge	
23.	Folding Double Leaf	
24.	Sliding Door	
25.	Revolving Door	
26.	Door with Projected Hinges	
27.	Rolling Shutter External	
28.	Rolling Shutter Internal	
29.	Rectangular Section	
30.	Round Section	
31.	Pipe or Tubing	
32.	Pipe or Tubing	
33.	Wood (Rectangular Section)	
34.	Rolled Shapes	

Abbreviations:

1.	B. B. M.	Burnt Brick Masonry
2.	C. M.	Cement Mortar
3.	D. P. C.	Damp Proof Course
4.	U. C. R.	Uncoursed Rubble
5.	C. R.	Coursed rubble
6.	D	Doors
7.	W	Windows
8.	V	Ventilators
9.	W. C.	Water Closet
10.	F. S. I.	Floor Space Index
11.	C. C. T. W.	Country Cut Teak Wood
12.	T. W.	Teak Wood
13.	M. H.	Man hole
14.	N. T.	Nahani Trap
15.	G. T.	Gully Trap
16.	G. L.	Galvanised Iron
17.	C. I.	Cast Iron
18.	R. C. C.	Reinforced Cement Concrete
19.	A. C.	Asbestos Cement

6.5 SCALES

For preparing proportionate drawings and to accommodate drawings of structures of various sizes in standard size of sheet, use of scales is done.

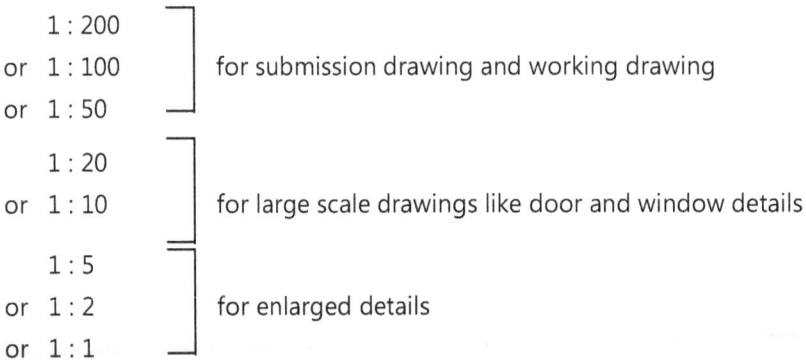

6.6 TITLE BLOCK

It is prepared in every drawing sheet at right hand bottom corner of sheet before or after drawings are prepared. This block clearly states, the name of drawing, number, date of preparation, prepared by, checked by, scale, name of architect and North direction etc.

Please refer Fig. 6.4 for title block for various sizes for different sizes of sheets.

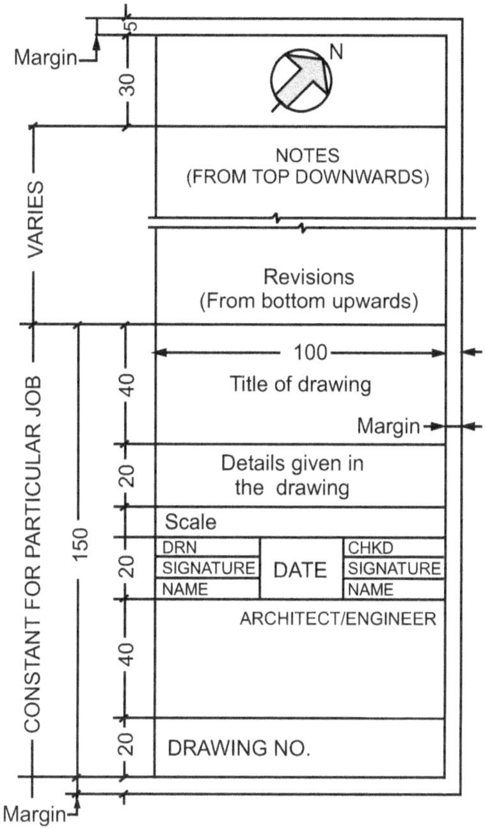

(a)

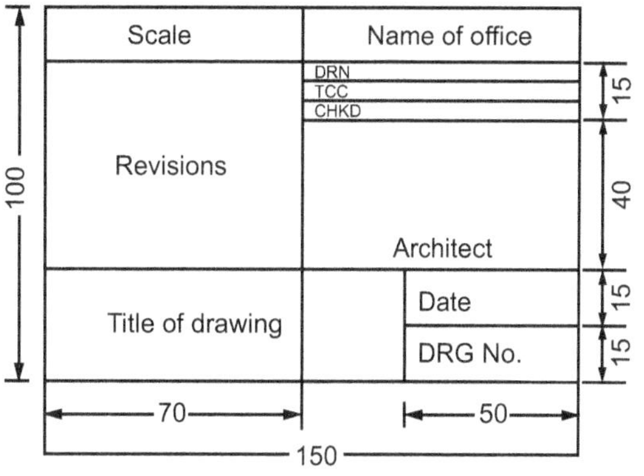

(b)

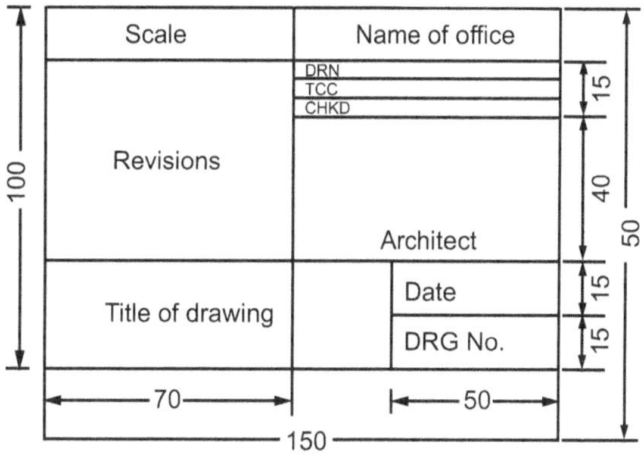

(c)

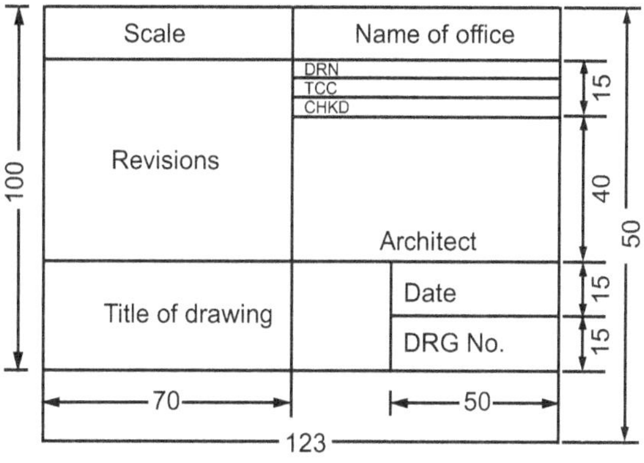

(d)

Fig. 6.4: Various types of title blocks

6.7 LINE - PLAN

It is a presentation drawing which is prepared by the architect and final plan is developed with the help of this. This plan also helps in preparing perspective drawing to be shown to the owner.

Before a plan is developed it is checked whether all the requirements of owner as well as basic requirements as per rules and bye-laws are included in line plan or not.

- This plan shows all the units and details which are to be erected while constructing the building.
- Dimension of units in this plan are clear inner dimensions.
- It can be drawn "Not to the Scale" also.
- By trial and error, various units are placed, according to their ideal location the area if possible which suits the shape of site. Thus, line plan is prepared. Please refer Fig. 6.5.

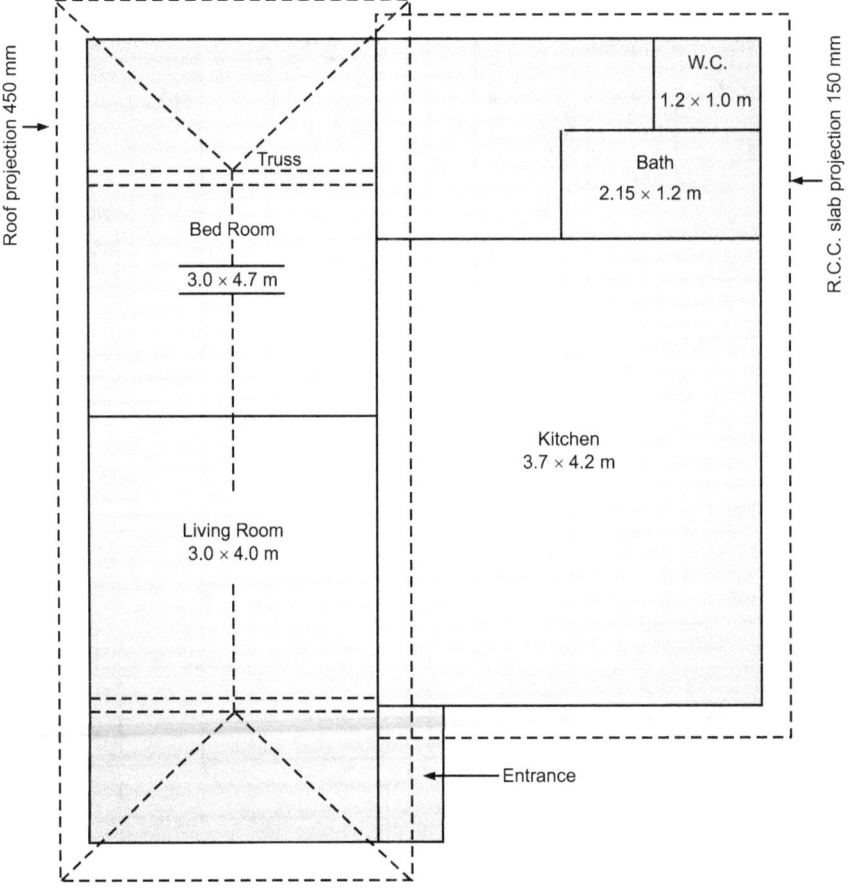

Fig. 6.5: Line – plan (not to the scale)

- Line plan is also prepared by assuming that whole building to be constructed, is cut with a horizontal section plane at sill level and then viewed from top. In this plan, wall thicknesses, doors and windows, chajjas etc. are not shown.

6.8 DEVELOPMENT OF LINE – PLAN

While developing the plan, line plan which is almost finalised with respect to arrangement of units is selected.

- Now plan is developed by keeping in mind the building to be constructed is cut with a horizontal section plane at sill level and viewed from top.
- While developing plan, elevation of all sides and perspective view should be kept in mind.
- While developing plan many other factors like shape of plot, North direction, wind and rain direction, main roads etc., should be considered.
- Thickness of walls (internal and external) depth and type of foundation, Number of stories is decided by knowing the type of structure whether load bearing type or framed type.

Like:

1. R.C.C. structure have external wall 230 mm thick and internal wall 150 mm thick.
2. In load bearing structure, external and bearing walls are 300 mm thick or more and partition walls are 200 mm thick.

Plans are drawn to the scales 1 : 50; 1 : 100 or 1 : 200.

[Scale is always represented as Representative Fraction (R. F.)].

$$R.F. = \left[\frac{\text{Distance on map or sheet}}{\text{Distance on ground}}\right]$$

[For drawings, R.F. is multiplied with distance on ground to know distance on map]

6.9 PLAN

This drawing shows length and width of building with rooms. A plan is prepared on a tracing paper or a sheet. A plan must include the following details:

1. Wall thickness and column size.
2. Area of each unit with size.
3. Name of the unit.
4. Location of W. C., bath, wash basin, urinals, sink etc.
5. Stair case (steps with landing, with up and down directions).
6. Location of door and windows (use symbols) direction of swing.

7. Passages, varandah, corridor etc.
8. Roof projections, slab projections, chajja projections etc.
9. In presentation drawings interior arrangement of furniture can also be shown (like sofa-set, chair, table, bed, kitchen platform, cub-board etc.)
10. External dimensions.
11. Plinth projection (if provided).
12. North direction.
13. Title [i.e. plan, Ground floor plan or typical floor plan (when more than two floors are similar in all respects in a building)].
14. Section lines.
15. Scale.

Method of Drawing Plan:

Start drawing the plan from the left hand bottom corner. Draw all external walls and thickness of walls as per the details of construction, care should be taken that the inner dimensions of rooms should remain same as shown in line plan.

Draw the location of doors and window with symbols, as per the dimensions, from schedule of doors and windows, suitably.

Show all the details enlisted above. While giving dimensions in plan, all external dimensions and dimensions from wall surface to doors and windows should be given in load bearing structure. In framed structure dimensions should be from centre of column or centre of door and window. In case of first floor plan or other, top floors, wall thickness or column size is reduced, so these changes should be shown. Location of stairs and roof details should be shown.

6.10 ELEVATION

This drawing represents the different views looking from different direction, when building will be constructed. For drawing this, all heights i.e. plinth height, sill height, ceiling height, window height, door height, thickness of lintel, thickness of slab, height of parapet etc., must be known.

Method of Drawing Elevation:

Elevation is drawn just above the plan by projecting lines from it. Now show G. L., plinth level, window sill, door and window's top level, lintel level, ceiling level, top level etc. Projected lines from plan show the location of walls, door and window steps, chajjas, roof with top of ridge, eaves, common rafters etc. After projecting doors and windows coming in elevations their detailed type should be shown. Design of grills also be shown by refering schedule of doors and windows. As far as dimensions are concerned, minimum dimensions should be shown in elevation. Because these dimensions will be shown in sections. Some dimensions can be shown like vertical heights of different levels. Title for elevation must be shown that from which side it is drawn. Along with this, notes and symbols of exterior material on the wall should be provided.

6.11 SECTIONS

For constructing a building various details are required. About the length and width, these are available from plan. Heights of different parts of building is shown in elevations. But details which are neither available in plan nor in elevations are drawn in sections by drawing suitable section lines in plan indicating all details.

Preferably section line should pass through W.C. and bath and stair-case. This gives all interior details of height of steps, height of landing, height of stair case, thickness of lintel, height of dado, height of window in W.C., details of roof etc. sections are two types generally.

1. Longitudinal section when building is imagined to be cut along the length.
2. Cross section when building is imagined to be cut along the width.
3. Section may be straight or offset. Section lines should be shown in ground floor plan and other floor plans also. Location of section line should be approximately at the same place. Because section line in plan represents a vertical section plane cutting the whole building.

Every section line must have arrow heads on its both ends. This arrow head shows that the building is cut and seen in the direction of arrow. The observer can stand on section line and he can see in the direction of arrows, whatever details are seen should be drawn according to type of section. These details must contain details from foundation to parapet. For section of a building with typical floor plans for number of stories, long break lines can be shown.

A very important thing that dimension of each and every part should be shown clearly and notes should be mentioned wherever required.

[For plan, elevation and sections of various buildings and their component parts refer sketchings].

Please refer Fig. 6.7, 6.8, 6.9 with reference to Fig. 6.6.

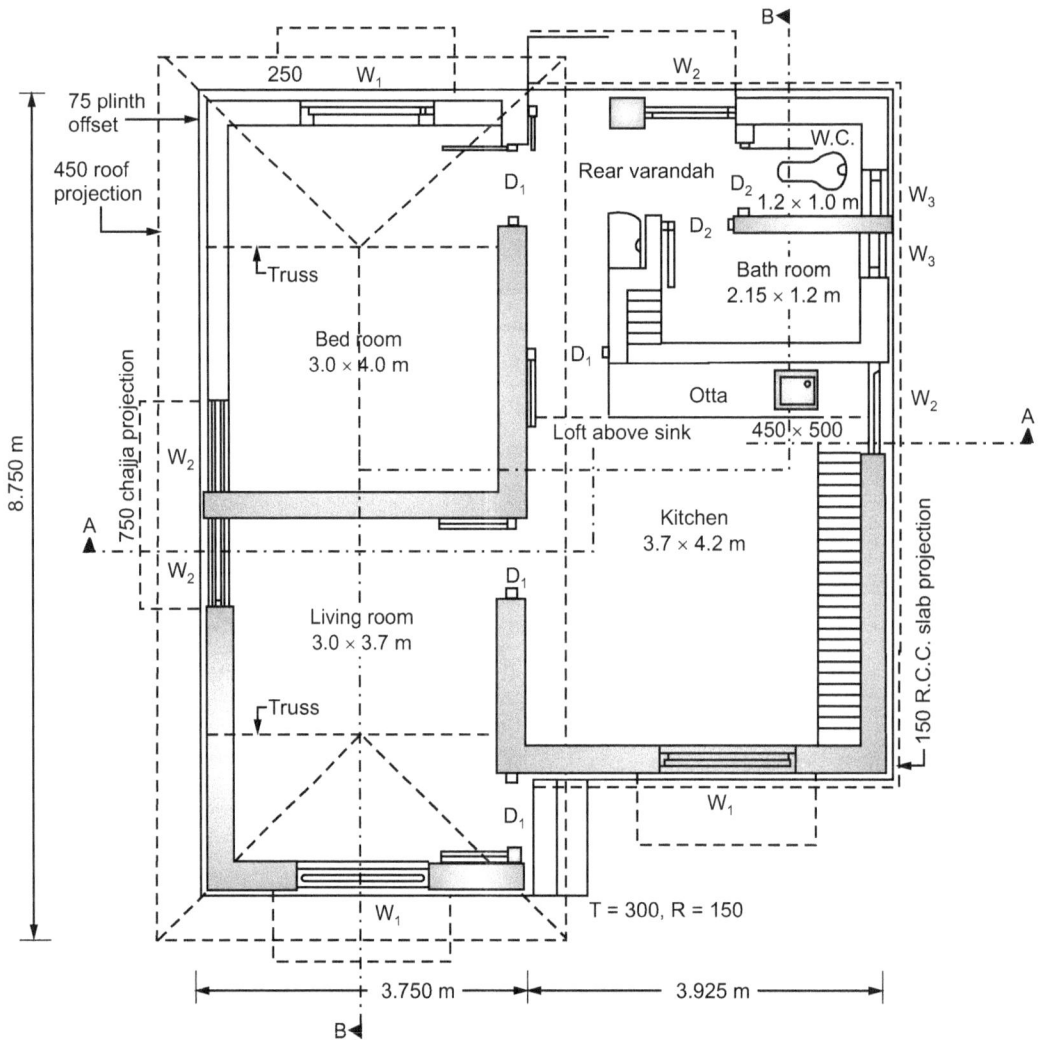

Fig. 6.6: Plan

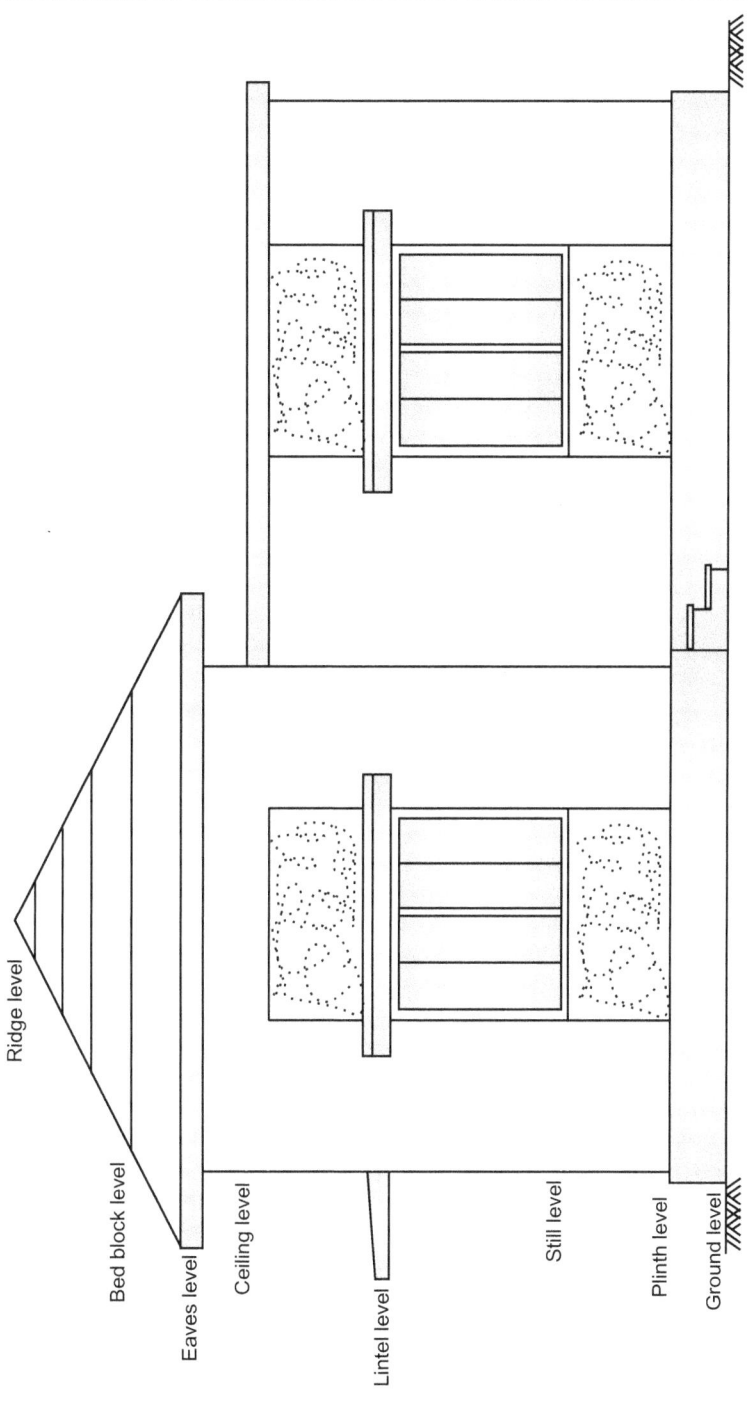

Fig. 6.7: Front Elevation

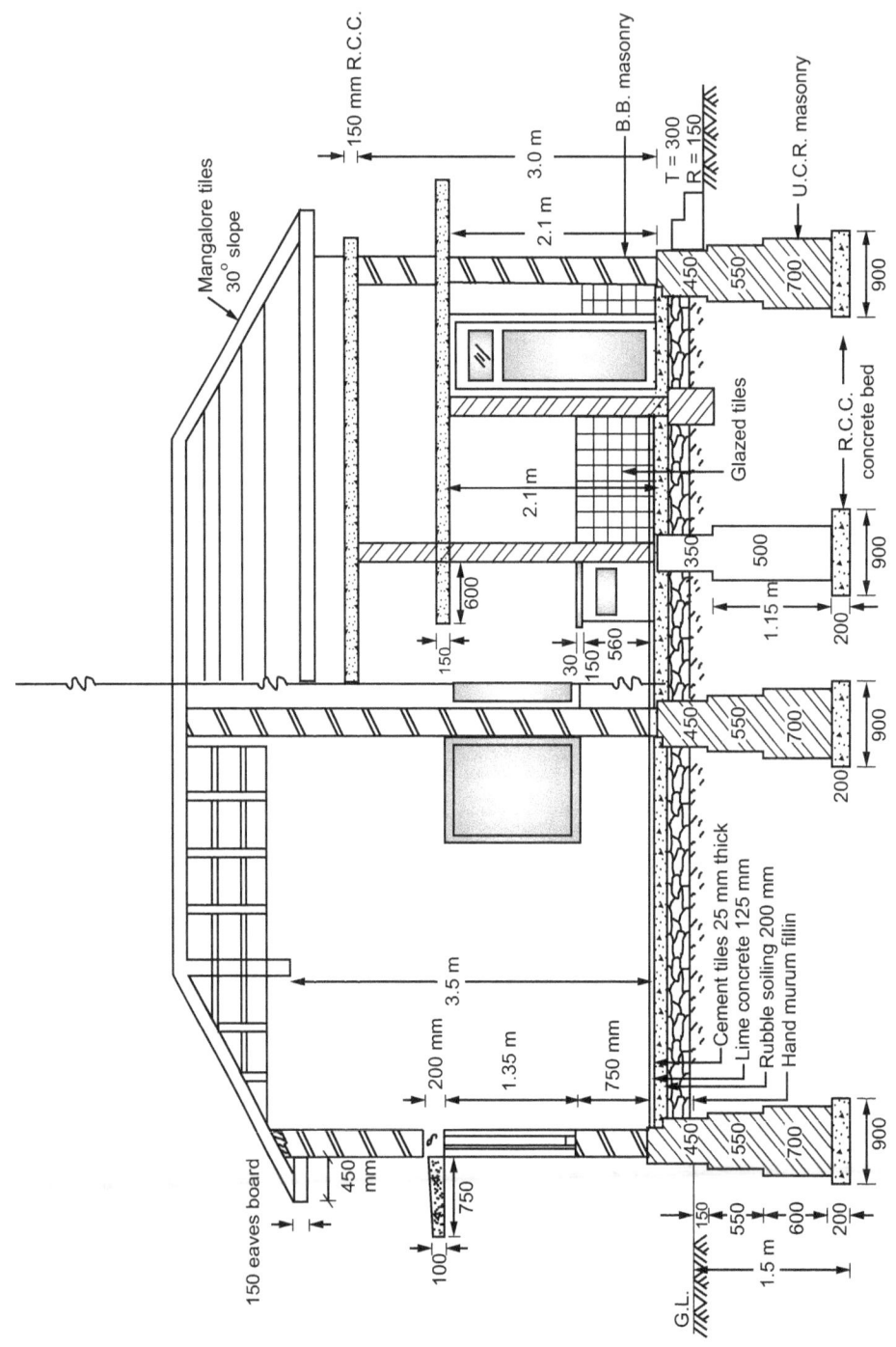

Fig. 6.8: Section B-B

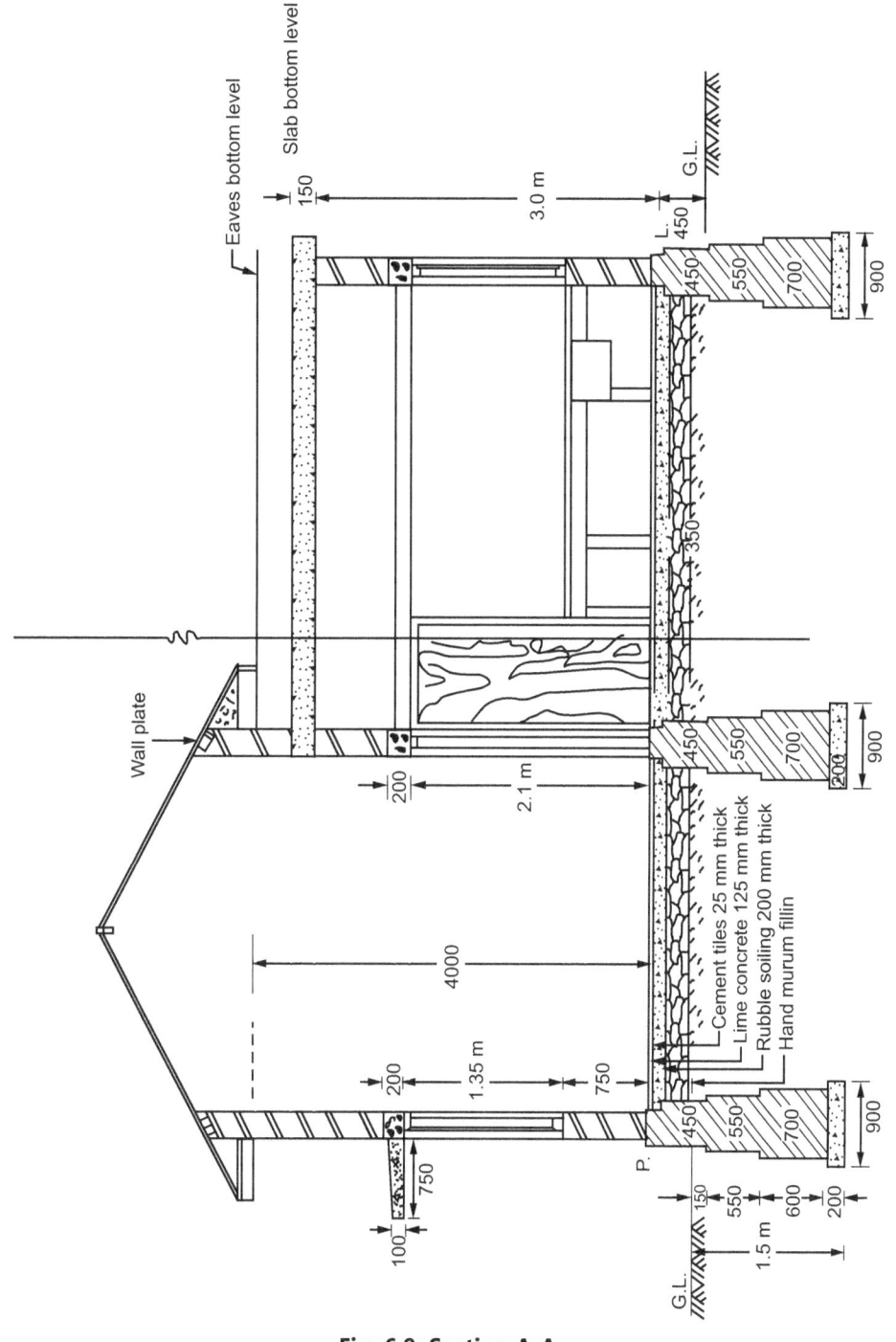

Fig. 6.9: Section A-A

6.12 SCHEDULE OF DOORS AND WINDOWS

Doors are provided in buildings for access, privacy and safety of different rooms. Windows are provided for ventilation and lightening in different rooms.

Generally, doors in a room should not be more than two and windows in each room should be provided as per the rules $\frac{1}{10}$th to $\frac{1}{20}$th of area of floor as per the climate, where building is constructed.

Types of doors which are provided in various types of buildings at different locations, like entrance, internally, shops etc. are as follows:
1. Battened leged and braced (timber) single or double shutter: For low cost housing.
2. Framed and panelled (timber) single or double shutter: For external and internal doors in residential building.
3. Flush doors (single shutter): For external doors.
4. Partly glazed and partly panelled (timber and glass) single shutter: For W.C., bath and stores.
5. Fully glazed doors (glass) single or double shutters: Office buildings.
6. Rolling shutter (steel): For garage, shops for large openings.
7. Collapsible doors (Iron): Jewellery shops, and in balcony and at entrance, in houses for safety.
8. Sliding doors (timber, iron or aluminium): Shops, offices and public buildings.
9. Revolving doors: Restaurants, hotels, airports, departmental stores etc.

Types of Windows:
1. Fan lights: Above the doors.
2. Glazed window: Residential and public buildings.
3. Casement window: In educational buildings.
4. Bay window: In residential buildings.
5. Louvered window: In W.C. and bath (where privacy is required as well as ventilation and light is required).
6. Dormer window: In pitched roofs etc.

Fixtures and Fastenings for Doors and Windows:

Various fastening and fixtures of doors and windows are as under:
1. Hinges: minimum three for each door shutter, minimum two for each window shutter.
2. Tower bolts: One for each door and one for window.
3. Barrel bolt: One for each door (if required) and one for window.
4. Aldrop: One for each door.
5. Hook and eye: One for each window shutter.
6. Handle: One for each shutter of door and windows.

Preparation of Schedules:

While preparing schedule of doors and windows all details about their size, type, symbol, location and description with remarks should be there. Table showing fastenings and fixtures should also be prepared.

For schedules of doors and windows please refer Table 6.1 (a) and (b).

Table 6.1 (a): Schedule of doors and windows

Sr. No.	Item	Symbol	No.	Size	Description	Remarks
1.	Door	D	1	1000 × 2000	Flush door with T. W. frame, single	External door.
2.	Door	D_1	2	900 × 2000	Fully panelled door in T. W. frame, single shutter type.	Internal door.
3.	Door	D_2	2	800 × 2000	Partly panelled and partly glazed door single shutter type.	In W.C. and bath.
4.	Window	W	3	1500 × 1300	Fully glazed window.	In Living rooms
5.	Window	W_1	4	1000 × 1300	Fully glazed window. With ventilators at top	
6.	Window	W_2	2	500 × 800	Louvered window.	In W.C. and bath
7.	Ventilator	V	2	500 × 300	Pivoted at centre horizontally	In Hall, Kitchen

Table 6.1 (b): Schedule of fastenings and fixtures

Sr. No.	Item	Type and Descriptions	No.	Remarks
1.	Hinge	Butt type, brass size 100 mm long.	9 12	3 for each shutter of door, 2 for each shutter of window.
2.	Tower bolt & barrel bolt	120 mm long, Aluminium - 3, Brass - 3	6	2 for each shutter at top and bottom.
3.	Handle	1 decorative type and other ordinary type.	7	4 for external door and other for internal doors.
4.	Safety chain and night latch	Stainless steel	1 each	For door at entrance.

6.13 AREA STATEMENT

This detail is required in drawings and must, to show with every building set to state the areas utilised.

This statement of area is prepared in a table and all types of areas like plot area, built up area, permissible built up area, carpet area, plinth area, F.S.I. (Floor Space Index) should be clearly shown.

Areas should be shown in m^2. In remark column of this statement table, remarks about bye-laws should be mentioned if required. Please refer Table 6.2.

Table 6.2: Schedule of area

Sr. No.	Area heading	Area in mm^2	Remarks
1.	Plot area	300	15 m × 20 m size plot, survey no. MNG/221062, plot no. 15489.
2.	Permissible built up area	100	$1/3^{rd}$ of plot area or according to to F.S.I.
3.	Built up area	61.36	Area of all units, with wall thickness.
4.	Plinth area	61.36	Area of building at plinth level. [It is equal to built up area if building is single storeyed].
5.	Carpet area	38.64	Usable area of all units excluding wall thickness and sanitary blocks.

For preparing area statement, after knowing plot areas, by following the rules and bye-laws, margins are left around the plan of building and site plan is prepared showing all details. The plan is divided (convenient geometric figures to calculate the areas as shown in Fig. 6.10.

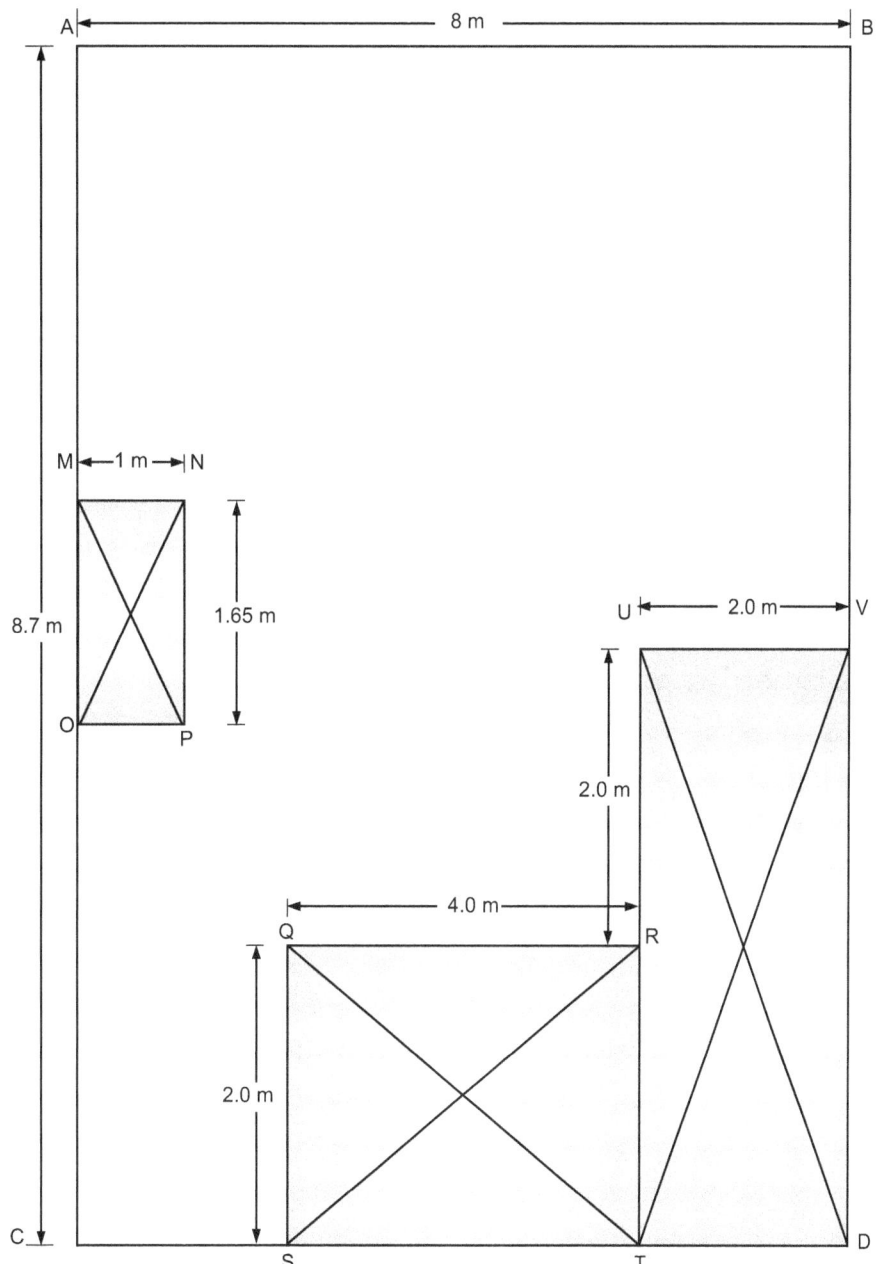

Fig. 6.10: Calculation of area of plot or building's built up area

Area of Fig. 6.10 of plan AB VU RQ SC
= Area ABCD - Area MNOP - Area QRTS - Area UTDV
= $(8 \times 8.7) - (1.65 \times 1) - (2 \times 4) - (2 \times 4) = 51.95 \text{ m}^2$

Measured Drawing:

Measured drawings are prepared by taking measurements of all component parts of a building. These drawings are prepared for the following purposes:
1. To be familiar with the construction details.
2. To study the views like elevations from different locations.
3. To study the dimensions of different parts like door, windows, roof etc., in proportion.
4. To give the training to any person for knowing about plinth, stair, column, beam, slab, roof, door, window, thresholds etc.
5. To give an idea of different style of architecture.

Measured Drawings are Drawn in the Following Steps:
1. Visit the site and note down the construction details like type of structure, details of foundation according to trend or as per old design sheets. Write construction notes.
2. Draw elevations of all sides.
3. Take all internal and external measurements and draw sketch plan.
4. Mark section line to give more or maximum details in section and draw section.
5. It is advisable to draw plan, elevation and section on graph paper first and then on sheets.

6.14 ABSTRACT FROM I.S. - 962 – 1967

Code of Practice for Architectural and Building Drawings:

6.14.1 Size of Drawing Sheets

Designation	Size in mm	Designation	Size in mm
A_0	841 × 1189	A_3	594 × 841
A_1	420 × 594	A_4	297 × 420
A_2	210 × 297	A_5	148 × 210

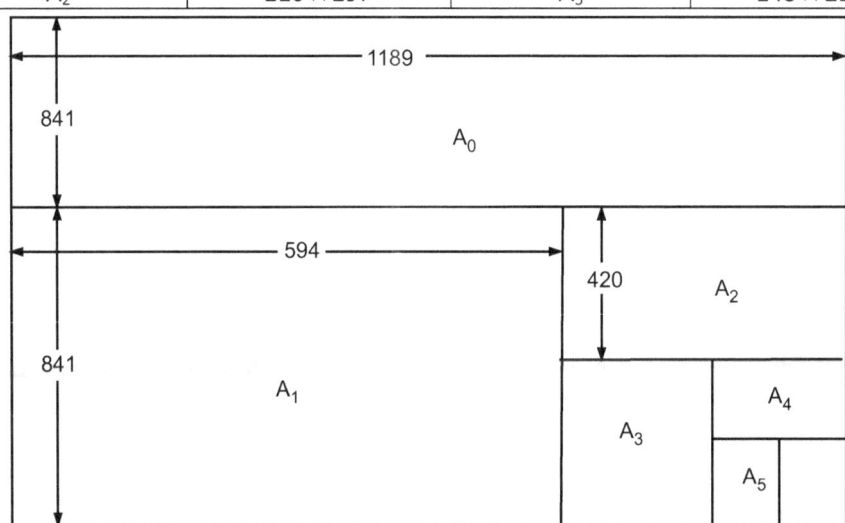

Fig. 6.11 : Sizes of drawing sheets

6.14.2 Size of Drawing Boards

Designation	Size in mm
B_0	1500×1000
B_1	1000×700
B_2	700×500
B_3	500×350

6.14.3 Margins

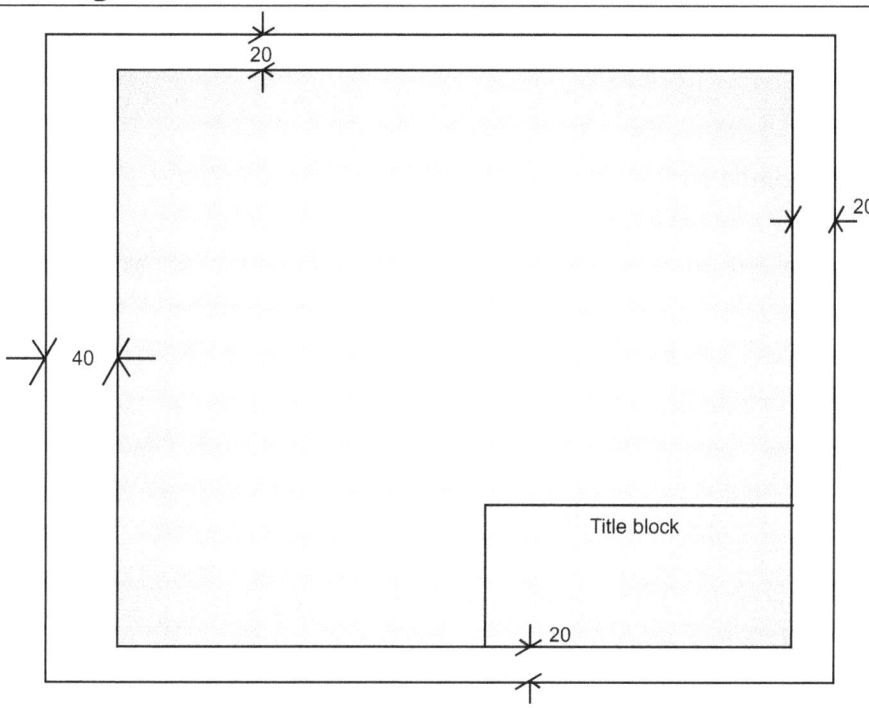

Fig. 6.12: Margins

All margins in case of full imperial size sheets are as shown in Fig. 6.12. A 40 mm margin on left hand side is left for binding in files.

In case of smaller sheets, the left hand margins may be 10 to 20 mm and remaining 10 mm.

6.14.4 Title Block

This block is very important since it presents details like title of drawing, name of organisation and firm, drawing number, scale, date of drawing etc.

It should be placed at the bottom right hand corner of the sheet where it is seen easily when the prints are folded. The title block shall have space provided for the dated initials of technical staff preparing, checking, and tracing the drawings and for the signatures of officers approving the design.

The size of the title block shall be 150 × 100 mm for large sheets, 150 × 50 mm for small sheets and also 123 × 50 mm for further small sheets.

Refer Fig. 6.4 (a, b, c, d).

6.14.5 Numbering of Drawing Sheet

In case of large civil engineering project works, where several series of drawings, for example, architectural drawings, structural drawings, construction drawings, plumbing drawings, electrical drawings and mechanical drawings are made then the drawing number shall be given either as A, B, C, D, E etc. or sheet number 3 of 10 (3/10). This gives the sheet number, as well as total number of sheets for that project. The sheet number shall be given at right hand top corner in vertical filing and at top right hand corner as well as bottom left hand corner in rolls.

Additional Information:

1. Job or order number.
2. Material list shall be placed immediately above the title block and includes construction notes, schedule of reinforcement, quantity required etc.
3. North point shall be clearly indicated in the right hand top corner of the drawing.

6.14.6 Reproduction of Drawings

Original drawings and tracings are normally preserved carefully and copies are used in workshops or on sites. The following copies are in use:

1. Blue print or Ammonia prints.
2. Photo-copy or Xerox.
3. Copies made on matt or rough paper with water colours.

6.14.7 Folding of Prints

The method of folding the prints of drawings is shown in Fig. 6.13 for storing in filing cases and attaching them. Following points should be observed while folding and unfolding the prints.

1. All maps and plans are folded to 297 × 210 mm size for convenient record in office files.
2. There is no necessity to open up the sheet to see what it refers to as the title block is visible which gives full details of it.
3. Plans may be opened out easily by holding firmly the top left hand corner and pulling the bottom right hand corner.
4. Always fold vertically first, fold horizontally next, and title block should be on the top most fold.

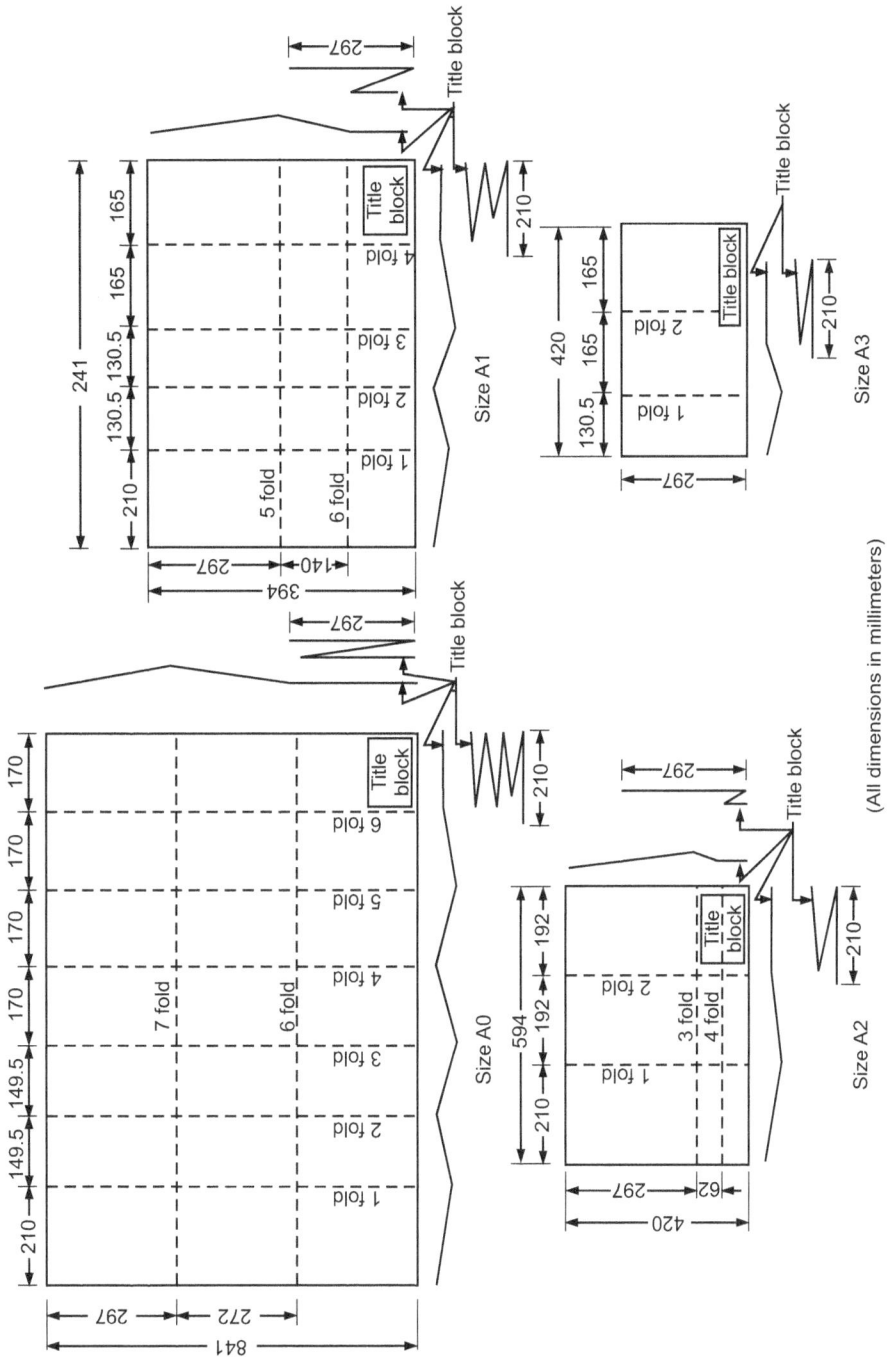

Fig. 6.13: Folding of prints

6.14.8 Reinforced Concrete Work

Numbering of beams and columns of reinforced concrete building structures shall be done, as C_1, C_2, C_3, C_4 and B_1, B_2, B_3 .... starting from right towards left. Beams shall be shown in double lines representing their width and their sizes by their overall dimensions. Beams below the slab shall be shown in dotted lines.

Slabs shall be numbered in the plan horizontally, starting at top left-hand coiner and finishing at the bottom right-hand corner.

The sizes of columns, slab thicknesses and details of stairs leading upto the level concerned shall also be indicated in the plan.

6.14.9 Colouring the Plan

Master plans, zone plans etc. may be coloured as specified in Table 6.3.

Table 6.3: Colouring the plan

Sr. No.	Item	Site Plan		Building Plan	
		Dye-Line Print	Blue Print	Dye-Line Print	Blue Print
(1)	(2)	(3)	(4)	(5)	(6)
(i)	Existing work	Black (outline)	White	Black	White
(ii)	Proposed work	Red filled in	Red	Red	Red
(iii)	Drainage and sewage work	Red dotted	Red dotted	Red dotted	Red dotted
(iv)	Water supply works	Black dotted	Black dotted	Black dotted	Black dotted
(v)	Work proposed to be dismantled	Yellow hatched	Yellow hatched	Yellow hatched	Yellow hatched
(vi)	Open spaces	No colour	No colour	–	–
(vii)	Plot lines	Thick, black	Thick, black		
(viii)	Permissible building lines	Thick, dotted black	Thick, dotted black	–	–
(ix)	Existing street(s)	Green	Green	–	–
(x)	Future street(s), if any	Green dotted	Green dotted	–	–

6.15 DETAILED DRAWINGS

Detailed drawings of various component parts of a structure are drawn and prepared to utilised them for work of supervision, preparing estimates, calculation of area for area statement, etc.

Detailed drawings are more or less related to working drawings. A complete set of submission drawings includes working drawings, detailed drawings, construction notes, area statement specification of works (if any), for execution of a building other than getting it sanctioned from the authority concerned, it is must to produce all the details of its component parts in the form of detailed drawings.

The complete set of drawings include:
1. Plans: Ground floor and first floor and plan for other floors.
2. Elevations of all sides (Preferably from the front side).
3. Sections:
   (a) Passing through doors, windows, balcony and maximum rooms.
   (b) Passing through stairs and W.C., bath.
4. Foundation plan with section of footing.
5. Roof plan with schedule of roof detail or terrace floor plan.
6. Site plan with area statement.
7. Structural details of columns, beams, slab (If framed structure is there).
8. Details:
   (a) Doors and windows drawings with fixtures and fastenings.
   (b) Staircase with all details of rise, tread, width in section and plan.
   (c) Details of chajja.
   (d) Details of dado.
   (e) Structural details of stairs.
   (f) Sanitary and water supply fixtures by drawing a house drainage plan separately showing details of drain pipes, gully traps, man holes, chambers for inspection and location of overhead tank for storage of water.
   (g) A plan showing electrical installation can also be drawn to show details of electric points in the house.
- All such drawing are drawn to the suitable scale (1 : 50, 1 : 25 or 1 : 10 etc.).
- All detailed drawings must contain each and every dimension, notes, data regarding materials used.
- Detailed drawings must be very carefully prepared as these will be used for preparing estimates as well as for site supervision. Incorrect and incomplete detailed drawings causes delay in progress of work, disputes and loss of time, also increase in expenses.

6.16 METHODS OF PREPARING DETAILED DRAWINGS

Methods of preparing drawings is explained in this chapter in details along with suitable drawings required.

6.16.1 Drawing Foundation Plan

Foundation plan is used for setting out of building, on site. Accuracy in construction depends upon the correct setting out, i.e. correct measurements of foundation plan.

For Load Bearing Structure:

Before drawing a foundation plan, depth of hard strata is determined by trial-pit results, then width of foundation. (i.e. width of foundation trench) is decided by thumb rule according to wall thickness in load bearing structure and according to loads in framed structure.

Now start drawing foundation plan:
1. Draw centre lines for all walls in plan.
2. Show width of trench equally on either side of centre line.
3. Show internal and external dimensions.
4. Mark excavation lines.
5. Mark diagonal check which is required to be checked after setting out the foundation at site.
6. Show the section of footing used with dimensions along with foundation plan.

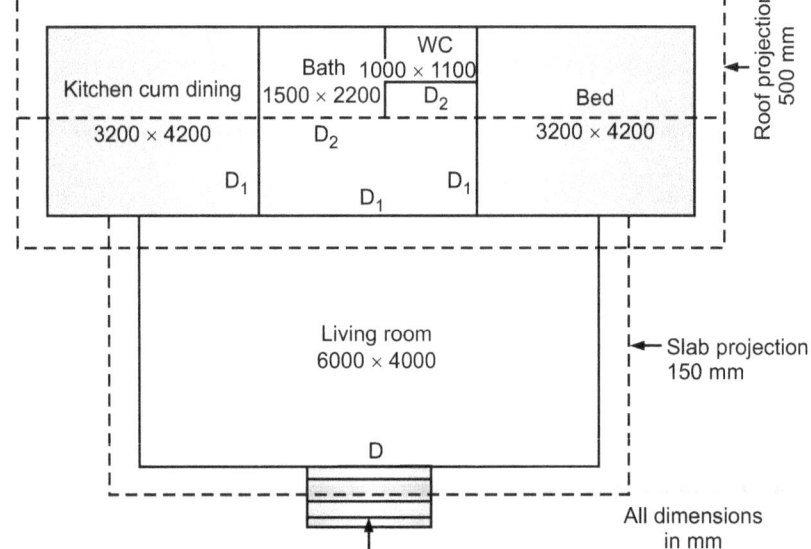

Details:
1. Depth of footing – 1100 W
2. Thickness of masonry – 300

Fig. 6.14 (a): Line plan (not to the scale)

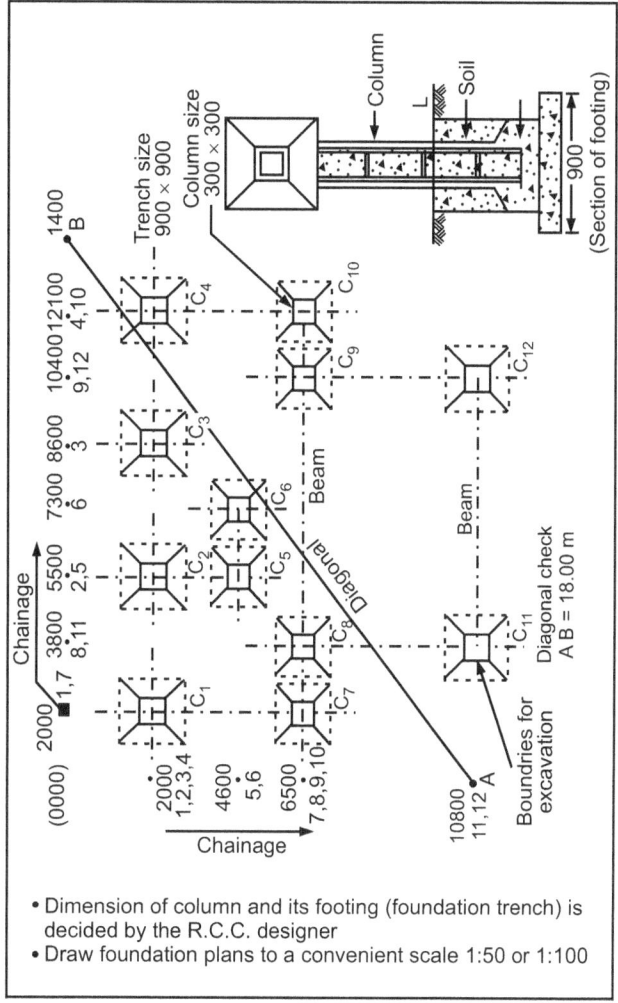

- Dimension of column and its footing (foundation trench) is decided by the R.C.C. designer
- Draw foundation plans to a convenient scale 1:50 or 1:100

- Dimension of column and its footing (foundation trench) is decided by the R.C.C. designer.
- Draw foundation plans to a convenient scale 1 : 50 or 1 : 100.

Fig. 6.14 (b): Foundation plan for framed structure

6.17 ROOF PLAN AND TERRACE FLOOR PLAN

Roof plan is prepared or drawn to get, the details of roof components - Roof for the building may be (1) Pitched roof, (2) Flat roof. For pitched roof, various types of roof covering materials are used like Mangalore tiles, A.C. sheets, G.I. sheets etc. For flat roof, materials used is R.C.C. This roof is also called slab. It can be a brick steel roof.

6.17.1 Roof Plan for Pitched Roof

A pitched roof is constructed either of wood work or steel members. In case of residential buildings it is constructed with wooden members like Trusses, Ridge, Valley, Hip, Gable, Purlins, Common rafter, Wall plates, Jack rafters, Eaves board, Gutter for drainage of rain water etc.

1. In roof plan all the members should be shown clearly.
2. All the members must be marked with their name and cross section.
3. All external dimensions of roof plan must be shown.
4. Along with this plan schedule of wood-work should be given including names of members, cross sections, lengths, quantity and number of Mangalore tiles or number of A. C. sheets required to cover the roof.

Refer Fig. 6.15 and Table: 6.1. Refer Fig. 6.14 (a) for line plan.

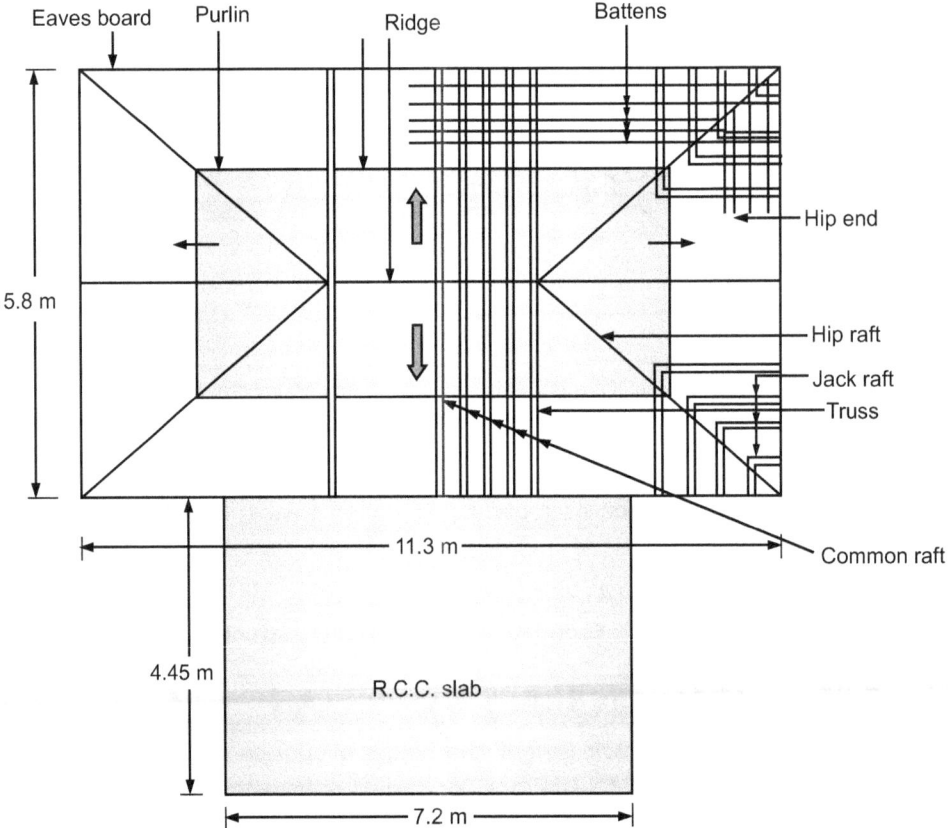

Fig. 6.15: Roof plan for pitched roof

Table 6.4: Schedule of wood work

Sr. No.	Item	Cross sections	Remarks
1.	Ridge	75 × 180	–
2.	Purlin	105 × 130	-
3.	Truss		
	(a) Tie beam	75 × 85	Different types of Trusses
	(b) King post	75 × 130	for different spans.
	(c) Strut	75 × 50	
	(d) Principal rafter	75 × 105	
4.	Hip rafter	75 × 135	–
5.	Jack rafter	75 × 155	Unequal in length.
6.	Common rafter	50 × 75	Equal in length 450 c/c.
7.	Battens (CCTW)	45 × 25	315 mm c/c.
8.	Eaves board	150 × 15	-

6.17.2 Roof Plan for Flat Roof

This roof is constructed as slab with R.C.C. material. Show the following details for such a roof plan:
1. R.C.C. slab projection (if any) must be shown.
2. Draw details of stair case room and parapet wall.
3. Show the position of water tank. (Generally over W.C. and Bath).
4. Show position of rain water pipes, direction of slope.
5. Mark external dimensions as this gives length and width of Terrace slab.

To draw roof plan for framed structure and for R.C.C. slab, following terrace details must be shown:
1. Size of terrace with slab projections.
2. Rain water pipes position.
3. Position of water Link.
4. Position of stair case room etc.

Remaining procedure to draw this will be same as explained.
Refer Fig. 6.15 (R.C.C. slab part).

6.18 SITE PLAN

A plan showing the location of a structure with respect to some permanent features. It gives an idea of site, its location and details. It is drawn to a scale of 1 : 500 or any other convenient scale.

It include the following details:
1. Shape of building with external dimensions.
2. Plot size and number (SVY).
3. Plots in vicinity.
4. North direction.
5. Marginal distance on front, rear and sides of building from plot boundary.
6. Compound wall or fencing.
7. Main gate, Trees, Electric poles.
8. Sanitary disposed or sewer lines and water supply line.
9. Roads, with width.
10. Permanent structure, Temple etc. Refer Fig. 6.16 for site plan.

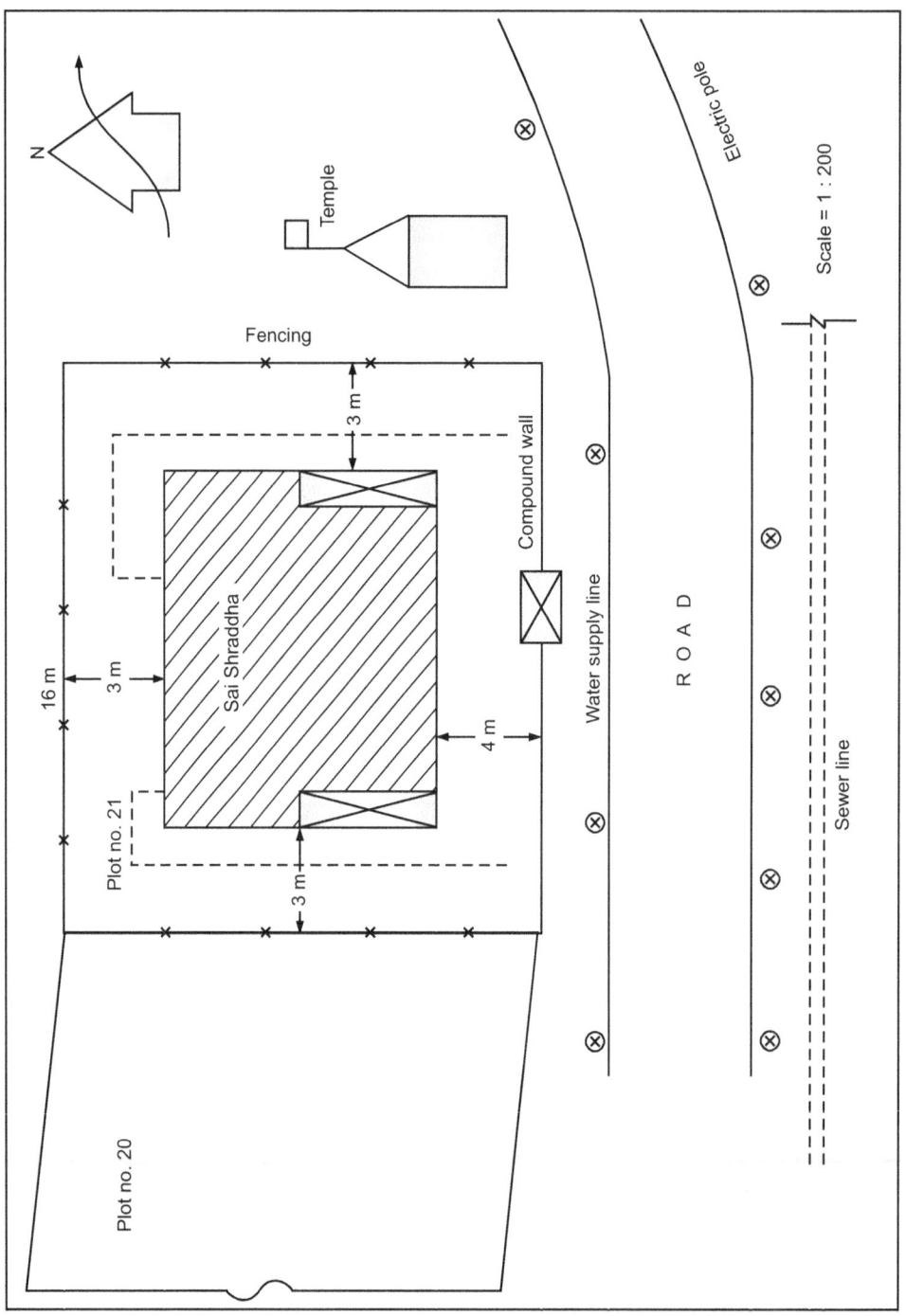

Fig. 6.16: Site plan

Area Statement:

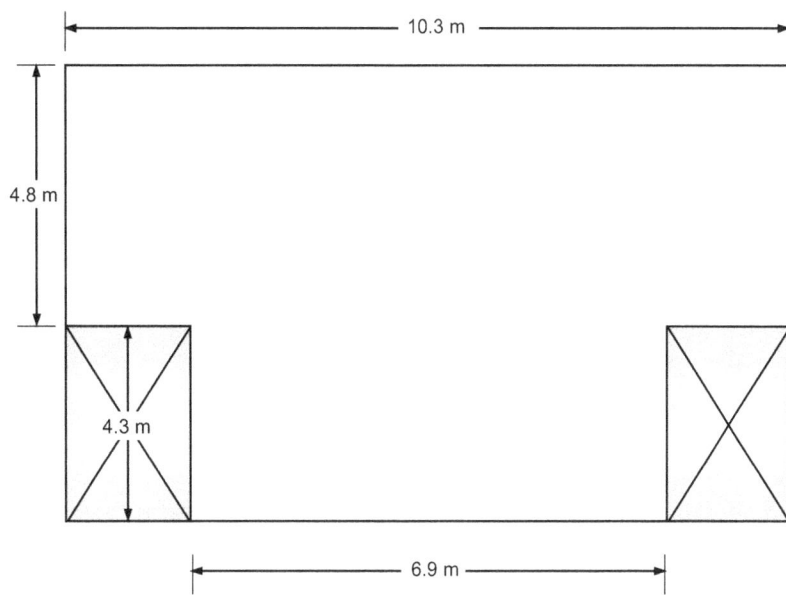

Fig. 6.17: Area plan

$$\text{Area} = \text{Complete Rectangle} - \text{Area of crossed}$$

$$\text{Plinth area} = 10.3 \times (4.8 \times 4.3) - \left[4.3 \times \left\{\frac{10.3 - 6.9}{2}\right\} \times 2\right]$$

$$= 93.73 - 14.62 = 79.11 \text{ m}^2$$

Table 6.5: Area details

Sr. No.	Item	Area in m²	Remarks
1.	Plot area	295.03	–
2.	Built-up area (permissible)	98.34	1/3 of plot area
3.	Area constructed (Built-up area)	79.11	–
4.	Plinth area	79.11	Similar to area constructed as building in single storeyed.
5.	Carpet area	60.37	Excluding W.C. bath and wall thickness.

6.19 OTHER DETAILS

Details regarding construction of various components are shown in detailed drawing like:
1. Structural details of footing, column, beam, slab etc.
2. Doors and windows, with fixture and fastenings details.
3. Stair case details with Rise, Tread, width etc.
4. Details of chajja etc.
5. House drainage plan and electrical installation plan for details of sanitary fittings and electrical fittings respectively.

IMPORTANT POINTS

- Types of Drawings.
- Various types of lines required in construction.
- Graphical symbols for construction materials.
- Abbreviations and scadfcdfles.
- Title block, line-plan, elevations and sections.
- Schedule of doors and windows, types of windows and fixtures and fastenings for doors and windows.
- Detailed drawings and its set for construction.
- Methods of preparing detailed drawings, foundation plan.
- Roof plan and its types: (a) For pitched roof, (b) For flat roof.

QUESTIONS

1. What are the objectives of framing development control rules?
2. What are the criteria for minimum area of plot?
3. What is F.A.R.? What are the areas exempted while calculating F.A.R.?
4. Why open spaces around any building should be left?
5. What is building line and control line?
6. What is FAR? State its necessity.
7. What is building line and control line? Explain their importances.
8. It is decided to plan a single storeyed hospital building. Enlist the essential amenities and areas for the different units. Explain also, with sketch, how you will apply principle of grouping, while preparing a flow diagram.
9. Enumerate the various area calculations in building and explain any one in detail.
10. Explain the necessity of building byelaws.
11. What is the difference between built-up area and carpet area?
12. Explain any one of the following :
    (i) Building line and control line. OR
    (ii) Rules regarding height regulations of buildings.
13. Explain the following terms with sketches :
    (i) Building line.
    (ii) Control line.
    (iii) Marginal distances.
14. State the bye-laws regarding road width and height of building.
15. What is Floor Area Ratio (F.A.R.)? State which areas of construction are excluded while calculating floor area ratio.
16. Write a detailed note on building line and control line. Mention its distances for all types of roads.
17. Discuss the importance of built-up area, plinth area, and carpet area.

■■■

UNIT 3

Chapter 7
PLANNING OF APARTMENT

7.1 INTRODUCTION

Apartment house, also called apartment block, or block of flats, building containing more than one dwelling unit, most of which are designed for domestic use, but sometimes including shops and other non-residential features.

Apartment buildings have existed for centuries. In the great cities of the Roman Empire, because of urban congestion, the individual house, or domus, had given way in early imperial times to the communal dwelling, except for the residences of the very wealthy. Four stories were common, and six, seven, or eight-story buildings were occasionally constructed.

7.2 MINIMUM FLOOR AREA AND HEIGHT OF ROOMS

	Floor Area	Height (m)
Living	10 sq.m. (100 sq. ft) breadth mm 2.7 m or 9")	3.3 (11)
Kitchen	6 sq.m. (60 sq. ft)	3.0 (10")
Bath	2 sq.m. (20 sq. ft)	2.7 (9")
Latrine	1.6 sq.m. (16 sq. ft)	2.7 (9")
Bath and Water Closet	3.6 sq.m. (36 sq. ft)	2.7 (9")
Servant Room	10 sq.m. (100 sq. ft)	3.0 (10")
Garage	2.5 × 4.8 m (8" × 16")	3.0 (10")
Min. Height of Plinth for Main Building	–	0.6 (2")
Min. Height of Plinth for Servant Quarters	–	0.3 (1")
Min. Depth of Foundation	–	0.9 (3")
Thickness of Wall	20 cm to 30 cm (9" to 13.5")	–
Damp Proof Course	2 cm to 2.5 cm (3/4" to 1")	Thick full width of plinth wall

Byelaws Regulations for Apartments:
- Line of building frontage and minimum plot sizes.
- Open spaces around residential building.
- Minimum standard dimensions of building elements.
- Provisions for lighting and ventilation.
- Provisions for safety from explosion.
- Provisions for means of access.
- Provisions for drainage and sanitation.
- Provisions for safety of works against hazards.
- Requirements for off-street parking spaces.
- Requirements for landscaping.
- Special requirements for low income housing.
- Size of structural elements.

7.3 ARRANGEMENT OF ROOMS IN APARTMENTS

1. Living Room
2. Kitchen
3. Store Room
4. Bed Room
5. Office Room
6. Bath and W.C.
7. Dressing Room
8. Verandah
9. Stair Case

1. **Living Rooms:** This area is for general use. Hence the living and drawing room should be planned near the entrance south east aspects. During colder day the sun is towards the south and will receive sunshine which is a welcoming feature. During summer sunshine the northern side and entry of sunrays from southern or south – east aspects do not arise.
2. **Kitchen:** Eastern aspects to admit morning sun to refresh and purity the air.
3. **Reading Room/ Class Room:** North aspects this makes more suitable since there will be no sun from north side for most part of the year.

4. **Bed Room:** Bed may also be provided with attached toilets, there size depends upon the number of beds, they should be located so as to give privacy and should accommodate beds, chair, cupboard etc., and they should have north or – west south – west aspect.

5. **Bath and W.C:** Bath and W.C are usually combined in one room and attached to the bed room and should be well finished. This should be filled with bath tub, shower, wash-hand basin, W.C., shelves, towels, racks brackets etc., all of white glazed tiles. Floor should be mosaic or white glazed files. Instead of providing all bed room with attached bath and W.C separated baths and latrines may also be provided.

6. **Verandah:** There should verandah in the front as well as in the rear. The front verandah serves setting place for male members and weighting place for visitors. The back verandah serve a ladies apartment for there sitting, working controlling, kitchen works etc., verandah project the room against direct sun, rain and weather effect. They used as sleeping place during the summer and rainy season and are used to keep various things verandah also give appearance to the building. The area of a building may vary from 10% to 20% of the building.

7. **Stair Case:** This should be located in a easily accessible to all members of the family, when this is intended for visitors it should be in the front, may be on one side of verandah. It meant for family use only, the staircase should be placed the rear. The stairs case should be well ventilated and lighted the middle to make it easy and comfortable to climb. Rises and threads should be uniform through to keep rhythm while climbing or descending.

   Some helpful points regarding the orientation of a building are as follows:
   - Long wall of the building should face north south, short wall should face.
   - East and west because if the long walls are provided in east facing, the wall.
   - Absorb more heat of sun which causes discomfort during night.
   - A verandah or balcony can be provided to wards east and west to keep the rooms cool.
   - To prevent sun's rays and rain from entering a room through external doors and windows sunshades are required in all directions.

8. **Orientation:** After having selected the site, the next step is proper orientation of building. Orientation means proper placement of rooms in relation to sun, wind, rain, topography and out look and at the same time providing a convenient access both to the street and back yard.

The factors that effect orientation most are as follows:
- Solar heat
- Wind direction
- Humidity
- Rain fall
- Intensity of wind site condition
- Lightings and ventilation

9. **Solar heat:** Solar heat means sun's heat, the building should receive maximum solar radiation in winter and minimum in summer. For evaluation of solar radiation, it is essential to know the duration of sunshine and hourly solar intensity on exposed surfaces.

10. **Wind direction:** The winds in winter are avoided and are in summer, they are accepted in the house to the maximum extent.

11. **Humidity:** High humidity which is common phenomenon is in coastal areas, causes perspiration, which is very uncomfortable condition from the human body and causes more discomfort.

12. **Rain Fall:** Direction and intensity of rainfall effects the drainage of the site and building and hence, it is very important from orientation point of view.

13. **Intensity of Wind:** Intensity of wind in hilly regions is high and as such window openings of comparatively small size are recommended in such regions.

14. **Site Conditions:** Location of site in rural areas, suburban areas or urban areas also effects orientation, sometimes to achieve maximum benefits, the building has to be oriented in a particular direction.

15. **Lighting:** Good lighting is necessary for all buildings and three primary aims. The first is to promote the work or other activities carried on within the building. The second is to promote the safety of people using the buildings. The third is to create, in conjunction to interest and of well beings.

16. **Ventilation:** Ventilation may be defined as the system of supplying or removing air by natural or mechanical mean or from any enclosed space to create and maintain comfortable conditions. Operation of building and location to windows helps in providing proper ventilation. A sensation of comfort, reduction in humidity, removal of heat, supply of oxygen are the basic requirements in ventilation apart from reduction of dust.

7.4 ADDITIONAL DRAWINGS FOR REFERENCE

Set No. 1:

Two storeyed drawings for reference

Table 7.1

REFERENCES		
D	Door	1.20×2.10 m
D_1	Door	0.90×2.10 m
D_2	Door	0.75×2.10 m
W	Window	1.50×1.20 m
W_1	Window	1.20×1.20 m
W_2	Window	0.90×1.20 m

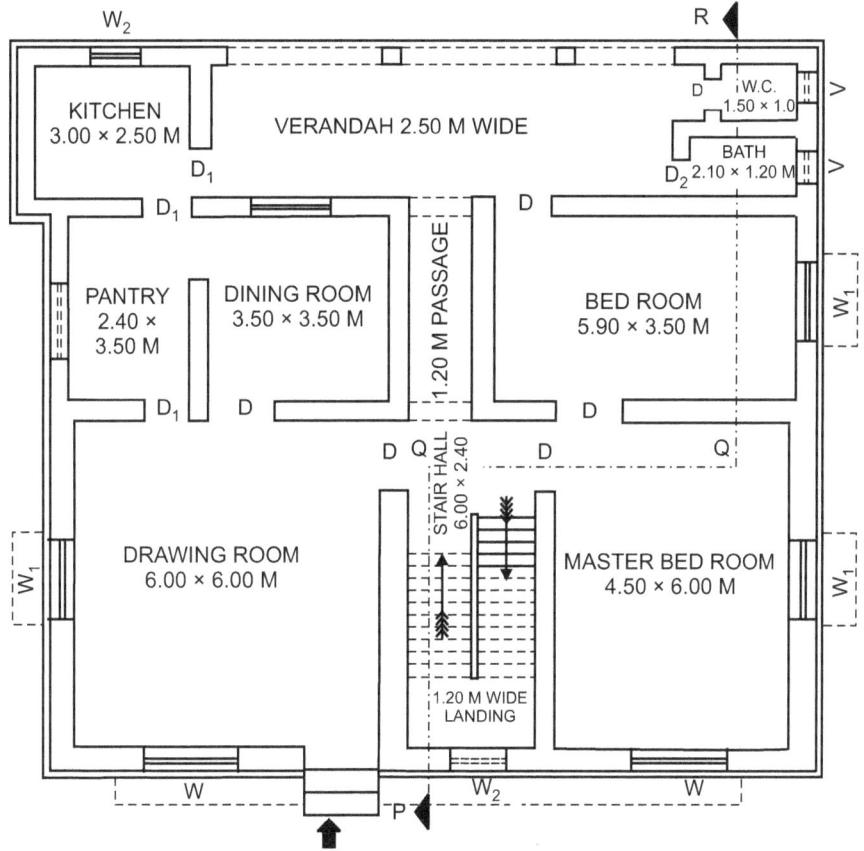

Fig. 7.1: Ground floor plan

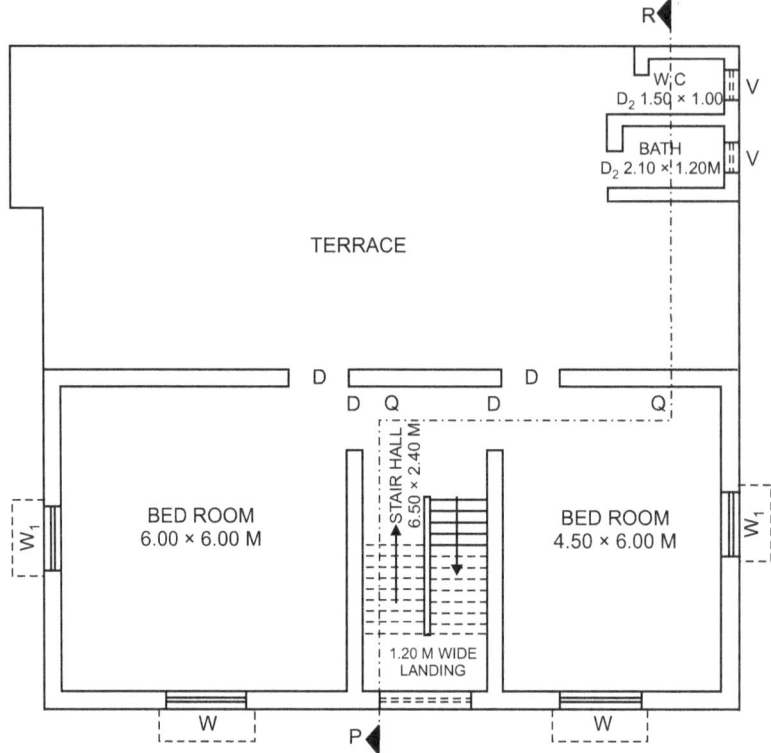

Fig. 7.1 (b): First floor plan

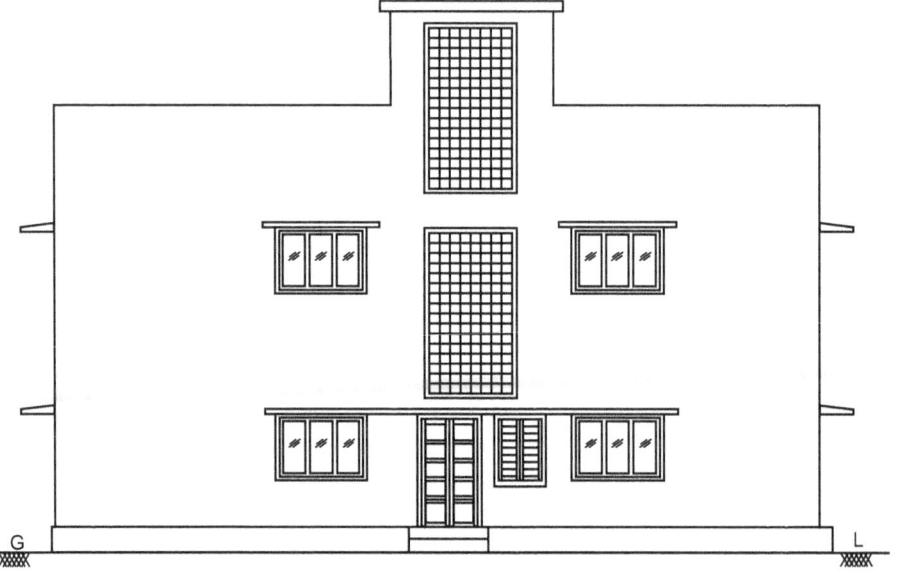

Fig. 7.1 (c): Front elevation

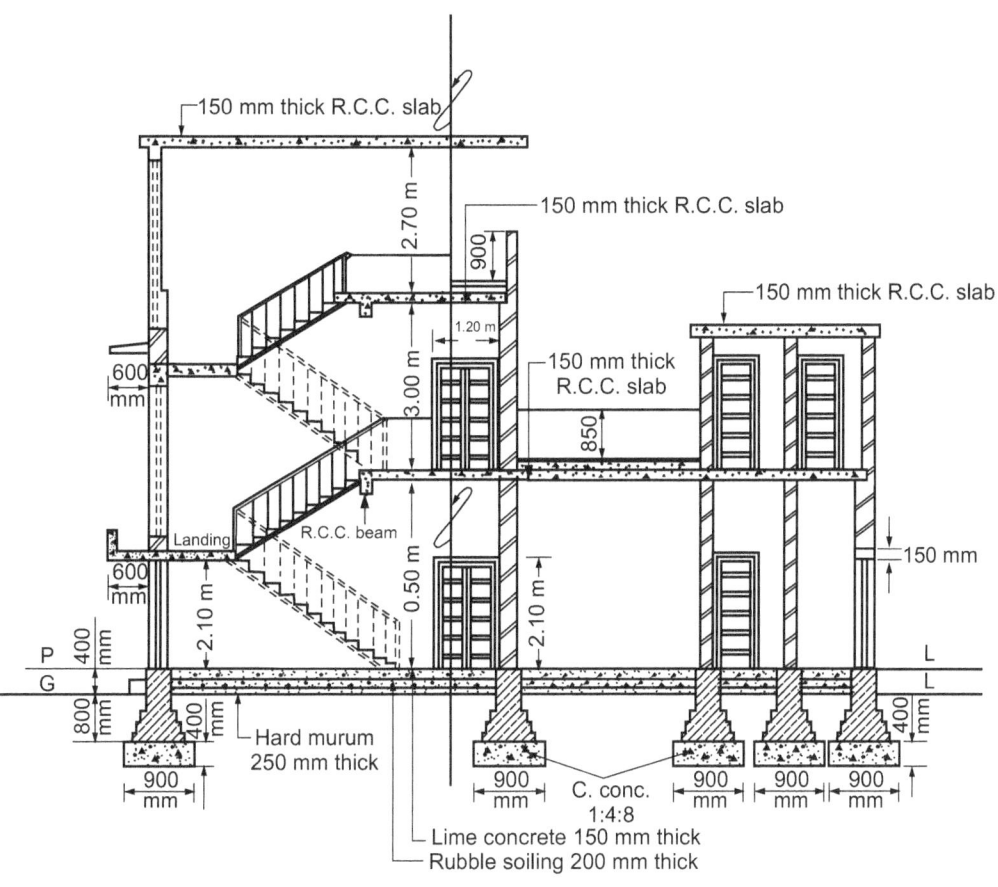

Fig. 7.1(d): Section on PQR

Set No. 2:

Planning of a residential building single storeyed, flat roof type, load bearing structure with detailed drawings. Refer Fig. 7.2 (a) to 7.2 (h). [The details are given in Table 7.2].

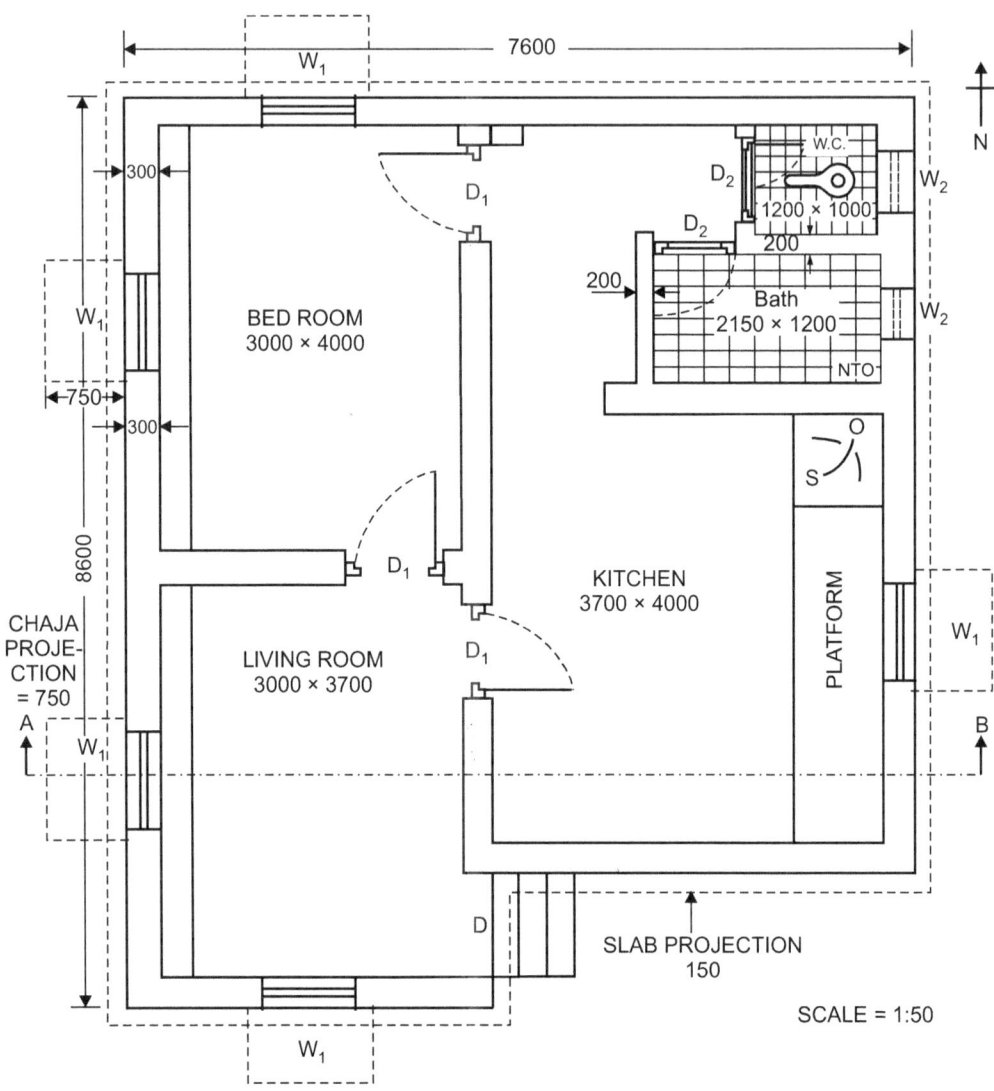

Fig. 7.2 (a): Plan of residential building

Table 7.2: Construction notes

(1)	Structure is load bearing type.
(2)	Foundation is at 1000 mm depth.
(3)	Sill height = 800 mm.
(4)	Ceiling height = 3000 mm
(5)	Thickness of slab = 120 mm.
(6)	Provide doors and windows suitably.
(7)	Rise = 160 mm and Tread = 250 mm and Width of stairs = 1300.
(8)	Chajja projection = 750 mm.
(9)	Slab projection = 150 mm.
(10)	U.C.R. Masonry in cm (1 : 6) in plinth and foundation.
(11)	B.B.M. in cm (1 : 6) 300 thk. For masonry walls.

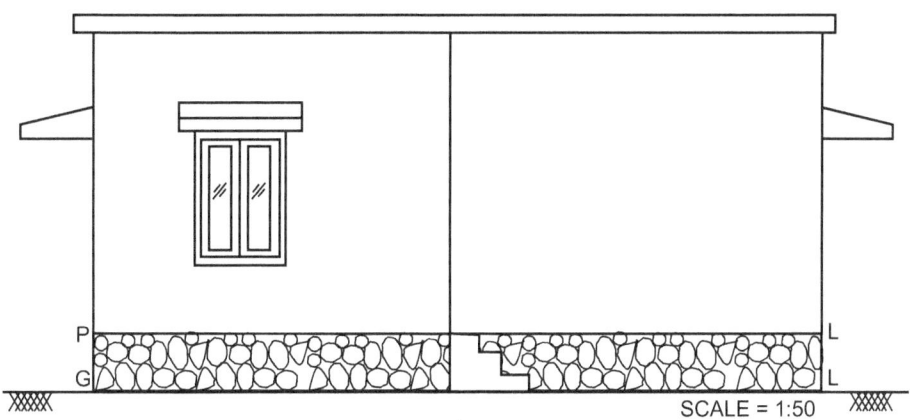

Fig. 7.2 (b): Elevation

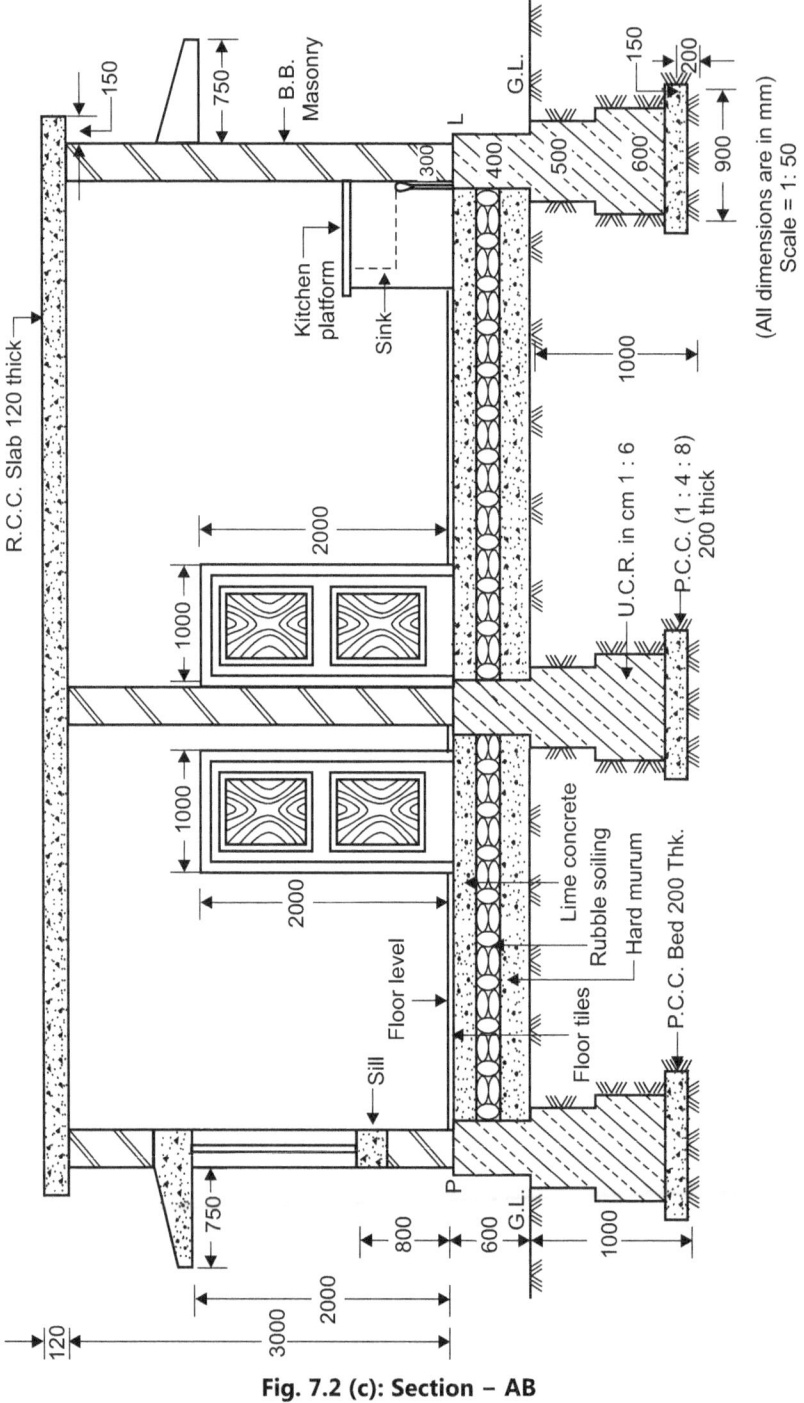

Fig. 7.2 (c): Section – AB

EP	Electric Pole
MH	Man Hole
IC	Inspection Chamber
GT	Gulley Trap

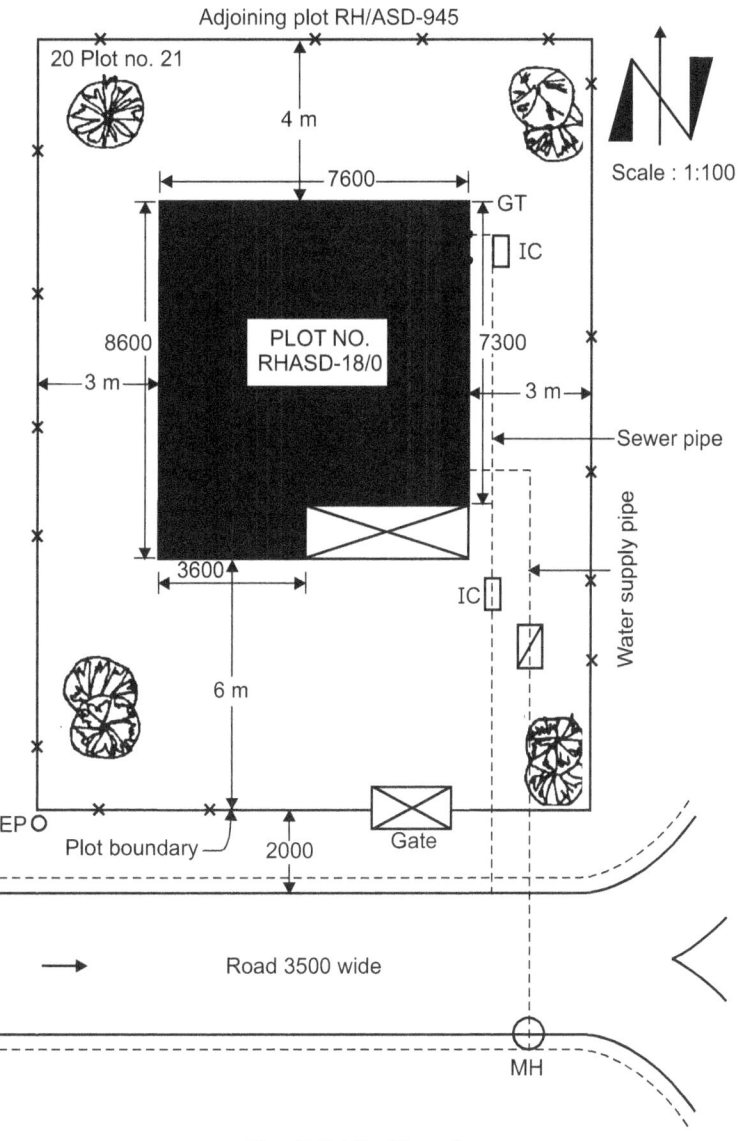

Fig. 7.2 (d): Site plan

Table 7.3: Area Statement

Sr. No.	Area	Area in mm²	Area in m²	Remarks
1.	Plot area	2.51×10^8	251.1	Plot No. 21
2.	Permissible built-up area	8.37×10^7	83.7	$1/3^{rd}$ plot area
3.	Built-up area	6.01×10^7	60.16	–
4.	Plinth area	6.01×10^7	60.16	–
5.	Carpet Area	4.23×10^7	42.32	Excluding W.C. and Bath

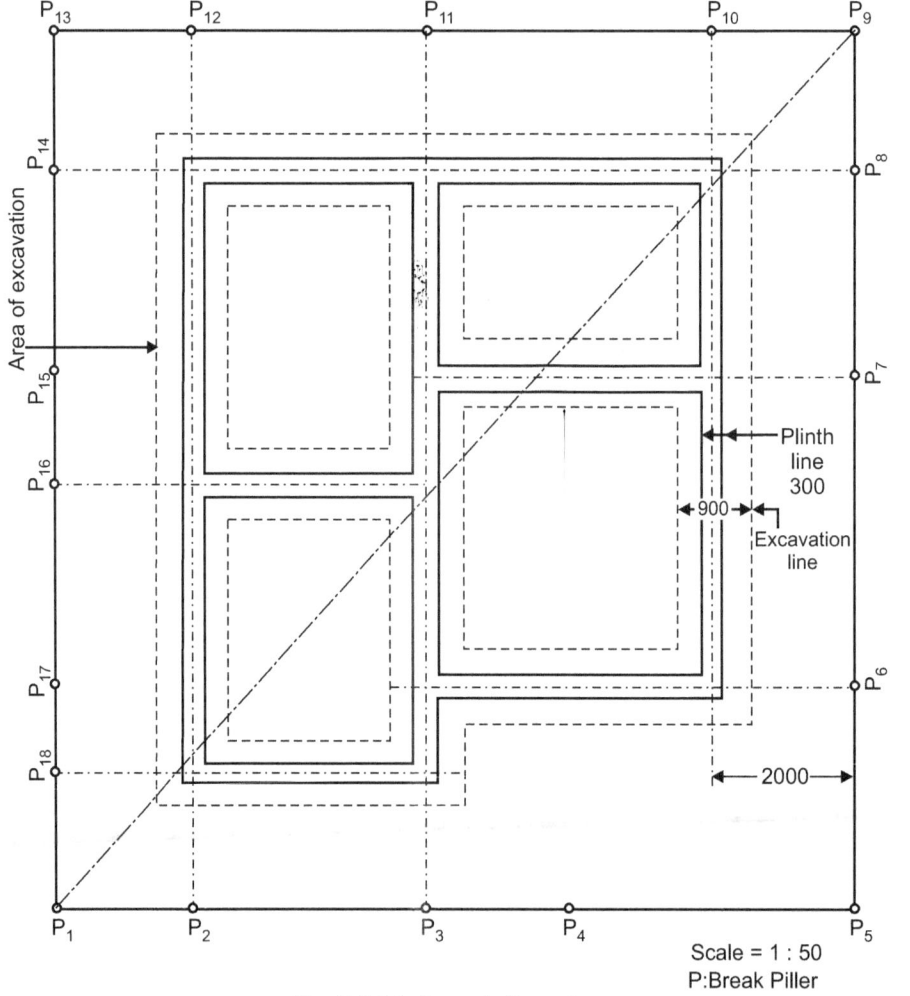

Fig. 7.2 (e): Foundation plan

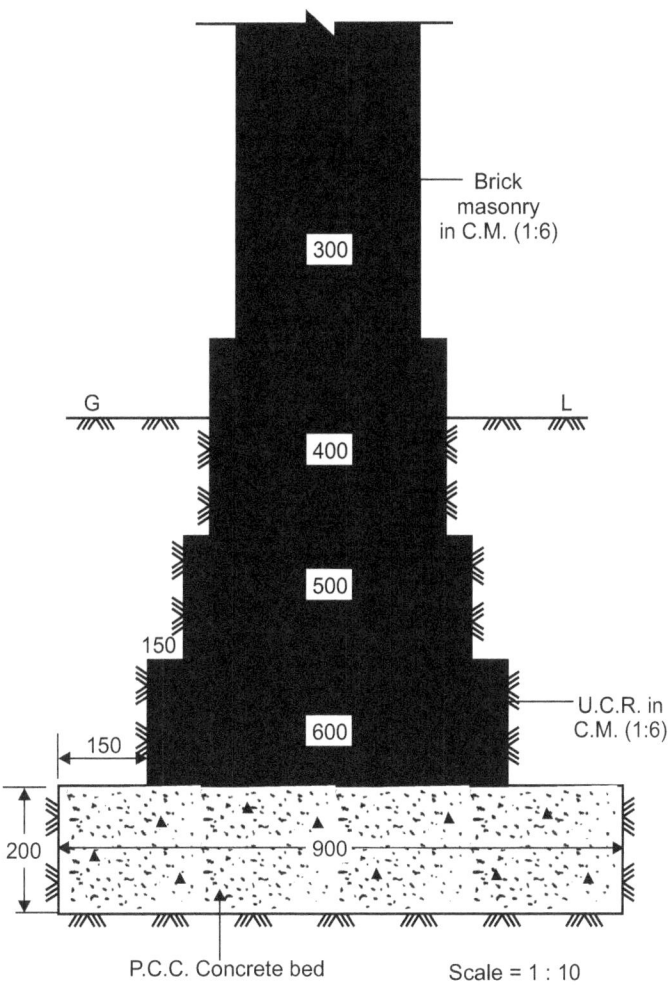

Fig. 7.2 (f): Section of foundation

Table 7.4: Schedule for Doors and Windows

Sr. No.	Item	Symbol	Size in mm	Qty.	Remarks
1.	Door	D	1000 × 2000	1	Teak wood fully panelled door
2.	Door	D_1	900 × 2000	4	Flush door
3.	Door	D_2	800 × 2000	2	Flush door
4.	Window	W_1	1200 × 1200	5	Glazed window with teak wood frame
5.	Window	W_2	500 × 1000	2	Lovered window

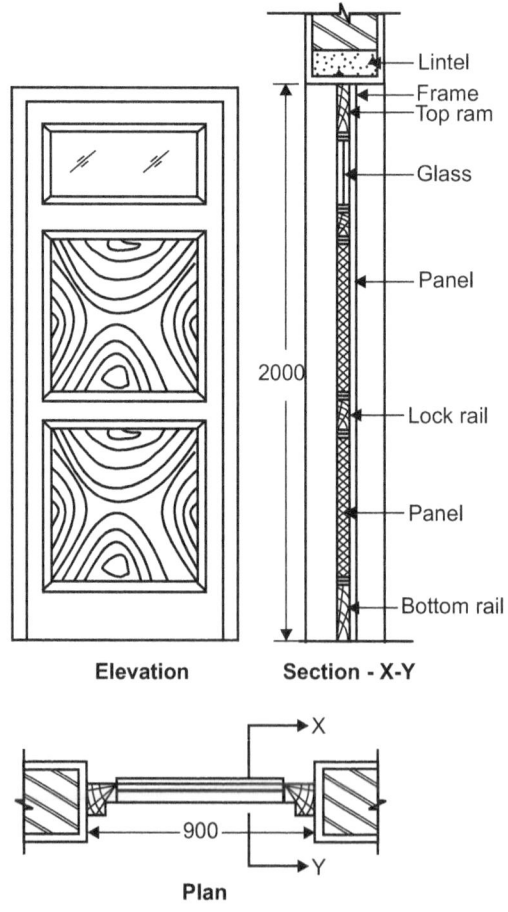

Fig. 7.2 (g): Partly glazed and panelled door

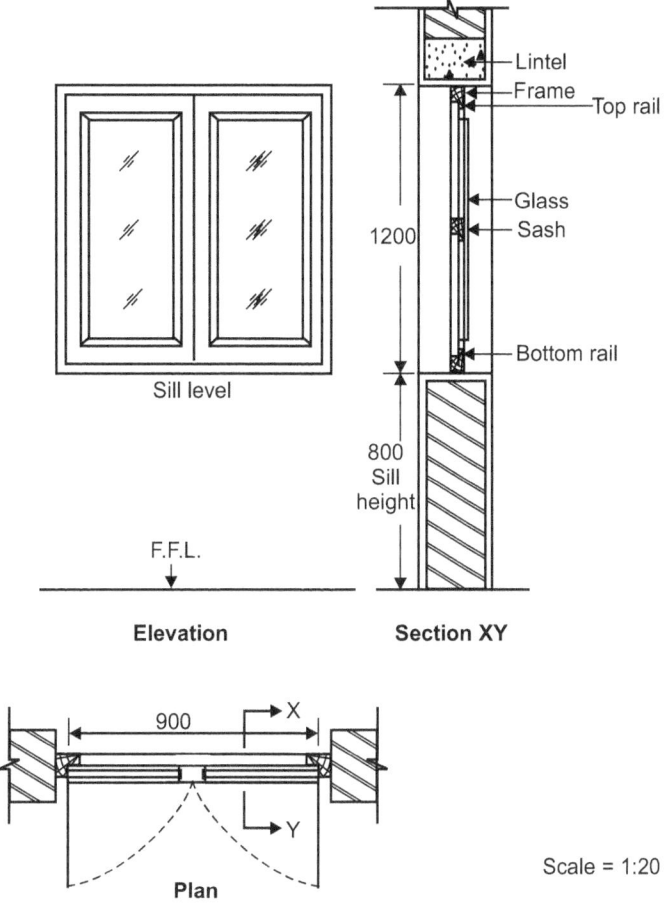

Fig. 7.2 (h): Glazed window

Set No. 3:

This planning will give a complete Idea to the students about various types of drawings of components in plan, elevation, section etc. because this depend upon types of building −

    (1)   Load bearing and partly framed structure.

    (2)   Flat roof cum pitched roof with lean roof.

    (3)   With different thickness of masonry. Refer Fig. 7.3 (a) to 7.3 (q).

Details of construction notes is given in Table 7.5.

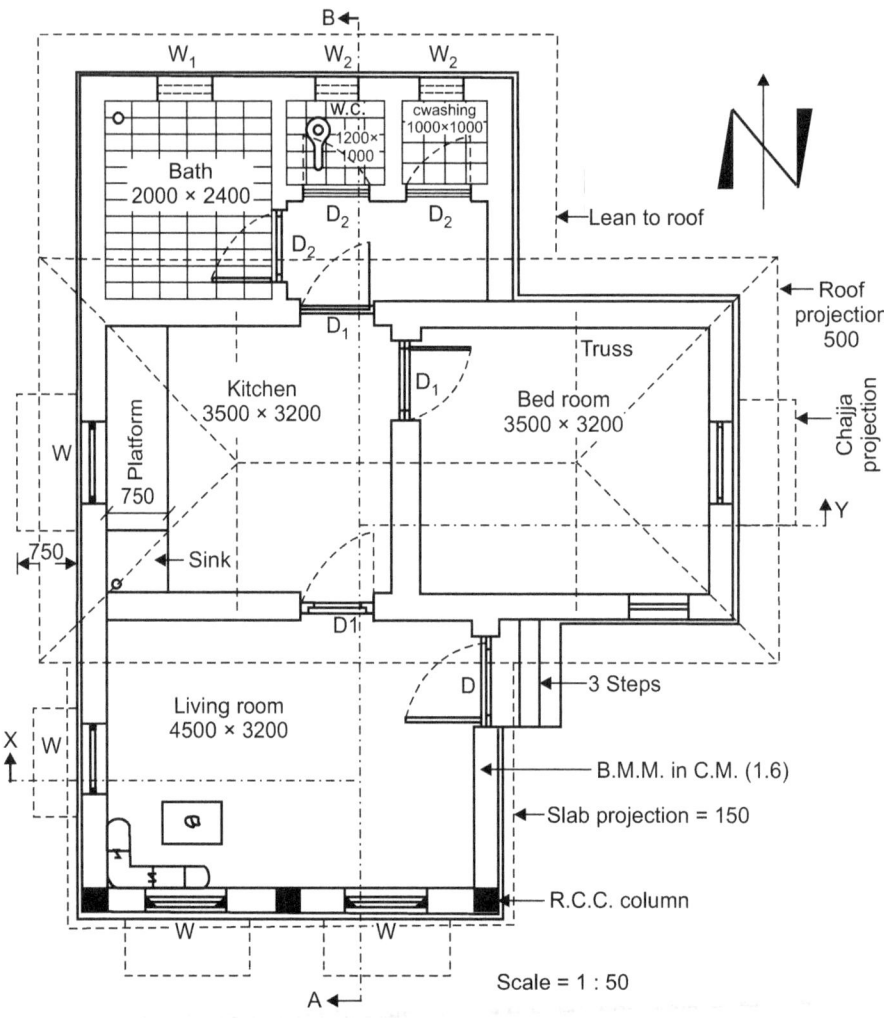

Fig. 7.3 (a): Plan

Fig. 7.3 (b): Elevation

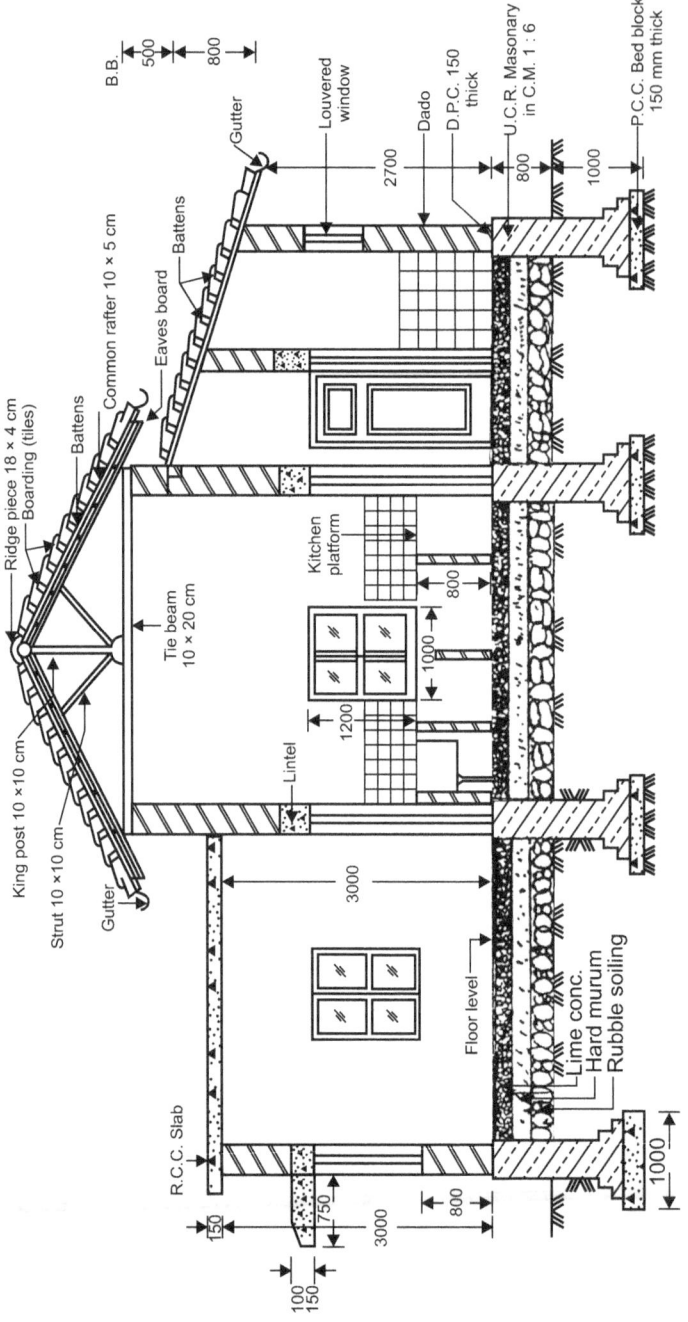

Fig. 7.3 (c): Section A-B

Table 7.5: Construction Notes

(1)	Foundation on hard strata at 1000 from G.L.
(2)	Structure is partly load bearing and partly framed.
(3)	Thickness of masonary wall 300 in bricks in cm. (1 : 6).
(4)	D.P.C. provided 150 thick at junction of floor and wall.
(5)	External plaster 10 mm thick is provided.
(6)	Cross-section of R.C.C. column = 300 × 300.
(7)	Ceiling level = 3000.
(8)	Bed block level = 4000 (from Floor level).
(9)	For lean-to-roof; height of wall = 3500 and Pillar = 2500
(10)	Mangalore tiles are provided for sloping roof.
(11)	Dado: 1 m height provided in W.C. in white glazed tile.
(12)	Provide doors and windows suitably.

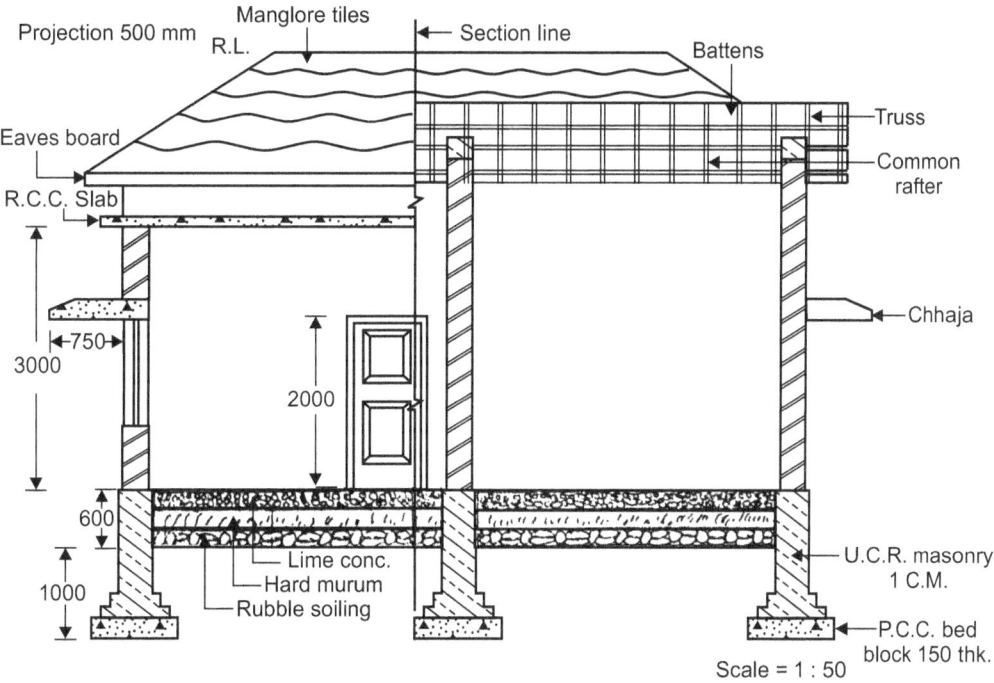

Fig. 7.3 (d): Section X–Y

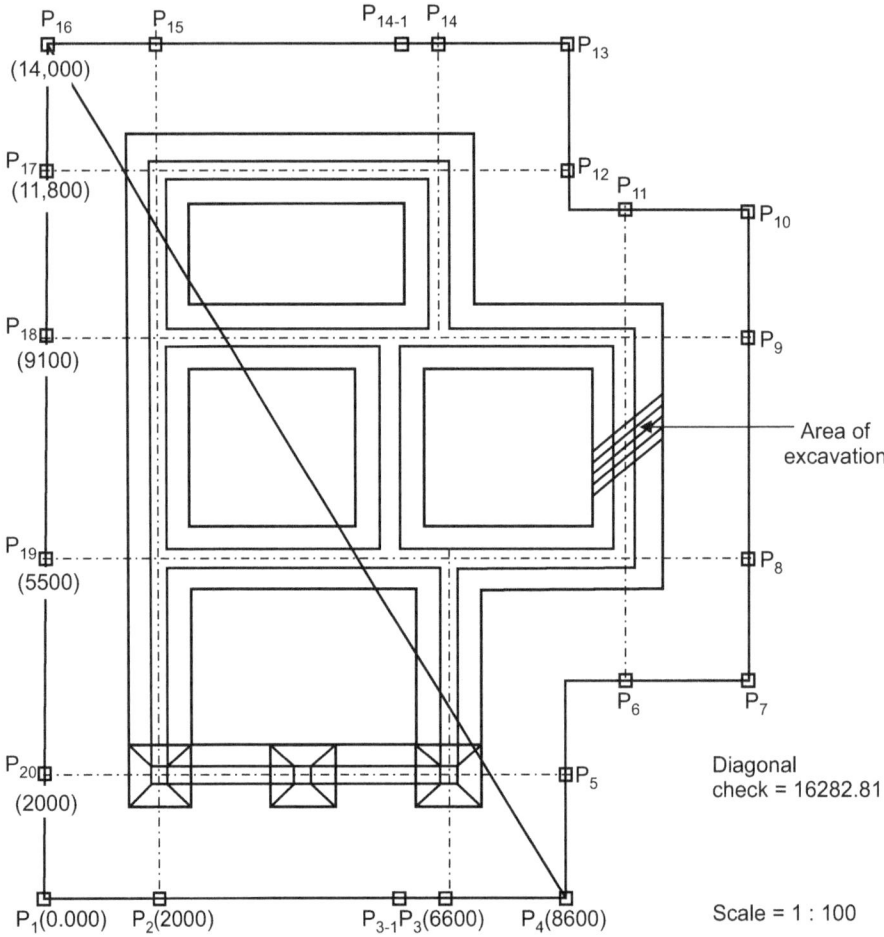

Fig. 7.3 (e): Foundation plan

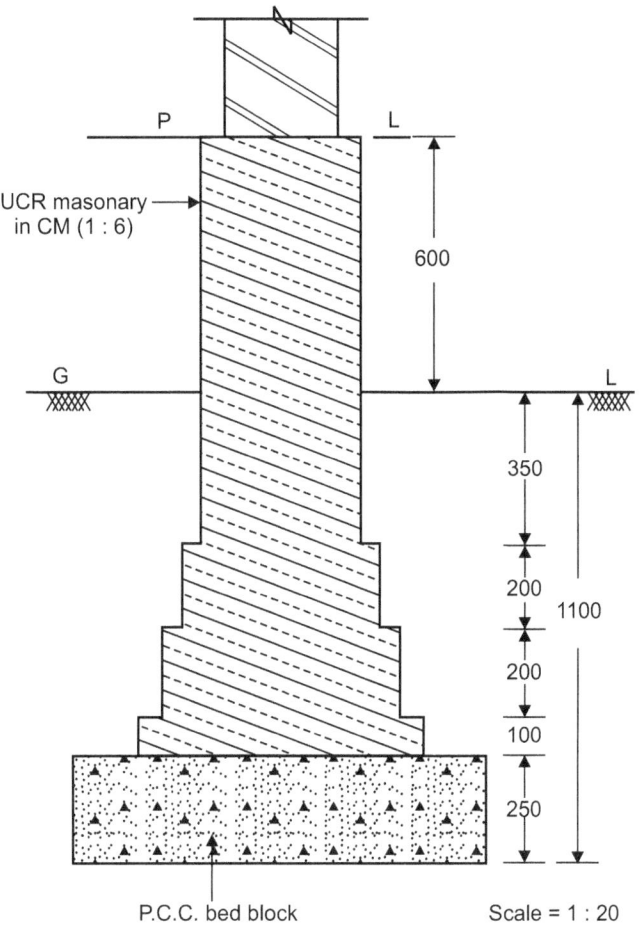

Fig. 7.3 (f): Section of wall footing

Table 7.6: Area Statement

Area	Area in mm²	Area in m²	Remarks
Plot area	278×10^6	278	Plot No. 32
Permissible built-up area	92.66×10^6	92.66	1/3rd plot area
Built-up area	6191×10^4	61.91	–
Plinth area	6191×10^4	61.91	–
Carpet area	39.2×10^6	39.2	Excluding W.C. and Bath

BUILDING DESIGN AND DRAWING (N.M.U.)   PLANNING OF APARTMENT

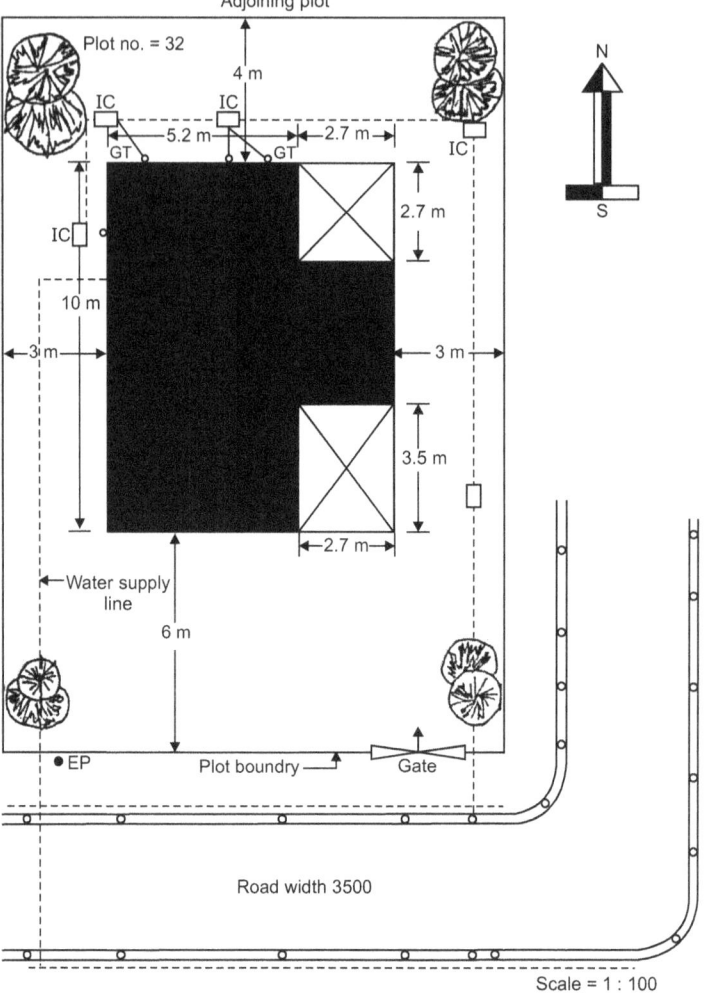

Fig. 7.4 (g): Site plan

IMPORTANT POINTS

- Apartments Planning.
- Minimum floor area and height of rooms.
- Arrangement of rooms in apartments.

QUESTIONS

1. What is meaning of apartments?
2. What factors are to be considered for planning of apartments?
3. Enlist minimum area for habitable rooms in apartments.

■■■

Chapter 8

PERSPECTIVE DRAWING

8.1 INTRODUCTION

Drawing is a language of Engineers. Drawings give a detailed idea about the structure, as it will appear. According to the need or purpose, the drawings can be classified as:

1. Isometric Drawing.
2. Oblique Drawing.
3. Perspective Drawing.

1. Isometric Drawing:

In the term isometric, prefix "iso" is taken from Greek word "isos" meaning equal. To draw isometric view, the object or structure is turned to make the three sides visible in such a way that they should lie on three equally divided axes about a centre. A pleasing view is obtained by keeping one axis vertical and other two axes at 30° angle with horizontal.

2. Oblique Drawing:

The top and side view of the object is shown by projecting oblique lines from a frontal orthographic view, i.e. elevation in an oblique drawing. Angles commonly used for such drawings are 30°, 45° and 60° depending upon the desired effect.

(i) If 30° angle is taken from horizontal axis, it gives more detailed view of sides. (single side).

(ii) If 45° angle is taken from horizontal axis, it gives a more clear idea of both the sides.

(iii) If 60° angle is taken from horizontal axis, it gives a clear picture of a top view of a structure.

3. Perspective Views:

The dictionary meaning of word 'perspective' is the proper relative position of objects as one perceives. Perspective is the only drawing which represents contemplated building as it would appear to spectator.

Perspective drawing: It is the representation of an object on a plane surface as it would appear to eye, when viewed from a fixed position.

A picture drawn by a man on a window glass, when he is looking through a window with one eye closed and other at a fixed position would be a perspective drawing. An architect is interested in knowing how the proposed structure will really look after completion, therefore perspective would represent existing things along with all possible details of building with the knowledge of a plane and solid geometry.

8.2 IMPORTANT TERMS IN PERSPECTIVE DRAWINGS

Following is the terminology used in practice to draw perspective drawings. (Refer Fig. 8.18)

1. **Station Point (SP):** It is a point where the eye of the observer is supposed to be located when the object is viewed for perspective drawing. The position of the station point carries lot of significance as general appearance of the perspective is dependent upon it. For large objects like buildings, the station point is usually taken at the eye level of the person i.e. about 1.5 m.

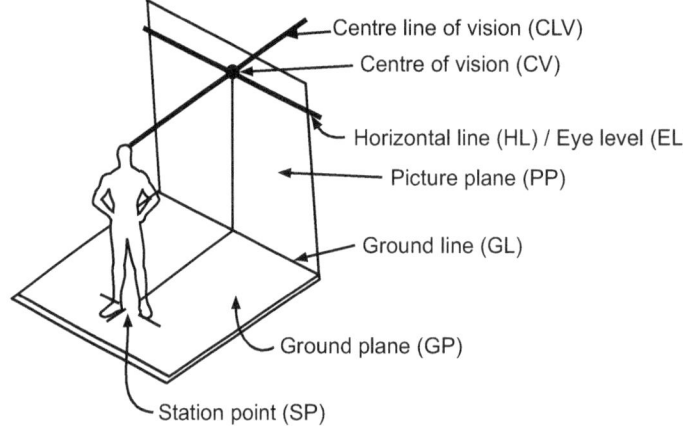

Fig. 8.1

Following general guidelines may be considered for obtaining a good position of station point:

(a) For small objects, the position of a station point should be such as to give a good view of top surface as well as side surface. For this, the distance of a station point from a picture plane may be taken equal to twice the greatest dimension of the object.

(b) For object having height and width more or less equal, the station point is so located that the angle between the visual rays from the station point to the outermost boundaries of the object is approximately 30°.

(c) It is preferable that station point should be so located in front of the object that the central plane passes through the center of intersection of the object.

2. **Picture Plane (PP):** It is an arbitrary transparent plane, which is always placed in vertical position between observer (station point) and the object to be viewed. It is like a curtain which gives the relative positions of different parts of the object sighted, for different distances of the object from the station point. The position of

the picture plane in relation to the object, determines the size of perspective view. Perspective view will always be shorter in size than the actual size of the object, except when picture plane coincides with the object, the size of perspective view will be same size as that of object.

3. **Line of Sight (LS):** It is the line drawn through the station point, joining to the centre of vision. It is also called as axis of vision or perpendicular axis.

4. **Horizontal Plane (HP):** It is an imaginary horizontal plane passing through the station point. It is always parallel to the ground line.

5. **Horizontal Line (HL):** It is the line formed by the intersection of a ground plane with picture plane. It is parallel to the ground line.

6. **Ground Line (GL):** It is a line developed by intersection of a ground plane with picture plane.

7. **Ground Plane (GP):** It is the horizontal plane on which the object is assumed to be situated.

8. **Centre of Vision (CV):** It is the point on picture plane. The point at which the line of sight strikes the picture plane is called the **centre of vision**. It always lies on the horizontal line.

9. **Centre Plane:** It is an imaginary vertical plane passing through centre of vision and the station point. It is perpendicular to both picture plane, and the ground plane and perpendicular axis contained in this plane.

10. **Angle or Cone of Vision:** The angle subtended at the eye, by the visible part of the object is known as cone of vision or angle of vision.

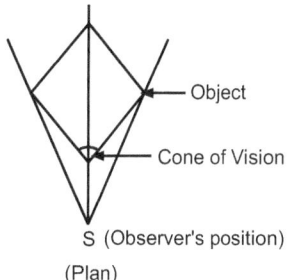

Fig. 8.2

11. **Vanishing Point:** It is an imaginary point situated at infinite distance from the point. In practice, the point at which the visual rays from eye cuts the picture plane is referred as the **vanishing point**. If we stand between the parallel rails of a long stretch of railway track, it would appear as if the rails meet far away at a point. This point of converge is called vanishing point.

8.3 PRINCIPLES OF PERSPECTIVE

Perspective drawing is based upon the conception that, between the eye of the observer and the object to be drawn, there is placed a transparent plane, a sort of a window pane called a "picture plane" on which the form of the object is projected.

For example, if a window plane is selected and the keeping the hand stationary trace the images seen through pane on the window pane. The result is perspective drawing. Refer Fig. 8.3 drawing perspective the following points must be noted:

1. The lines appear to be shorter than their actual length, and this effect increases as the distance of the object increases.
2. The picture of all points and lines on the picture plane coincides with the points and lines themselves.
3. Perspective of all parallel lines which are also parallel to the picture plane are themselves parallel.
   (i) Vertical lines such as trees, corners of building and poles appear truely vertical. That is perspective of the vertical lines are vertical or parallel to vertical lines.
   (ii) Perspective of horizontal lines which are parallel to the picture plane are horizontal except those at eye level, do not appear horizontal.
4. Perspective of all parallel lines; which are not parallel to the picture plane converge to a point (vanishing point).
   (i) Perspective of parallel line which are parallel to the vertically plane converge to a vanishing point on the vertical line.
   (ii) Perspective of horizontal line appear to vanish on the horizontal line or converge to a vanishing point on the horizontal line. A group of horizontal lines running in one direction in the perspective drawing appear to converge to a single point. Another group of horizontal lines having different direction have different vanishing point downward which they converge.
   (iii) Perspective of horizontal lines to the picture plane converge to the centre of vision, i.e. in this case centre of vision is the vanishing point. Refer Fig. 8.3.

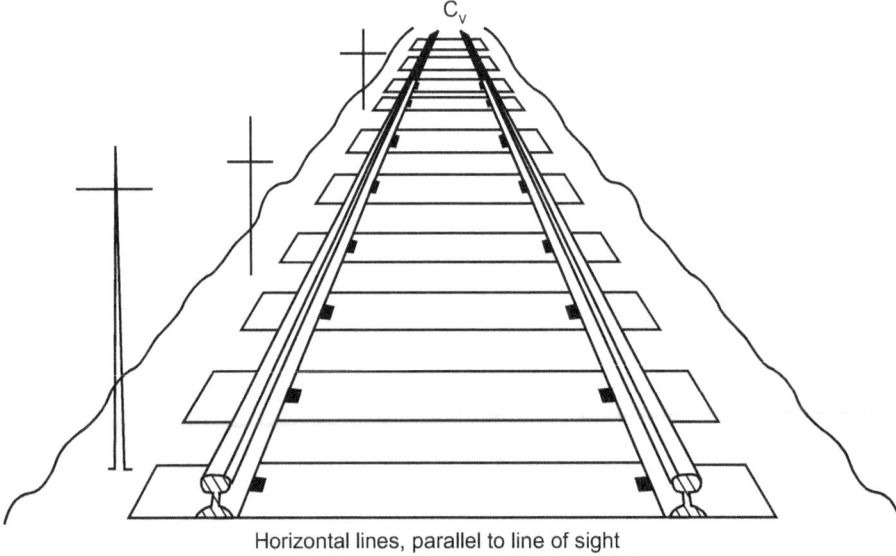

Horizontal lines, parallel to line of sight converge to a point "Centre of Vision" (C_v)

Fig. 8.3: Centre of vision

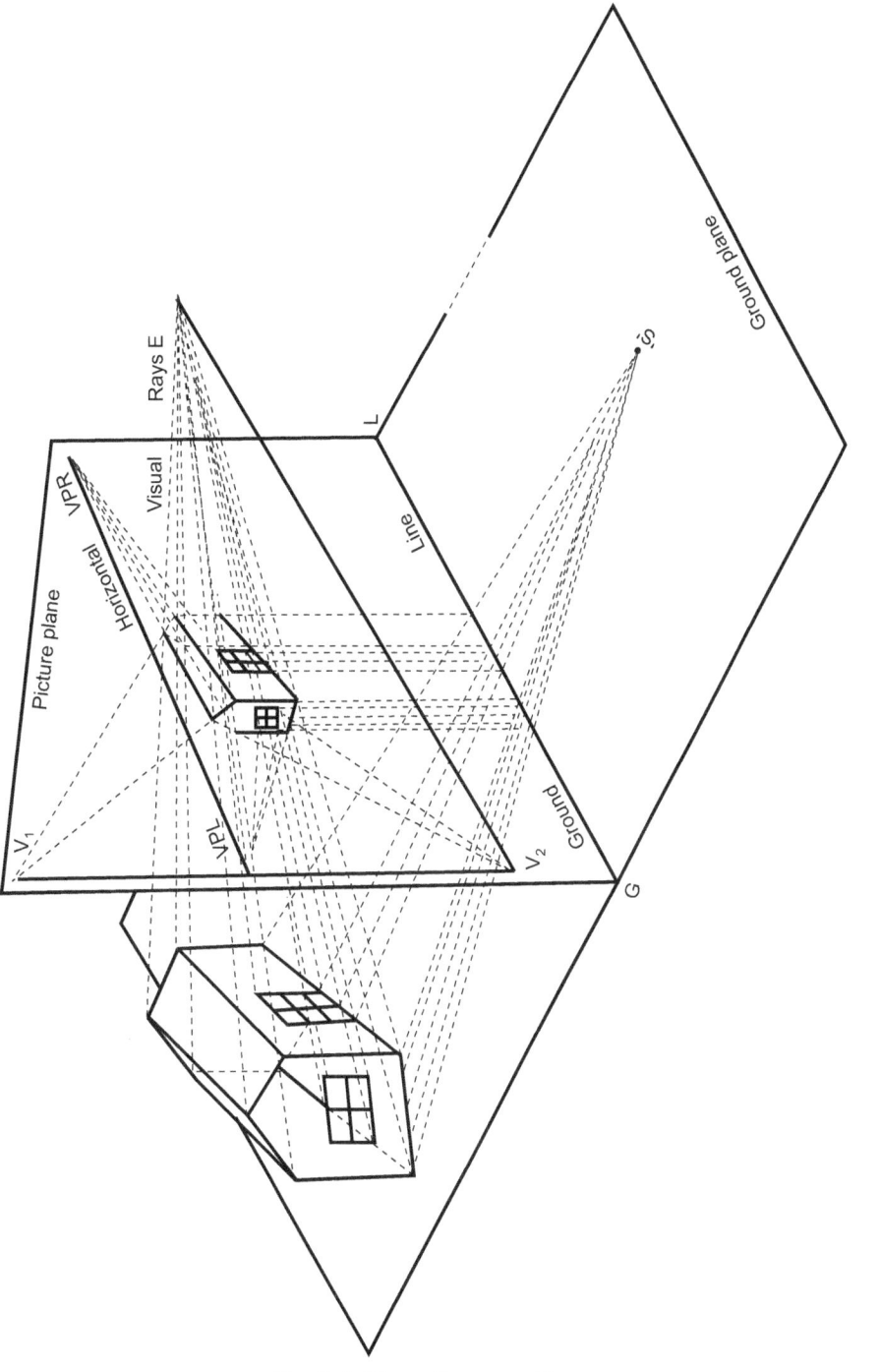

Fig. 8.4: Idea of perspective

8.4 TYPES OF PERSPECTIVE

Perspective views can be classified as:

1. Based on position of object with respect to picture plane.
2. Based on number of vanishing points.

8.4.1 Based on Position of Object with Respect to Picture Plane

1. **Parallel perspective:** When one or more faces of an object are parallel to the picture plane, than perspective of this object is called **parallel perspective**. This is same as one point perspective. Refer Fig. 8.5.

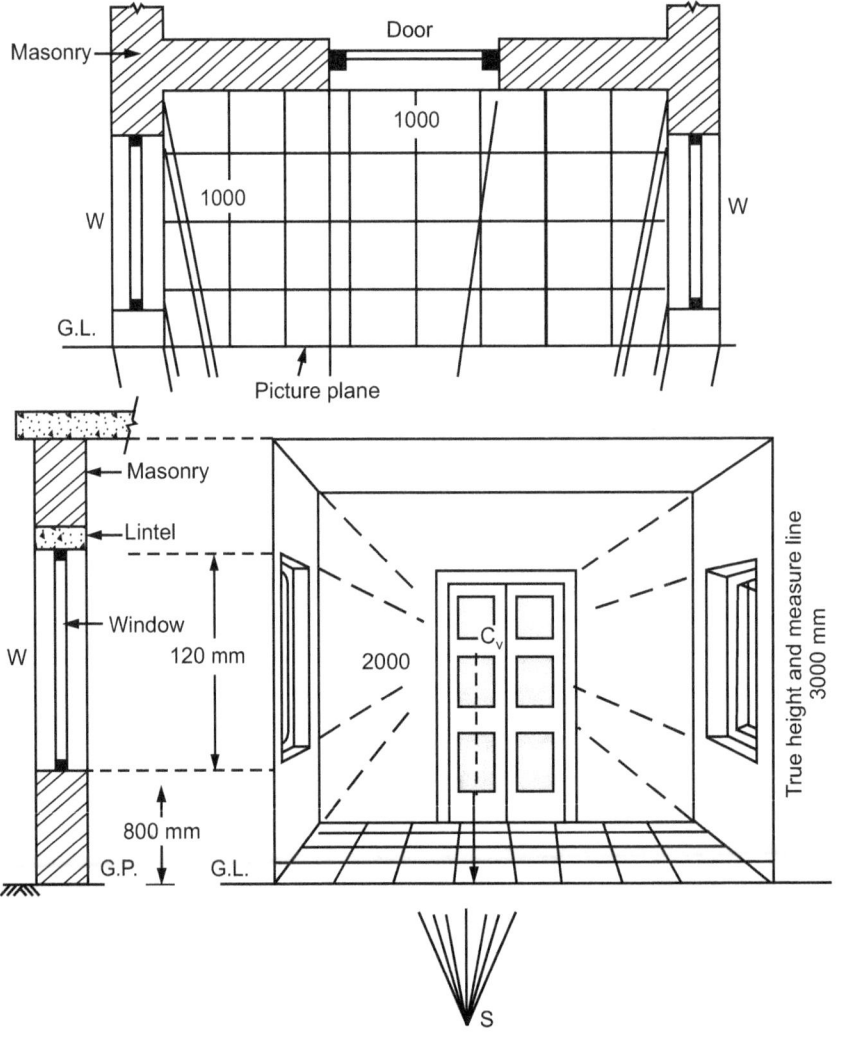

Fig. 8.5: Parallel perspective of an interior

2. **Oblique perspective:** When the faces of the object are inclined to the picture plane then the perspective of the object is called **oblique perspective**. This is similar to two point or three point perspective. Refer Fig. 8.6.

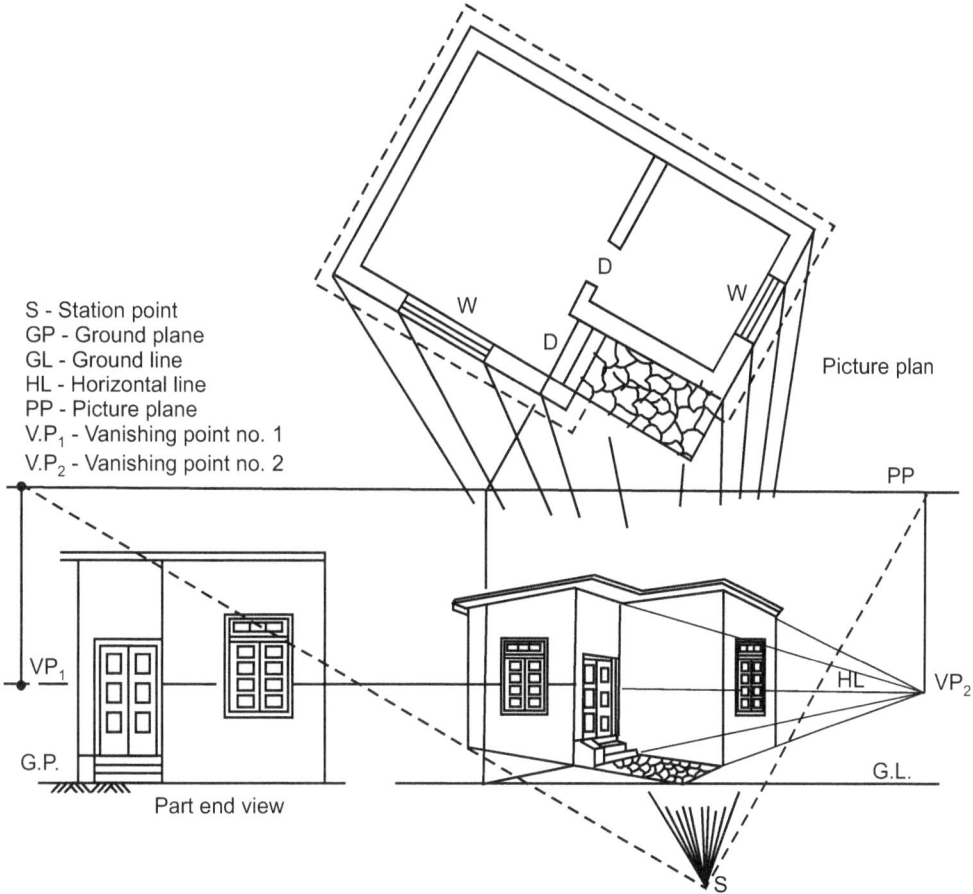

Fig. 8.6: Oblique perspective

8.4.2 Based on Number of Vanishing Points

1. **One point perspective:** In this perspective, there is only one vanishing point. In such views picture plane is parallel to two sets of lines out of the three sets. This perspective view drawn is called one **point perspective**.

   Here the picture plane is parallel not only to the vertical line, but also to one of the sets of horizontal lines and these horizontal lines appear as truly horizontal in the image. This perspective is used when only one plane of the object is of interest and perspective is needed only to suggest depth, like interiors of auditorium, interior decoration, front elevation. Refer Fig. 8.7.

2. **Two point perspective:** In this, there are two vanishing points. The picture plane is parallel to only one set of parallel lines out of these three sets of lines.

   The most general case of this is that the picture plane will be vertical and object is such that its vertical edges are parallel to the picture plane and its faces are inclined to it. In this case, vanishing points of the lines lies on the same horizontal line.

   Two point perspective is used for buildings. This is also called bird's eye view. Refer Fig. 8.25.

3. **Three point perspective:** In this case, the picture plane is tilted and not parallel to any of the principal lines of the object. Three point perspective is only useful when a sky-scrapper is viewed from a road or an aeroplane.

8.4.3 Shades and Shadows in Perspective Drawings

A perspective drawing is incomplete, if natural surrounding like roads, sky, garden, trees etc. are not shown.

Naturally, we observe the shadows of different object like chajjas, cantilevers, roof projections, trees, persons etc. Therefore, all these shadows are shown in perspective for pleasing appearance.

Sun rays are assumed to be parallel therefore a shadow is the part of the surface from which light is excluded by an opaque object.

Shade is the part of an object not exposed to rays of light.

Light is assumed to be appearing from upper left side of elevation of object. Therefore, shadow will fall on the right side and below the object. Shadow lines are drawn at 45° inclination in front elevation.

8.5 METHOD OF DRAWING ONE POINT PERSPECTIVE

First draw the plan of the object parallel to the picture plane as shown in Fig. 8.7. Now select a station point, S.P. at a suitable distance from the picture plane. Join all the angular points of the plan with station point, cutting picture plane at 1, 2, 3, 4. Draw vertical projections from point 1, 2, 3, 4 touching the ground line at a', b', d' and c'. Draw horizontal line parallel to ground line having the height equal to eye level. Select a vanishing point, V. P. on the line of sight EO and on horizon line. Join the point a' d' with V. P. cutting the vertical lines 2b' and 4c' at 5 and 6 respectively. Mark aa', dd' equal to h on vertical lines a 1, d' 1. Joining a, d with V. P. cutting the vertical lines drawn from b' c' at b and c. Complete the figure joining the point a, b, c and d.

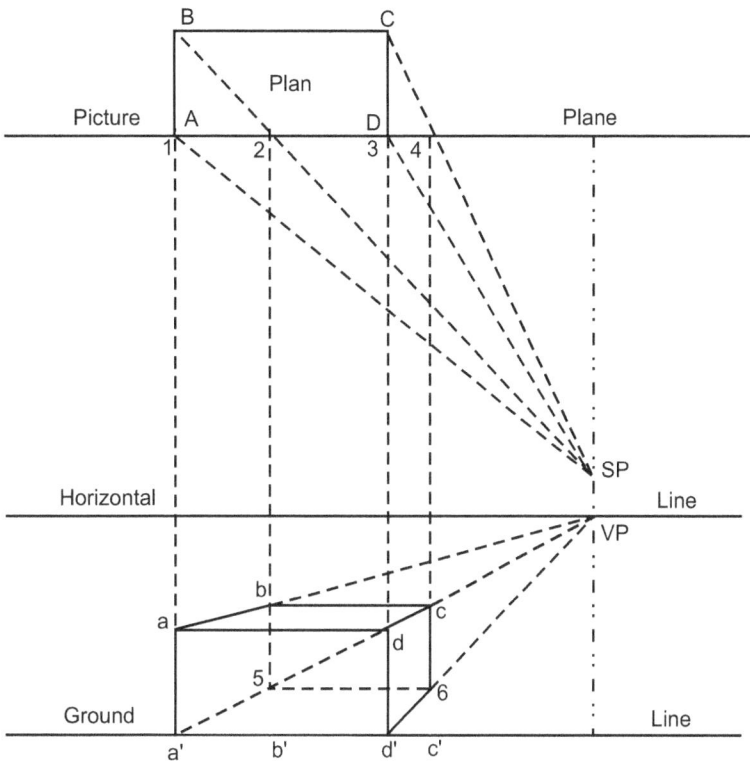

Fig. 8.7: One point perspective

8.6 METHOD OF DRAWING TWO POINT PERSPECTIVE

First draw the plan of the object making an angle of 30° or 45° with the picture plane. Draw the line of sight OE and mark the position of the station point S. P. From the station S draw lines parallel to 1, 4 and 1, 2 cutting the picture plane at V and V'. From these two points draw vertical projection cutting the horizon line which is drawn parallel to ground line and height equal to eye level at VPL and VPR. Hence, these are required vanishing points. Join the angular point of the object with station point and mark the position of these points where they pierce the picture plane. Draw vertical projection from these points. To find out depth of the object, produce the line 4, 1 cutting the picture plane. From this draw vertical projector on the ground line; on this vertical line cut the height of the object and join with the V.P.L., which gives the actual height that is 1. 1' in the vertical line drawn already. Now join 1, 4 to the V.P.L. and V.P.R. cutting the vertical line at 4, 4'. In this way complete the sketch as shown in Fig. 8.8.

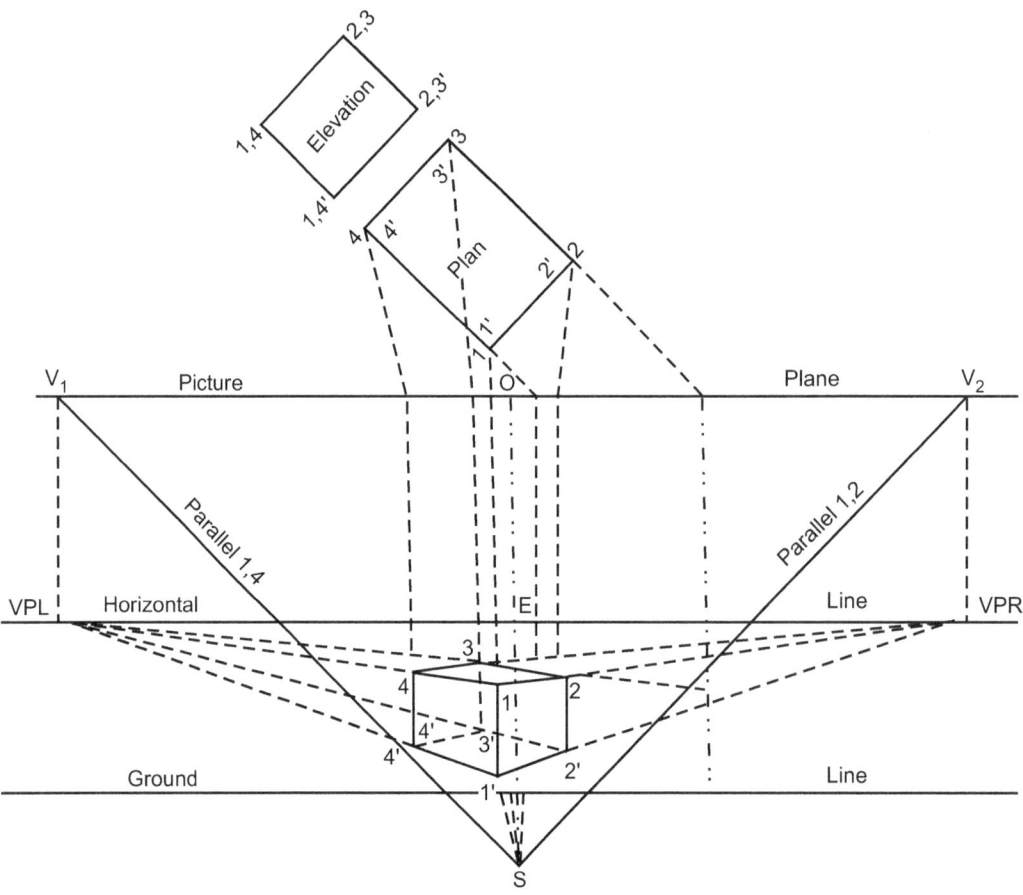

Fig. 8.8: Two point perspective

SOLVED EXAMPLES

Example 8.1 : Draw a two point perspective for a rectangular block 3 cm × 4.8 cm × 1.7 cm. The block is resting on a H.P on face 3 cm × 4.8 cm. The position of block is such that arc of the side of the plan is making 45° angle with the UP station point is 7.5 cm away from PP and height of eye is 3.5 cm. The nearest corner of block is 1 cm away from PP.

Solution:

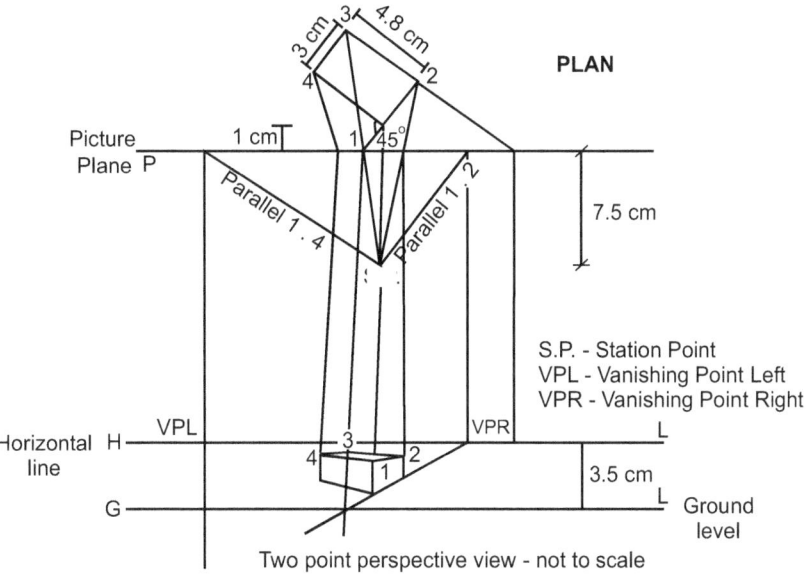

Two point perspective view - not to scale
Fig. 8.9

Example 8.2: The Fig. 8.10 shows the plan and elevation of an object. It is inclined at a angle of 30 degrees to the picture plane and touches the picture plane at "B". The observer is standing at a distance of 3.00 metre from the picture plane along the central visual ray. Assuming eye level at 2.00 metre above ground level, draw the perspective view to a suitable scale.

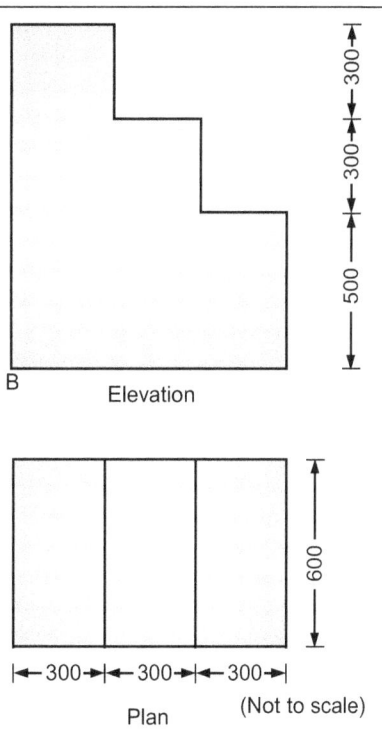

Fig. 8.10

Solution:

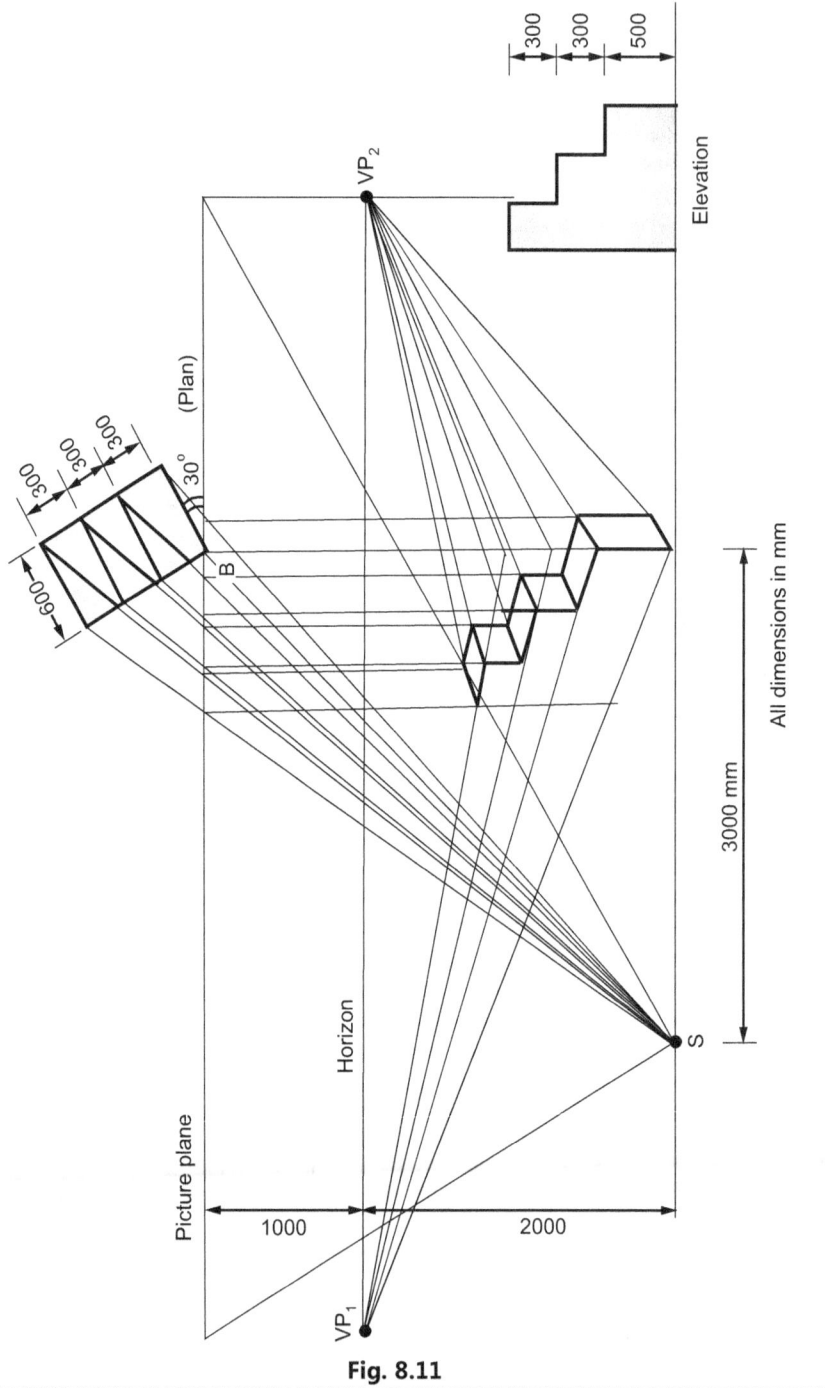

Fig. 8.11

Example 8.3: Draw parallel perspective of a cylindrical tower 4.5 metres high above plinth and 2.00 metres in diameter The tower is supported symmetrically on two square plinths 4 × 4 × 0.5 metres and 3 × 3 × 0.5 metres. Assume eye level 2.00 metres.

Solution:

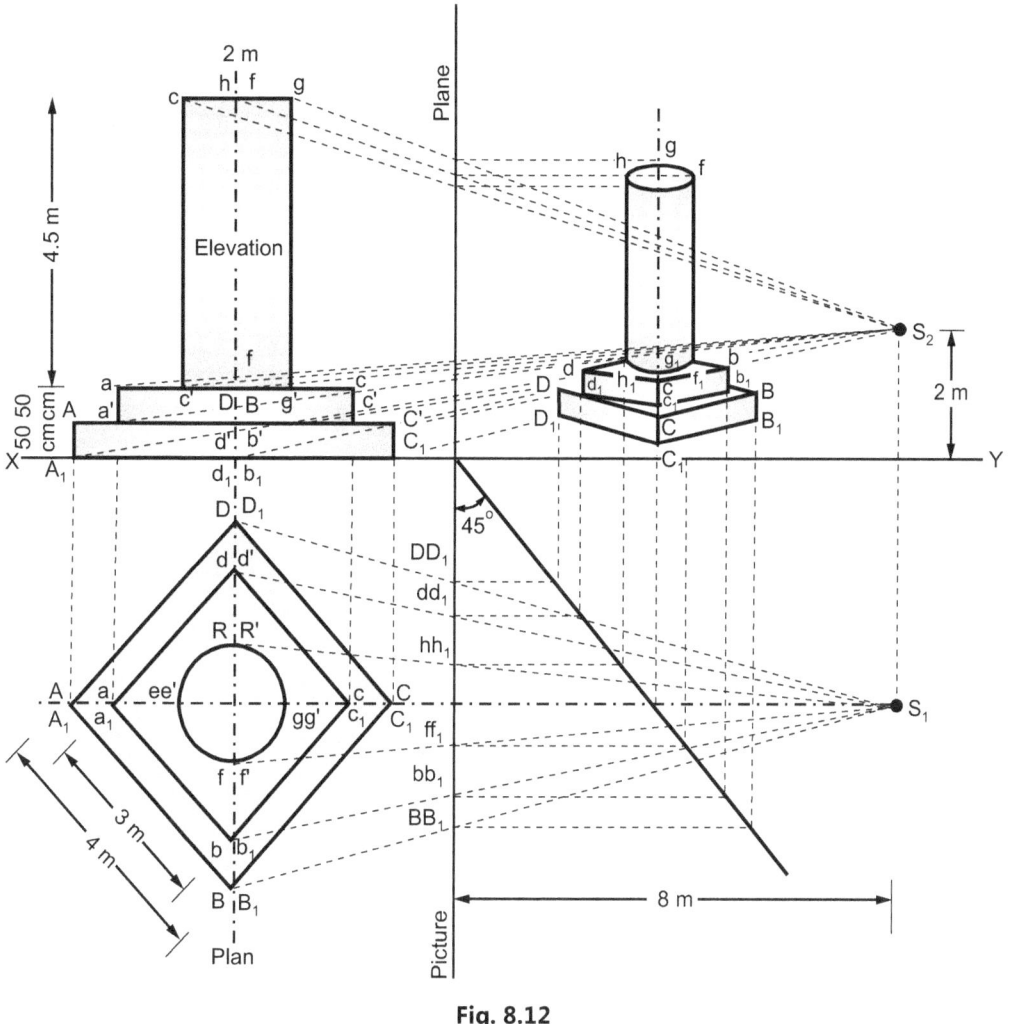

Fig. 8.12

Example 8.4: The Fig. 8.13 shows the plan of an object. Longer side of object is inclined at 30° to the picture plane and touches the same at A. The observer is at a distance of 10 m along the central visual ray. Assuming eye level at 1.5 m above G.L. Draw the perspective view of the object to some convenient scale.

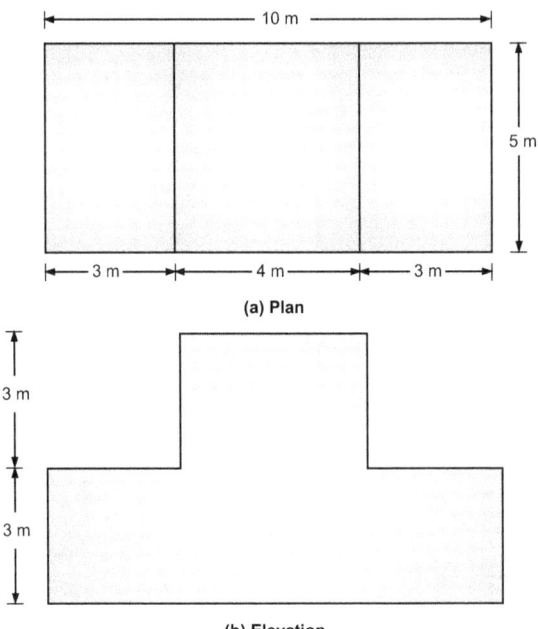

(a) Plan

(b) Elevation

Fig. 8.13

Solution:

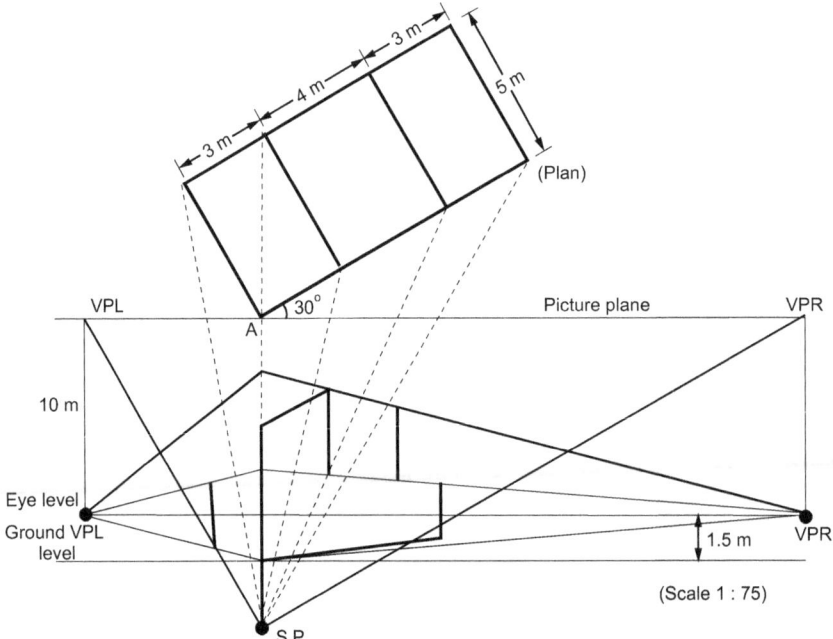

Fig. 8.14: Perspective view

Example 8.5: Draw the two point perspective view of a stone memorial pillar shown in Fig. 8.32 to a scale 1 : 2 or to same convenient scale.

The base block of pillar makes an angle of 30° with the picture plane and touches the same at A. The observer stands at a distance 3 m along the central visual ray. Assume eye level is at 1.5 m above G.L. Retain all construction lines.

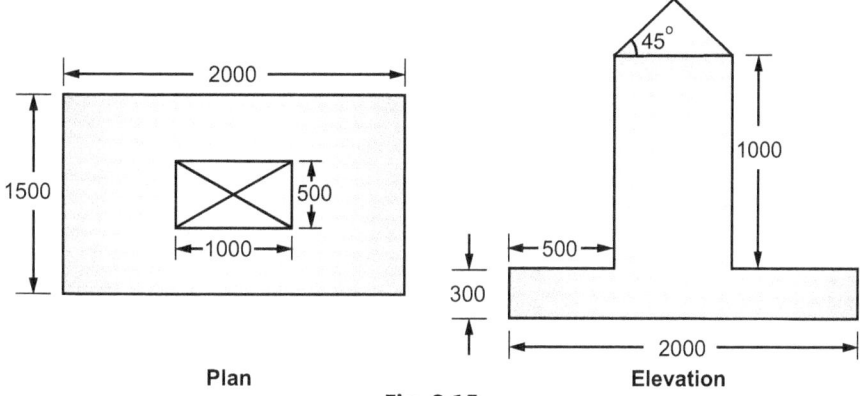

Fig. 8.15

Solution:

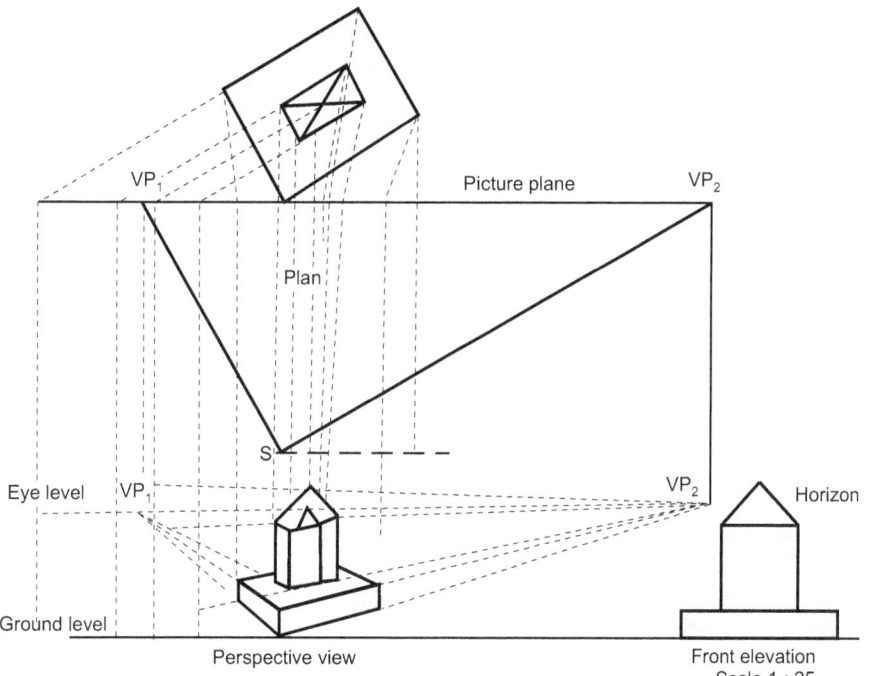

Fig. 8.16

BUILDING DESIGN AND DRAWING (N.M.U.) — PERSPECTIVE DRAWING

Example 8.6: Fig. 8.17 shown below shows the plan of Thresholds, one side of which is inclined at 30° to the picture plane and touches the same at A. The observer is standing at a distance of 2 m along the central visual ray. Assuming eye level at 1.5 m above G.L. draw the two point perspective view to scale of 1 : 20.

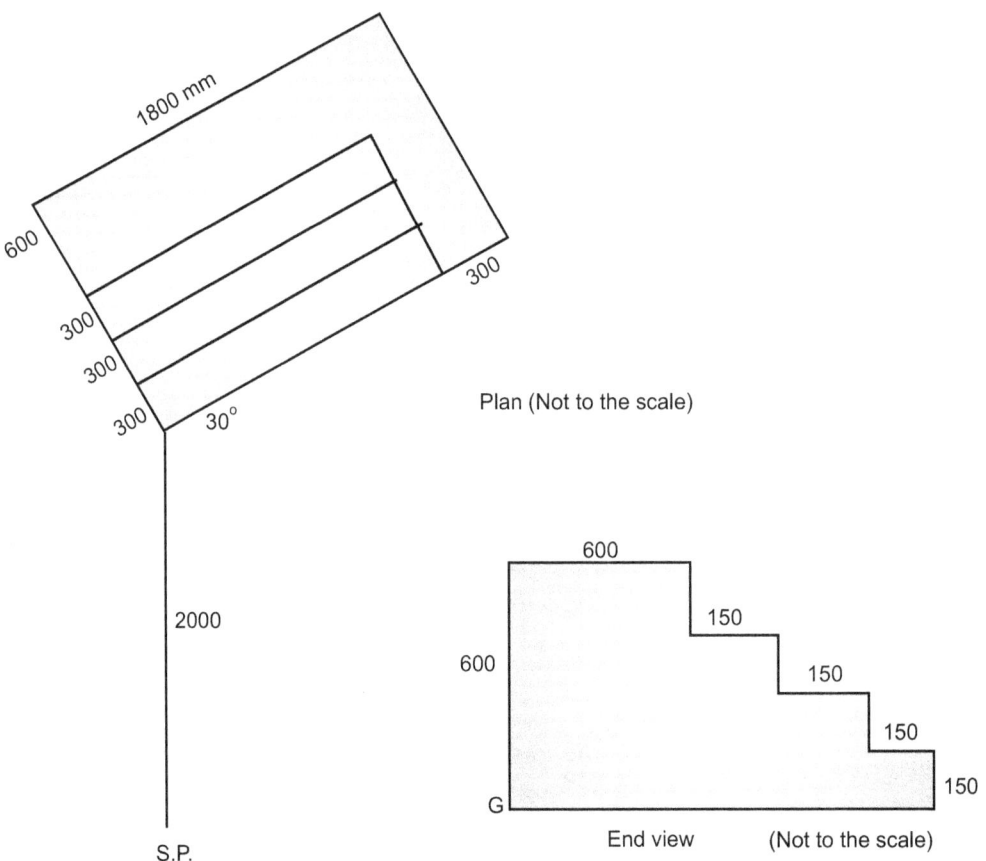

Fig. 8.17

Solution:

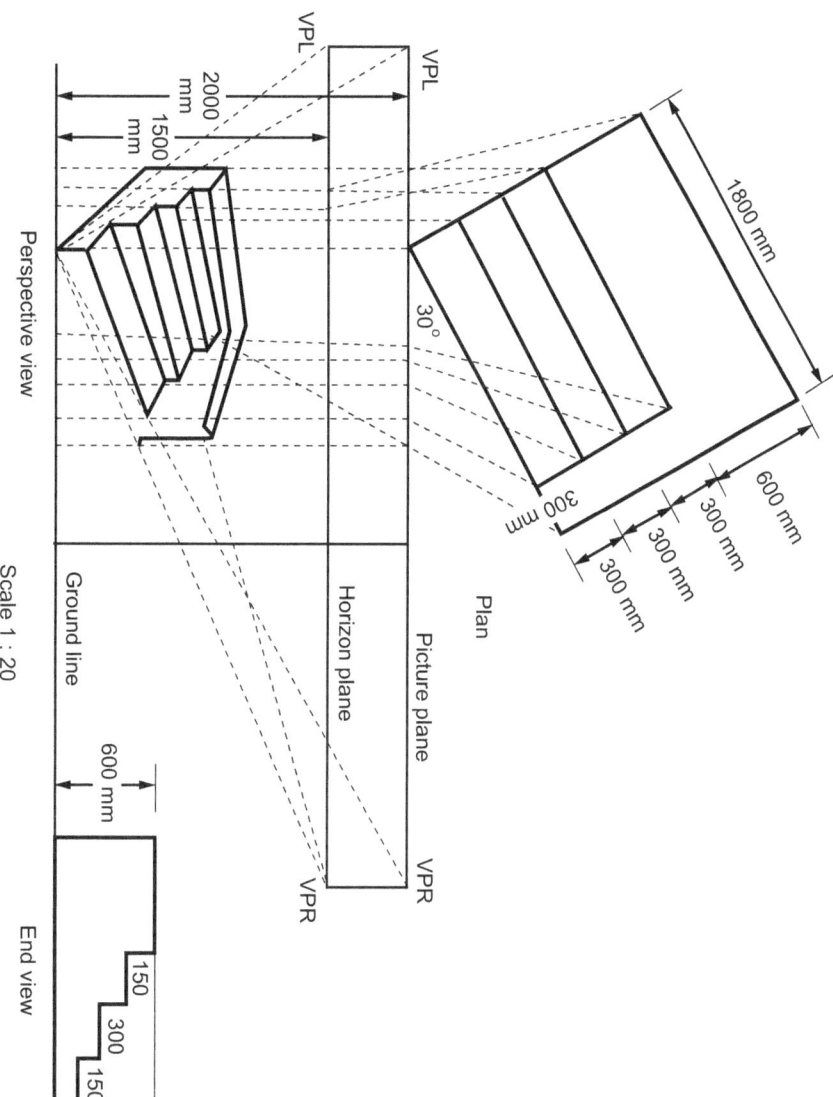

Fig. 8.18

QUESTIONS

1. Draw to a scale 1 : 50, the perspective view of the object shown in Fig. 8.19.

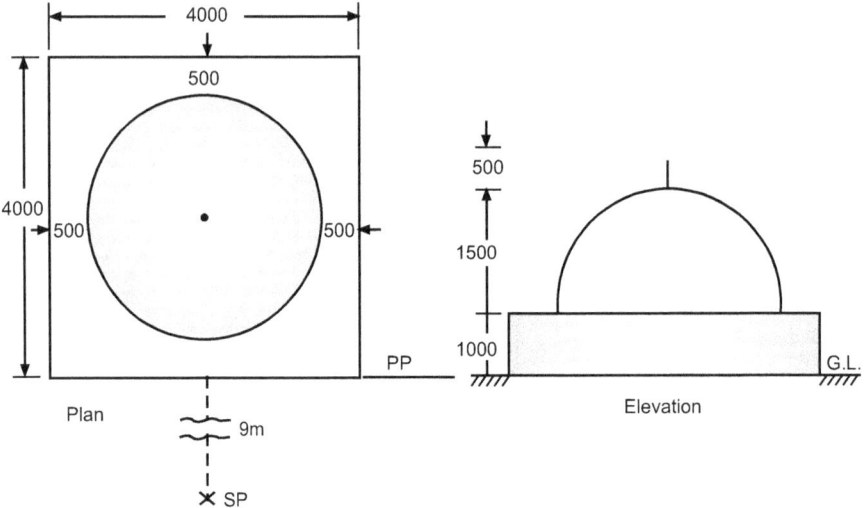

Fig. 8.19

4. Draw to a scale 1 : 100 or suitable, a two-point perspective view of the building shown in Fig. 8.20.

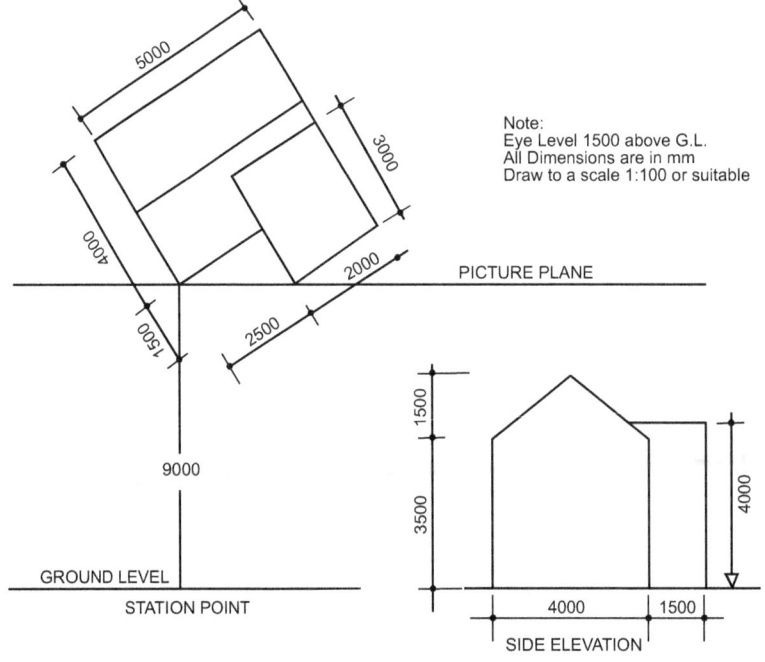

Note:
Eye Level 1500 above G.L.
All Dimensions are in mm
Draw to a scale 1:100 or suitable

Fig. 8.20

5. Draw to a scale 1 : 100 or suitable a two point perspective view of an object shown below, the position of eye level is 1.8 m above ground level.

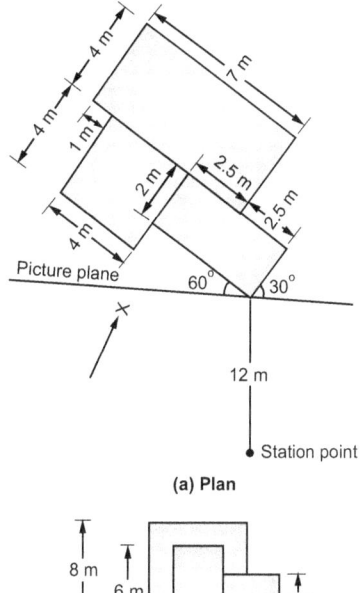

Fig. 8.21

6. Draw to a scale 1 : 100 or suitable a "Two Point Perspective" view of the overhead water tank. The plan and elevation is as shown in Fig. 8.22.
   Tilt the plan to 45° w.r.t. picture plane.
   Use the following details:
   (a) Tilt the plan to 450 with respect to the picture plane. The corner of the tank (in plan) must be touching the picture plane.
   (b) Select station point vertically below the plan from the point, where the inclined plane touches the picture plane. Take station at 7.2 m below picture plane.
   (c) Select eye level = 1.90 m above Ground level.
   (d) All dimensions are in mm.
   (e) Retail all construction lines.

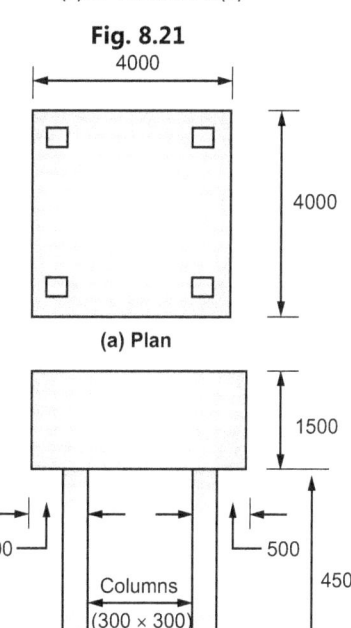

Fig. 8.22: Overhead water tank

7. Draw perspective view of the monument shown in Fig. 8.23.
   Scale 1 : 100 or suitable.

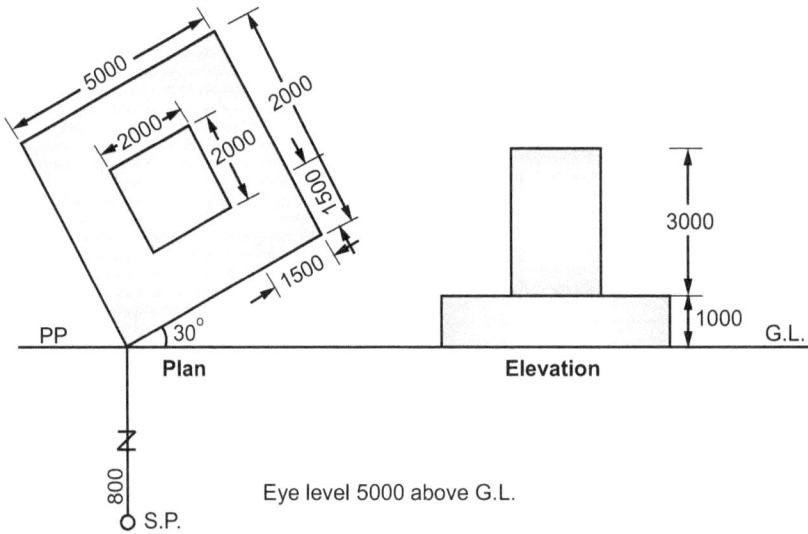

Fig. 8.23

8. Draw to a scale of 1 : 100 or suitable, a two point perspective view of the building shown in Fig. 8.24.

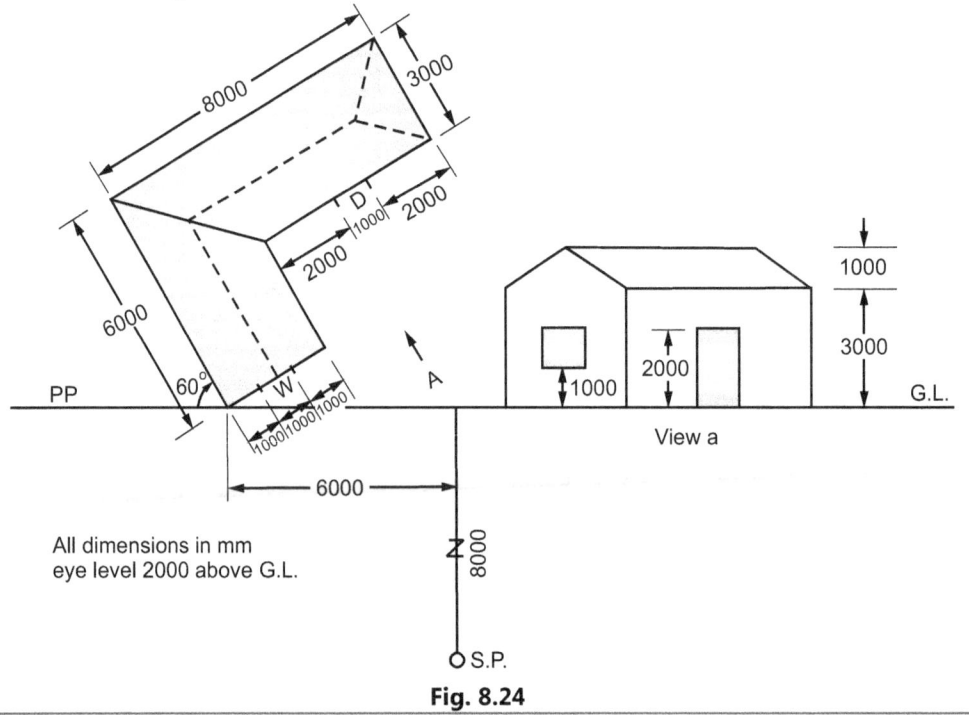

Fig. 8.24

9. Draw to a scale of 1 : 50 the perspective view of the object shown in Fig. 8.25.

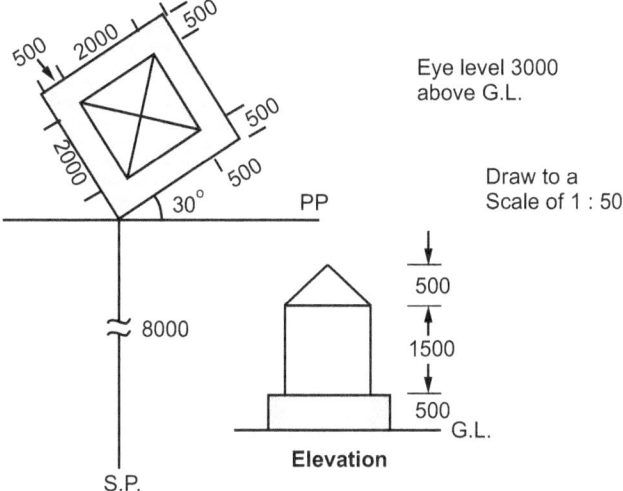

Fig. 8.25

10. Draw two point perspective view of the object shown in Fig. 8.26. Retail all construction lines.

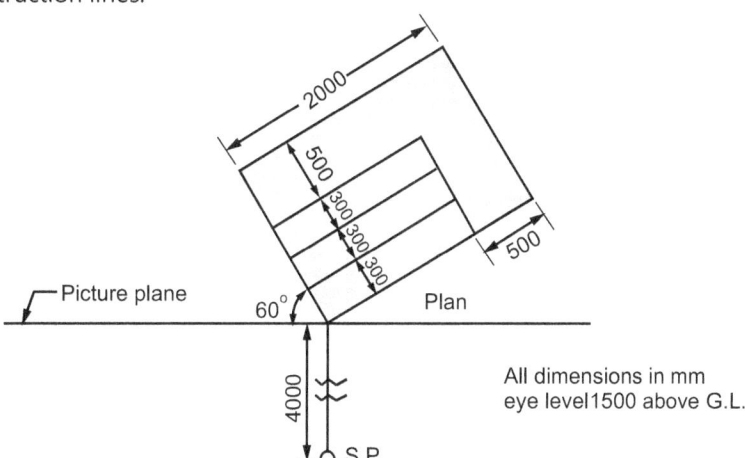

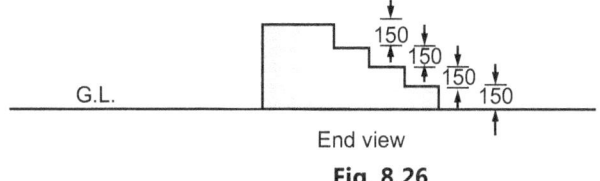

Fig. 8.26

11. (a) Explain one point and two point perspective.
    (b) Draw perspective view for the block shown in Fig. 8.27 with scale 1 : 200 or suitable.

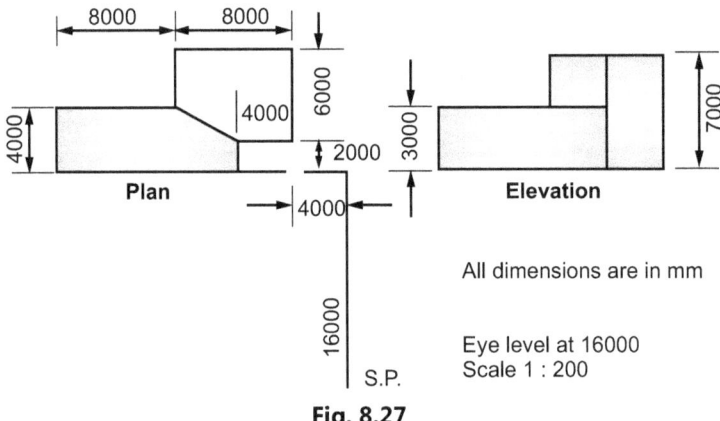

All dimensions are in mm

Eye level at 16000
Scale 1 : 200

Fig. 8.27

12. Draw a one point perspective view of the blocks shown in Fig. 8.28. Assume eye level as 3 m. Scale 1 : 50 or suitable.

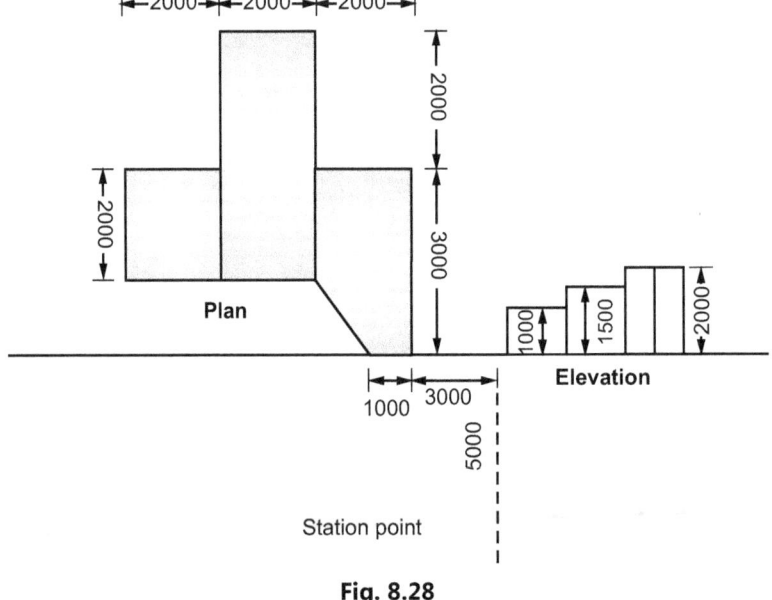

Fig. 8.28

UNIT 4

Chapter 9

PLANNING AND DESIGNING OF PUBLIC BUILDINGS - I

9.1 PLANNING OF PUBLIC BUILDINGS

The design of public building depends upon the nature of the building. Every building has a special character of it's own. The function of the building is to be ascertained initially. Then the different components or blocks or units are to be planned. The units are then joined together to form the whole building. The site of various units depend on the number of person that will be occupied in that room, furniture requirements, space required for circulation etc. There are no hard and fast rules to ascertain the dimension of each block or unit in these building. Minimum dimensions are needed to be fixed on the basis of space needs, thermal comfort, lightning, ventilation requirement etc. of that specified building unit.

9.2 TYPES OF BUILDINGS

National Building Code of India (Sp: 7-1970) defines the building as "any structure for what so ever purpose and of what's ever materials constructed and every part there of whether used as human habitation or not and includes foundations, plinth, walls, floors, roofs, chimneys, plumbing and building services, fixed platforms, balcony cornice or platform projection, part of a building or any thing fixed there to or any wall enclosing or intended to enclose any land or space and signs and outdoor display structures."

According to National Building Code of India (1970), buildings are classified based on occupancies, as follows.

- Group A : Residential buildings.
- Group B : Educational buildings.
- Group C : Institutional buildings.
- Group D : Assembly buildings.
- Group E : Business buildings.
- Group F : Merchandise buildings.
- Group G : Industrial buildings.
- Group H : Storage buildings.
- Group I : Hazardous buildings.

In this chapter, buildings belonging to group B to group F are discussed.

9.3 GROUP B: EDUCATIONAL BUILDINGS

These include any building used for school, college or day care purposes for more than 8 hours per week. Involving assembly for instruction, education or recreation and which is not covered in Group D. This includes a primary and secondary schools, arts, science, commerce, and law colleges, technical, medical and agricultural colleges or institutes.

Codal Minimum Provisions for Various Units:

According to IS: 8827-1978:

Classrooms:

(A) For primary schools age group I-IV standards.

    (i) For a class of 40 students per class 1.11 m^2/student.

(B) For Secondary/ Higher secondary school (Age above 10 years).

For a class room of 40 students per class - 1.2 – 1.5 m^2/student.

General sizes of rooms recommended are:

4.5 m × 6 m

5.5 m × 6.5 m

6.0 m × 7.2 m and

6.0 × 7.8 m

- Teachers room   –   14 m^2
- Drawing halls   –   Area 3-4m^2/student.
- Ceiling height of classroom – 4.2 m or more for area upto 60 sq.m.
- Ceiling height of classroom – 4.8 m or more for area more than 60 sq.m.
- Assembly hall   –   0.5 – 0.6 m^2/student.
- Laboratories   –   Area 3-4 m^2/student.
- Library   –   area 80 – 95 m^2 for 1500 students.

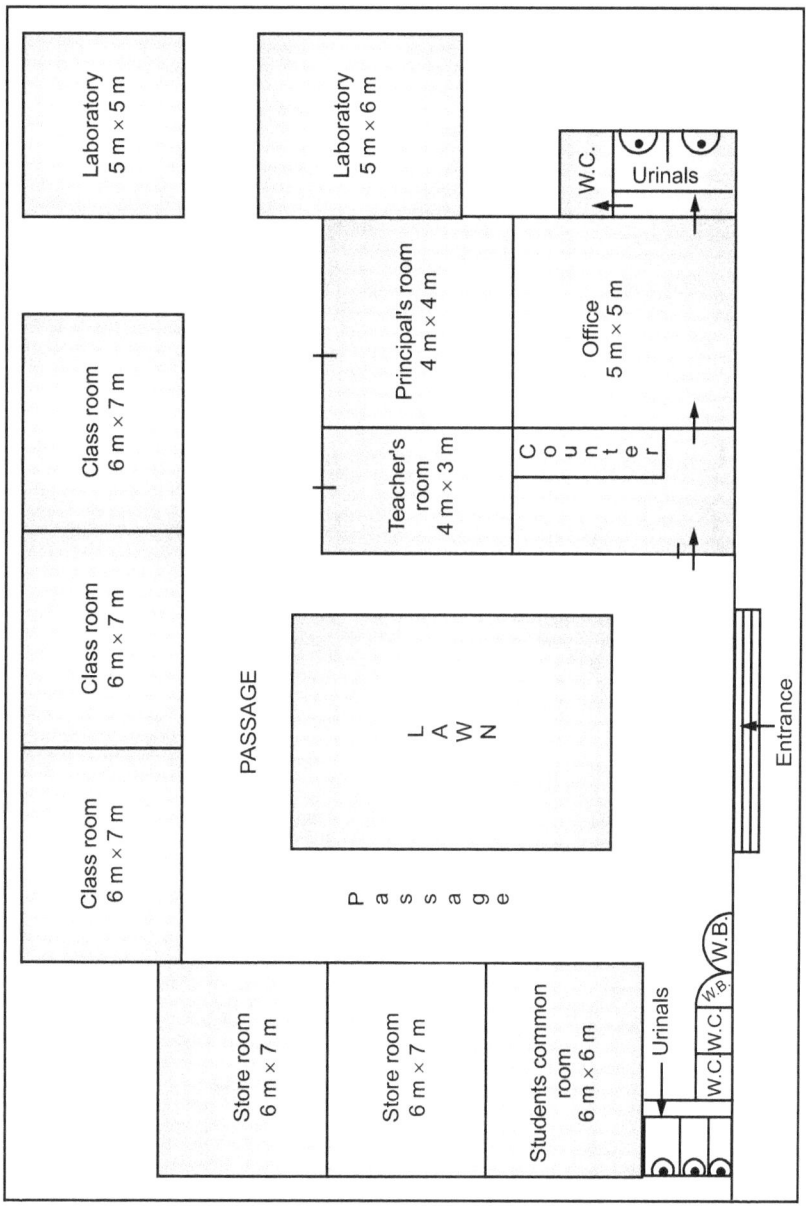

Fig. 9.1: Line plan of a School (not to the scale)

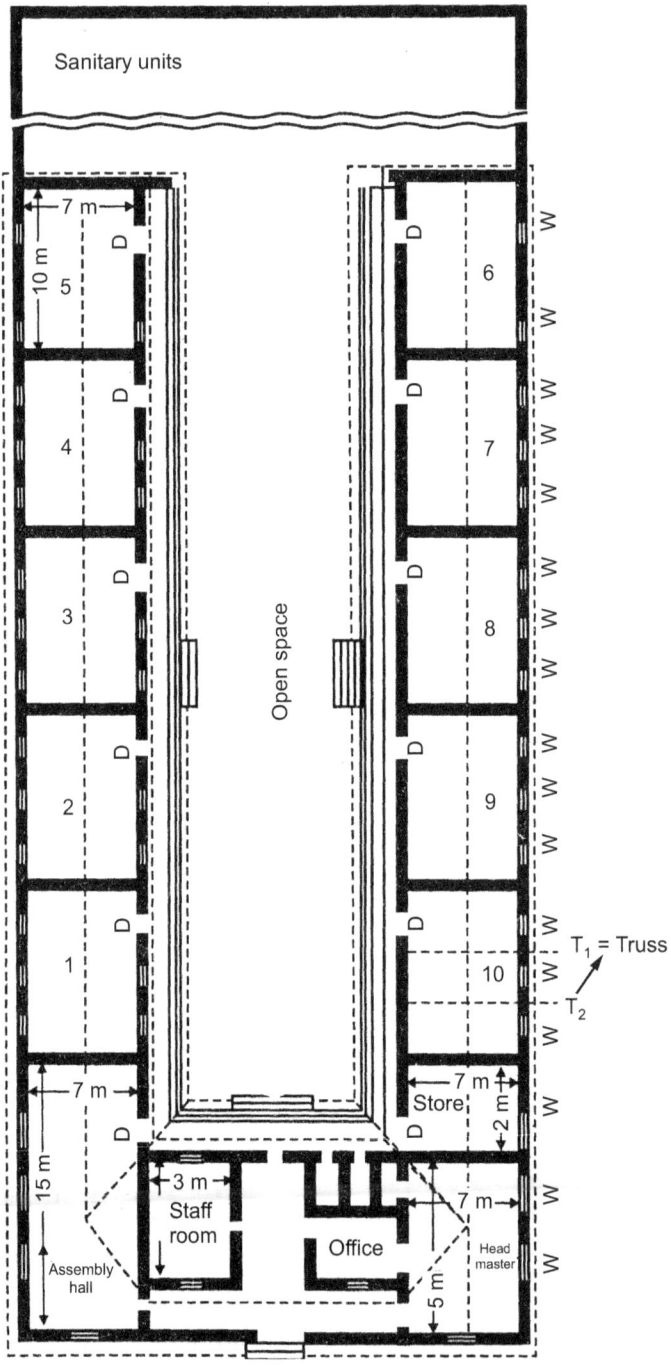

Fig. 9.2: Plan of Primary school

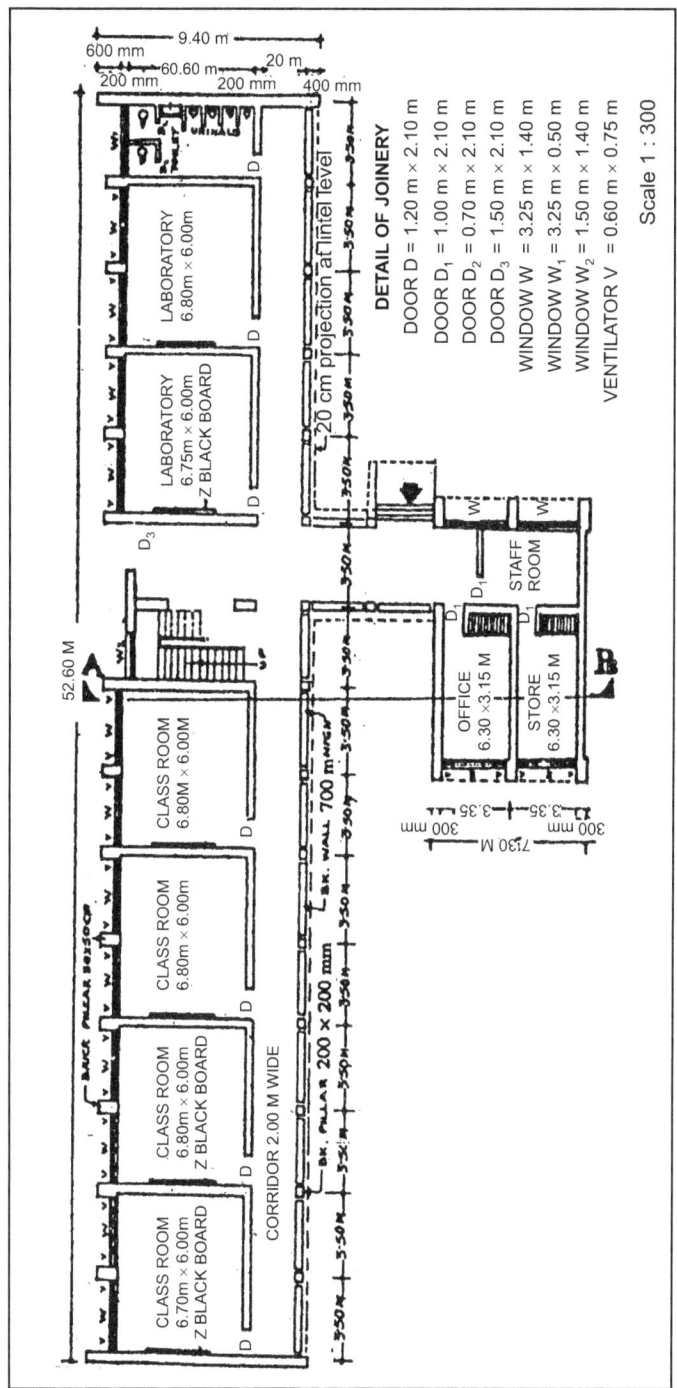

Fig. 9.3: School Building (Ground Floor Plan)

The sanitary blocks should be provided using the following rules:

Description	Male	Female
W.C.	1 for 40 students	1 for 25 students
Urinals	1 for 20 students	–
Wash Basin	1 for 40 students	1 for 40 students
Water taps	1 for 50 students	1 for 50 students

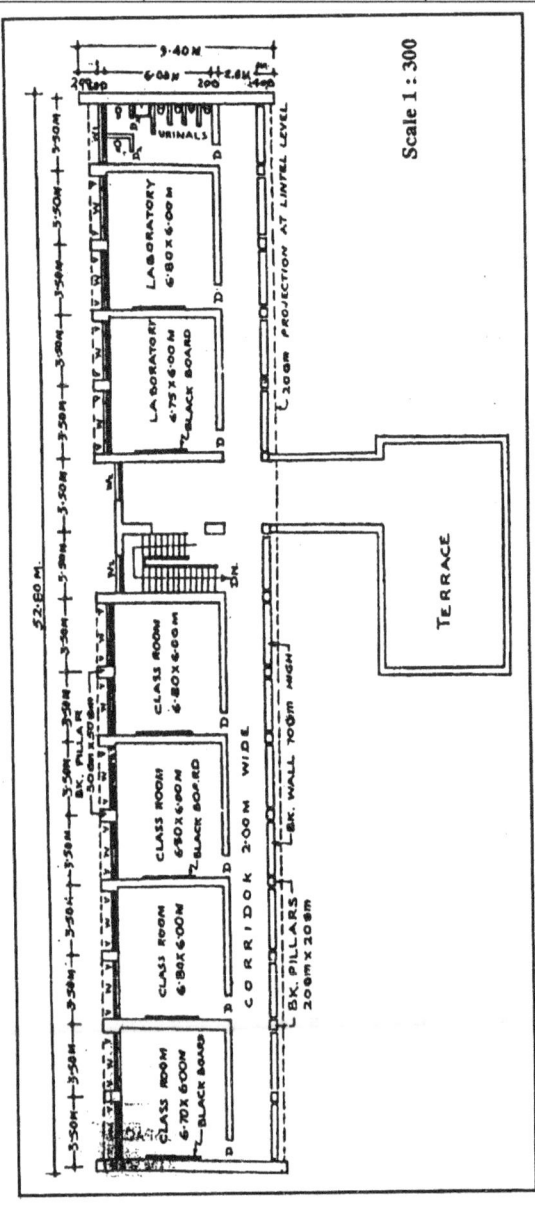

Fig. 9.4: First Floor Plan

Parking Requirements:
1. Cycles   - 1.1 m²/student.
2. Scooters - 3 m²/student.
3. Cars   - 25 m² per car.
4. Buses   - 60 m² per bus.

The area of parking should be calculated after assuming some percentage of students and staff using types of vehicles. (Refer Plate 17)

Points to be Considered for Planning:
1. In hot humid climate of our tropical country it is absolutely essential that the classrooms should not be constructed on two sides of a corridor and derive light from the north as far as possible.
2. The classrooms and other rooms should be planned in such a manner that there is no disturbance to classrooms while the other rooms are being used.
3. As far as possible, the principal's room should be located in is such a manner that classrooms are visible to him.
4. The principal's room and office should be close to each other and as well as near to the main entrance.
5. A common room with area 2.5 to 3.0 sq.m. per teacher would normally be provided.
6. The layout of classroom can be either L-shaped or rectangular pattern.
7. Care should be taken that the classroom in above fashion should form an enclosure.
8. The sanitary blocks and water taps should be placed in each wing in such a manner that they are easily accessible to all units.
9. Other important units are assembly hall, gymnasium, library, stackroom, administrative block and play ground.

9.4 GROUP C: INSTITUTIONAL BUILDINGS

These include any building or part there of which is used for purposes such as a medical or other treatment or care of persons suffering from physical or mental illness, disease or infirmity, care of infants, aged persons.

These buidings for health include various types of buidings from a small dispensary to a big hospital.

(A) Dispensary:

A dispensary is a place where medicines are prescribed and accordingly given out to the patients. Following units are required in a dispensary:
(i) Entrance/waiting area – 2.5 m wide (minimum).
(ii) Circulation area – passage, corridors etc.
(iii) Doctor's room/consulting room – 2.5 m × 4 m.

(iv) Dressing/Examination room/small O.T. – (3 × 4) m (one or two number).

(v) Drug store – 2.75 m × 3 m.

(B) Primary Health Centre:

Primary health centre is a place for medical examination and treatment. Usually, these centres are run by local bodies of government and their purpose is to provide medical advice and attention to general public.

- Entrance and waiting spaces
- Doctors room/consulting room   3 m × 3.6 m (one or two number)
- Examination room/dressing room   3 m × 4 m
- Operation theatre   4 m × 4.5 m
- Ward
  Maternity and General   8 – 10 m^2/bed
- Drug store   3.53 × 4.75 m
- Office   12m^2
- Residence quarters
  (i) Doctors   60 – 90 m^2/head
  (ii) Servants   40 – 60 m^2/head

Circulation Requirements:

Provisions for horizontal circulation:

Passage / corridor   1 – 2.5 m wide

Verandah   1.8 – 2.5 m wide

Provisions for Vertical Circulation:

Stairs and lifts can be provided for the effective circulation in each building:

(i) Stairs
  Width   1.2 m (minimum)
  Riser   130 – 150 mm
  Tread   300 – 325 mm
  Landing   1 – 1.8 m wide

Points to be Considered for Planning:

1. A waiting room should be provided for the visitors in front of doctor's room and one in front of a operation theatre for friends and relatives of the patient being operated.
2. The wards should be positioned in such a manner that they should have a good aspect and prospect requirements.

3. Sanitary blocks should be provided at the end of the corridor to keep away any bad smell.
4. Draw a line plan of primary school with the following data:
   (a) Classroom   6 m × 8 m   8 nos.
   (b) Headmasters room 5 m × 4 m   1 no.
   (c) Office   5 m × 5 m   1 no.
   (d) Staff room   6 m × 8 m   1 no.

   Assume other important details and state them clearly.

(C) Hospital:

A hospital comprises of units like out patient's department, nursing units, where patients are housed and led. Nursing units are having various wards, such as medical, surgical, casualty ward, children's ward and maternity ward. A good hospital should have large nursing units. There may be separate hospital or a unit for infectious diseases.

Following are the units in a hospital building with their sizes:

Out Patient Departments:

(a) Entrance and waiting space 1 – 2 m^2/person.
(b) Consulting rooms for various specialists like medicine, ENT, Eye, Dentistry, Gynaecology, Orthopeadic, Mental, Skin, Venereal diseases etc., each unit of size 12 to 15 m^2.
(c) Office   3 m × 4 m
(d) Emergency   4 m × 5.5 m
(e) Dispensary   4 m × 5 m

Sanitary Blocks:

Description	Male	Female
W.C.	1 for 100	2 for 100
Urinals	1 for 50	–
Wash Basins	1 for 100	1 for 100

Operation Theatre:

Operation Theatre - 4.5 m × 5.5 m
Sterilization Room - 3 m × 4 m
Doctor's Room   - 3 m × 4 m
Nurse's Room   - 3 m × 3 m
Waiting Space   - 3 m wide

Nursing Area (Wards):

Wards are gynecology, female, children, infectious diseases etc. The minimum sizes to be provided are as follows.

(a) Ward $\quad$ 8 – 10 m^2/bed and 30 cu.m space/bed

(b) Nurse's room $\quad$ 3 m × 4 m

(c) Sanitary Provisions:

	W.C.	1 for 8 beds.
	Bath	2 for 1 ward.
	Wash Basin	1 for 30 beds

Other Requirements:

(a) Radiology department.

(b) Laundry.

(c) Pathology laboratory.

(d) Circulation space: Horizontal and vertical circulation.

(e) Parking space.

(f) Casualty department.

(g) Kitchen and store.

(h) Drug store.

Points to be Considered for Planning of Hospital Furniture:

1. The numbers of beds to be accommodated in each ward varies largely with the type of wards and the total capacity of the hospital.

2. For convenience a ward may contain 20 – 24 beds. But in some cases wards have been provided to contain even 30 – 40 beds.

3. The space between the sides of a beds should be 0.9 m as a minimum.

4. A clearance of 1.2 m between the ends of a beds should be left.

5. A common size of a bed used in hospitals is 0.9 m × 2 m.

6. The sill of a windows should be placed not lower than 75 cm, as height of bed is usually 0.6 m.

9.5 HOTELS AND RESTAURANTS

9.5.1 Hotels

Space requirement for a hotel can be divided into (i) public area, such as entrance hall, lounges and dining halls, (ii) bed rooms, (iii) service area such as kitchen, laundries, air conditioning plant etc., (iv) restaurant attached (may or may not be).

The minimum requirements for hotels are as follows:

Entrance, reception, waiting hall.

Dining	2.0 – 2.5 m²/head
Kitchen	20 m² – 30 m²
Store	10 m² – 15 m²
Pantry	6 m² – 10 m²
Bed rooms:	
General bed	3.0 m × 4.5 m
Good size double bed	3.5 m × 4.5 m
General sizes	3.5 m × 5.5 m
	4.0 m × 5.5 m
Laundry	3 m × 4 m
Servant room	3 m × 4 m
Sanitary block	For servants separate
	Each near dining and entrance hall
	For every bed room (attached)

9.5.2 Restaurants

The approximate areas for each units of a restaurant are as follows:

Dining hall	2 to 2.5 m²/head
Pantry	4 m × 6 m
Kitchen	20 m² to 30 m²
Store	4 m × 3 m
Cook's room	3 m × 4 m
Preparation	4.5 m × 5 m

Points to be Considered for a Planning / Grouping of Units:
1. The kitchen and pantry shall open out into the dining halls by means of a service counter.
2. It is necessary that hygienic conditions should be maintained in the kitchen and pantry, so for this purpose sufficient light and good ventilation are needed.
3. A separate service entry to be provided to the store and to the main preparation area.
4. Toilets can be used by the restaurant users as well as the restaurant staff. Provisions shall be made so as to have proximity to the both area.
5. A separate washing space has to be provided for washing all the utensils, vessels etc.

9.6 GROUP E: BUSINESS BUILDINGS

These include any buildings or part of a building, which is used for the transaction of business (other than covered by building in Group F) for keeping of accounts and records and similar purposes.

In such a classification, library can also be classified because the principal function of library is to keep record of books.

(A) Library:
- (a) Entrance and moving space around delivery counter — 2.0 m wide (minimum)
- (b) Issue counter — Height 1.5 m – 1.8 m.
- (c) Sections in library — 3 m × 3 m (minimum)
    - Reference section
    - Serious reading
    - General reading (Magazine and Newspaper)
    - Stack room
    - Periodical section
- (d) Administrative area
    - Librarian room
    - Other staff area
    - Card index area
    - Record area

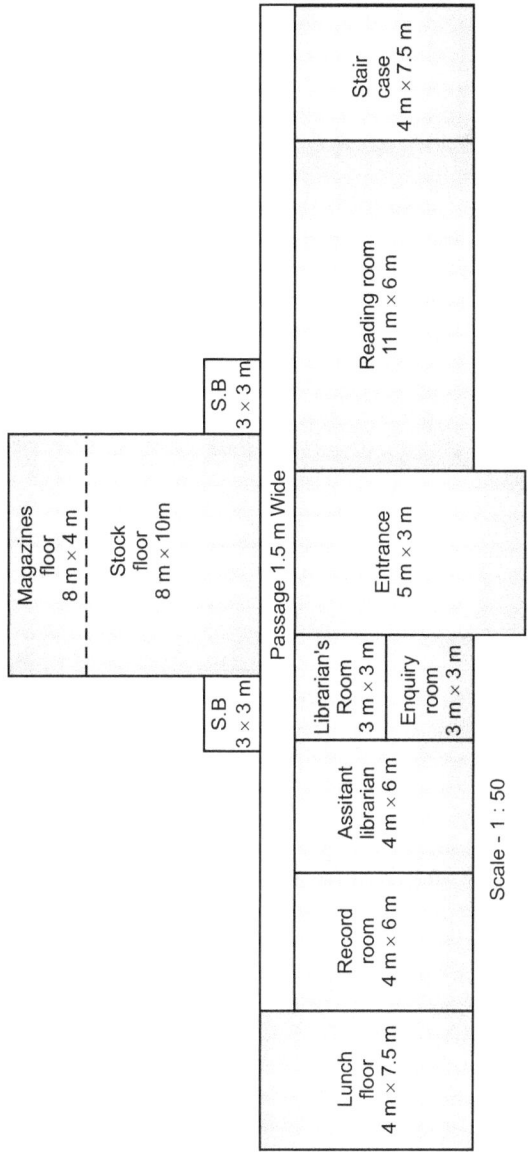

Fig. 9.5: Library building

Sanitary blocks:

Description	Male	Female
W.C.	1 for 200, upto 400 and above 400, 1 for every 250.	1 for 100 upto 200 above 200 1 for every 150.
Urinary	1 for 50	—
Wash Basin	1 for 200, upto 450 and above 400, 1 for every 250.	above 450, 1 for every 250.

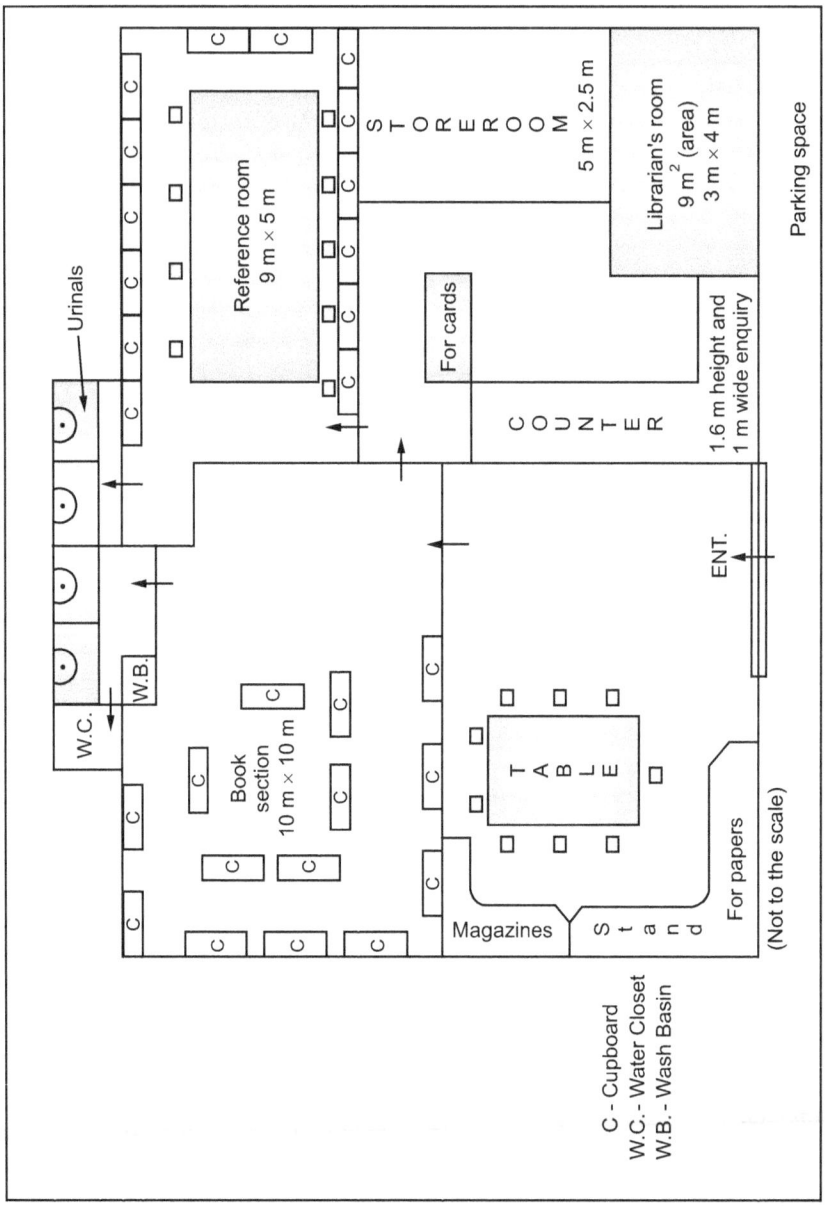

Fig. 9.6: Line plan of a library

Points to be considered for Grouping and Furniture arrangement:

1. In reading rooms tables are designed to accommodate four to eight persons each, together on either sides.
2. 0.75 m length per person is provided for table and allowing seats along both the sides it should be at least 0.9 m wide.
3. Height of tables is usually 0.75 m to 0.85 m from the floor.
4. Size of Newspaper stand is 1.2 m in length. The sloping face of a newspaper stand should have width of about 0.75 m and its lower end 0.9 m above ground.
5. The width of a lobby space required for moving around the newspaper stand should be 0.9 m and between two stands is 1.5 m.
6. Larger tables are required for reference reading than required for a periodical etc.
7. The size of racks and number of sections required for the particular library should be considered based on the type of institute and its capacity.

9.7 HOSTEL BUILDING

Entrance	3 m wide
Common room	
Rector office	
Security room	
Guest room	
Rooms	
Single seated	Area 9.5 m² / head
Two seated	Area 7.5 m² – 8 m² / head
Three seated	Area 7.2 – 7.5 m² / head
Circulation	1.8 m minimum
Recreation hall	2 – 3 m² / head
Dining hall	3 – 4 m² / head
Kitchen	9.5 m² minimum
Store	2 m × 3 m
Pantry	2.75 m × 3 m
Parking space	

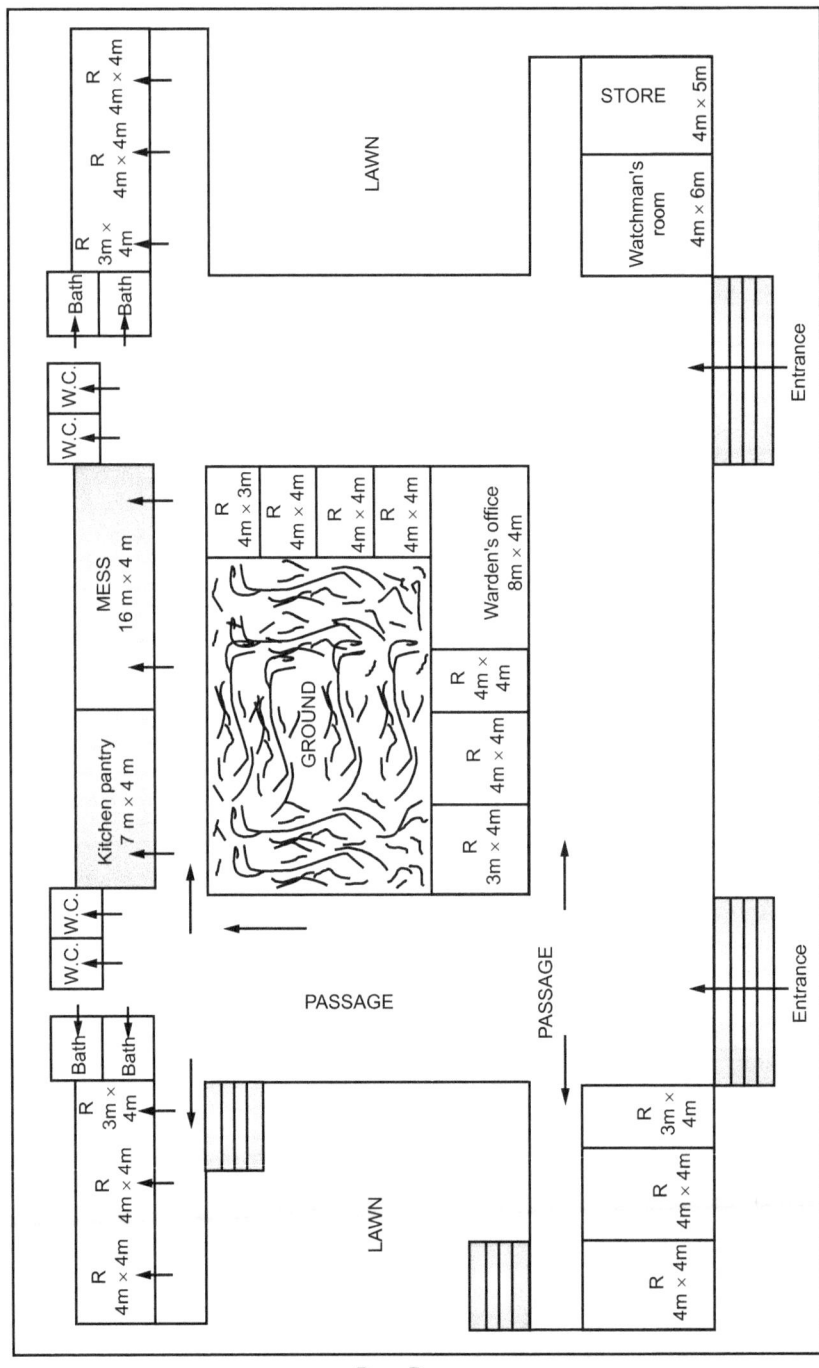

Fig. 9.7: Line plan of a Hostel

R → Room

Sanitary Blocks:

Description	Male	Female
W.C.	1 for 10	1 for 8
Bath	1 for 10	1 for 10
Urinals	1 for 25	–
Wash basins	1 for 10	1 for 10

IMPORTANT POINTS

- All rooms should be arranged or grouped in such a manner that there is a formation of an enclosure.
- The rectors room, store room, and other rooms like dining hall, common room, and kitchens area all should be taken as far as possible near to the entrance so that they do not disturb the hostel rooms.

QUESTIONS

1. A hospital to serve a population of 20,000 is to be designed on a site measuring 100 m × 150 m separate word for men and women W.C., Nurses room etc. are to be provided and detailed have to be worked out. Draw a line plan to a suitable scale.
2. Design a Hostel of your college. Make suitable assumption and state them clearly. Draw a typical furniture layout of a single bed in that.

    Plan a commercial bank in a city. Assume suitable data, clearly mention the data. Draw a line plan to a suitable scale.
3. It is proposed to construct a Public Health Centre with the following data:
    (1) Lounge: 30 sq.m.
    (2) Reception: 20 sq.m.
    (3) Administration office: 20 sq.m.
    (4) Doctor's cabins: 15 sq.m.
    (5) Nurse's room: 15 sq.m.

(6) Labour room: 15 sq.m.

(7) Wards two numbers: 20 sq.m each.

(8) Store: 15 sq.m.

With the help of a connectivity matrix and bubble diagram to a scale of 1 : 50 or suitable.

(a) Line plan showing location of doors and windows.

(b) Schedule of openings.

(c) Suggest suitable material for painting of walls.

UNIT 5

Chapter 10
PLANNING AND DESIGNING OF PUBLIC BUILDINGS - II

10.1 INDUSTRIAL BUILDINGS

Industrial buildings are the structures in which various types of materials are manufactured from raw materials, fabricated and processed etc. It requires space for storage of raw materials, for installation of machinery and plant, for storage of final product.

To prevent haphazard growth of industries in cities, industrial area should be well planned. It should be located away from residential areas and preferably outside the town.

Basic Requirements:

1. Raw materials available in near vicinity.
2. Source of water within reasonable distance.
3. Source of electric power close to railway station.
4. Easy transportation facilities.
5. Flexible tax policies.
6. Availability of finance on easy installments.
7. Land or plot with sizes for future expansion.
8. Space for storage of raw materials.
9. Space for installation of machineries.
10. Space for parking of vehicles and circulation.

Orientation and Lighting:

1. Shape of the plot and orientation of industrial building should be in close link.
2. In North, saw toothed North-light roof truss can be used.
3. For the regions to the South of Tropic of Cancer, North light roof truss is used.

4. Proper lighting in the factory is obtained by arranging factory sheds in East and West directions and by providing glass windows in Northern walls.
5. In no case, windows should be placed in Eastern and Western walls of the building.

Area of Plot and Other Spaces of Utilisation:
1. Total area of plot for industrial building should be according to the requirements with future expansion.
2. Area for installation of machineries of plant and storage of materials should be 60% of the total built-up area.
3. Area under roads inside the factory should not be more than 20% of area of plot.
4. Area of administrative building is 5% to 10% of built-up area.
5. Area of open space should be 8% of total area.
6. Work sheds should be of area minimum 50 sq.m to 500 sq.m.
7. Minimum height of plinth is 300 mm from top of road surface.
8. Height of bed block level and tie beam of roof is minimum 4.2 m from floor level.
9. Flooring in cement concrete or brick flooring or rubber flooring depending on the use of industry and nature of work.
10. Sizes of ventilators and windows should be according to rules of area of openings. This should be maximum 25% of floor area in hot and humid region and 15% of floor area in case of hot and dry region.
11. Pitch roof in C.I. sheet or A.C. sheet should be used.
12. There must be an arrangement of water supply, drainage, electricity, connection of plot with main roads at the initial stage only.
13. According to the functional requirement different sizes of sheds should be constructed in 10 m to 13 m span in general cases. Standard types of trusses should be used for pitched roof.
14. For small factories covered area is 50% of plot area.
15. Roads should be laid in width of 3.7 m. All roads should lead to the work sheds and from there must be connected to common road.

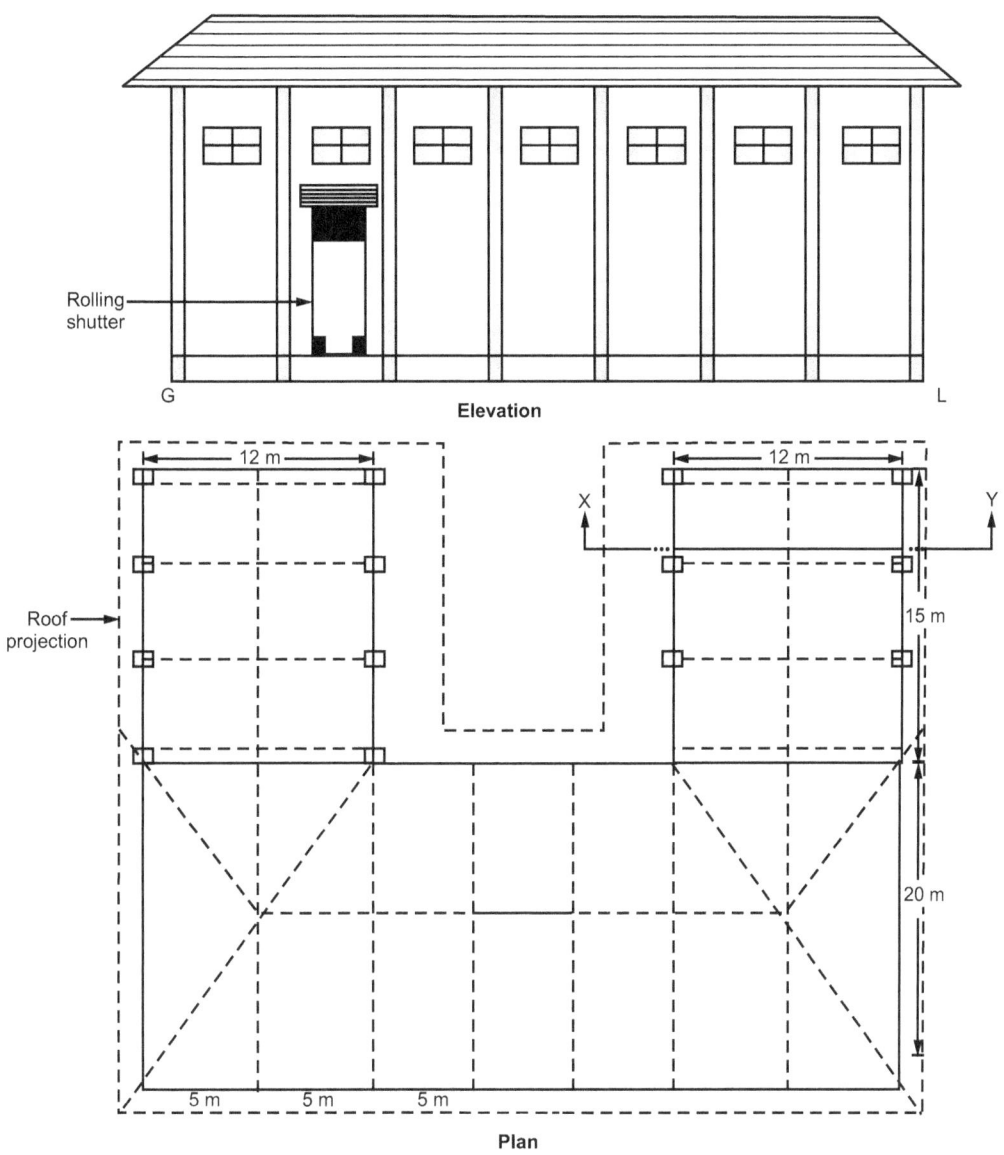

Fig. 10.1: Planning of dal mill

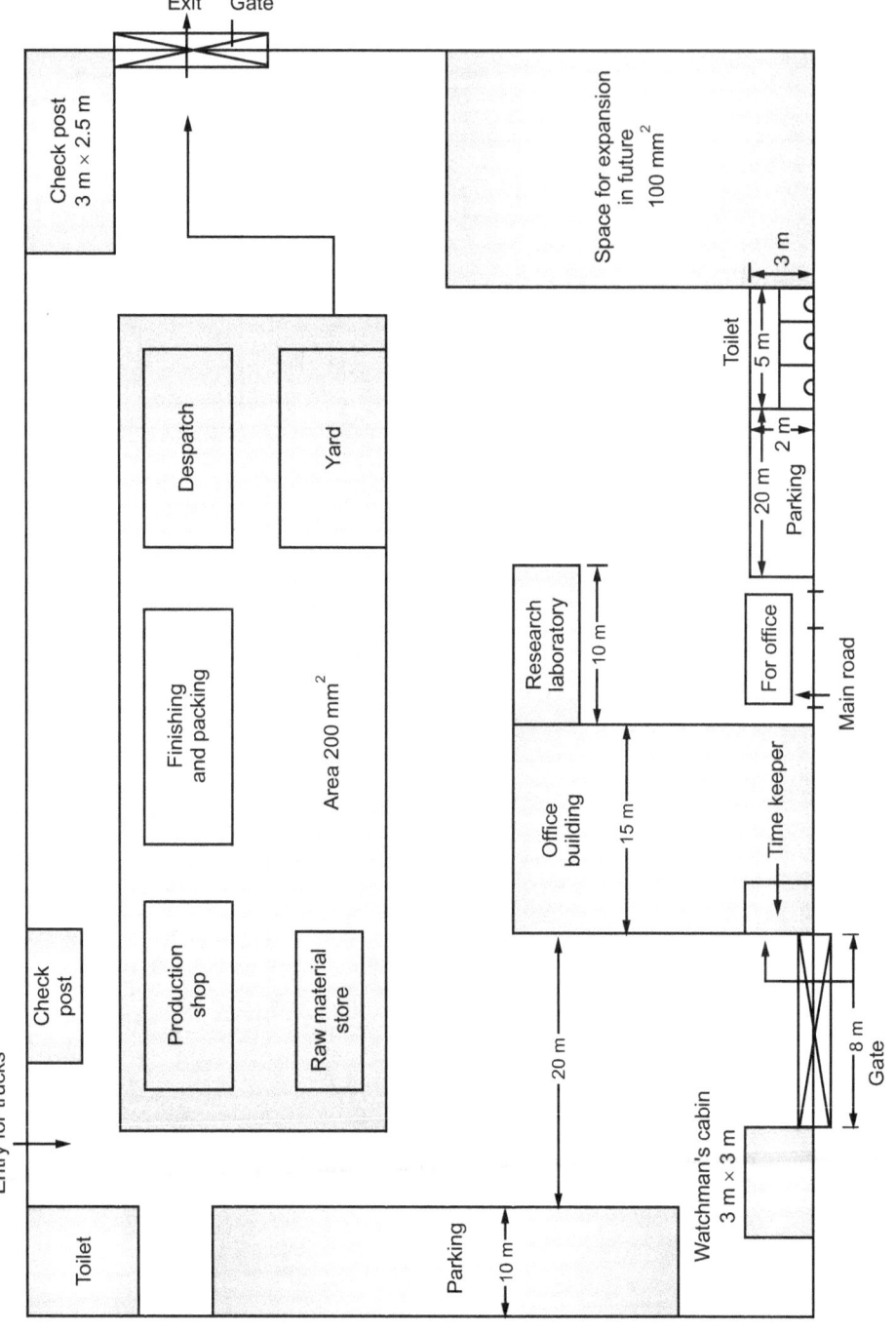

Fig. 10.2: General layout of an industrial building

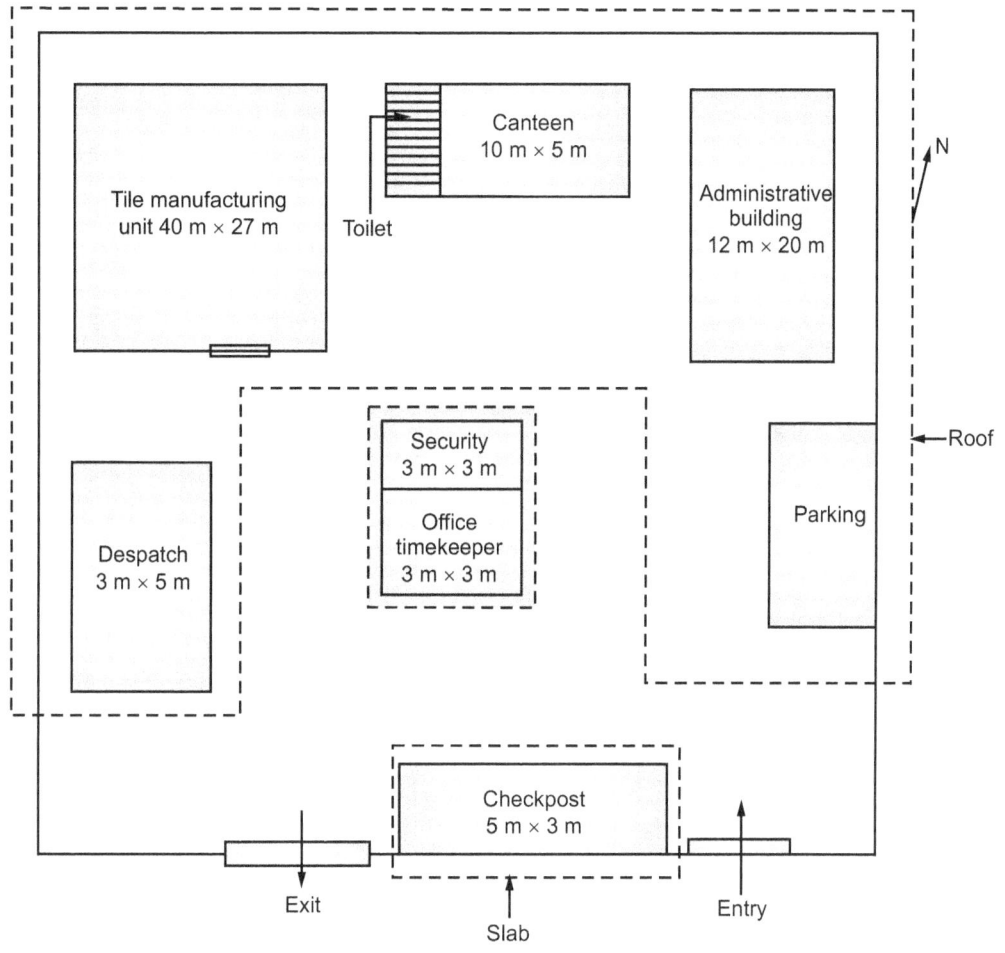

Fig. 10.3: Tile manufacturing factory

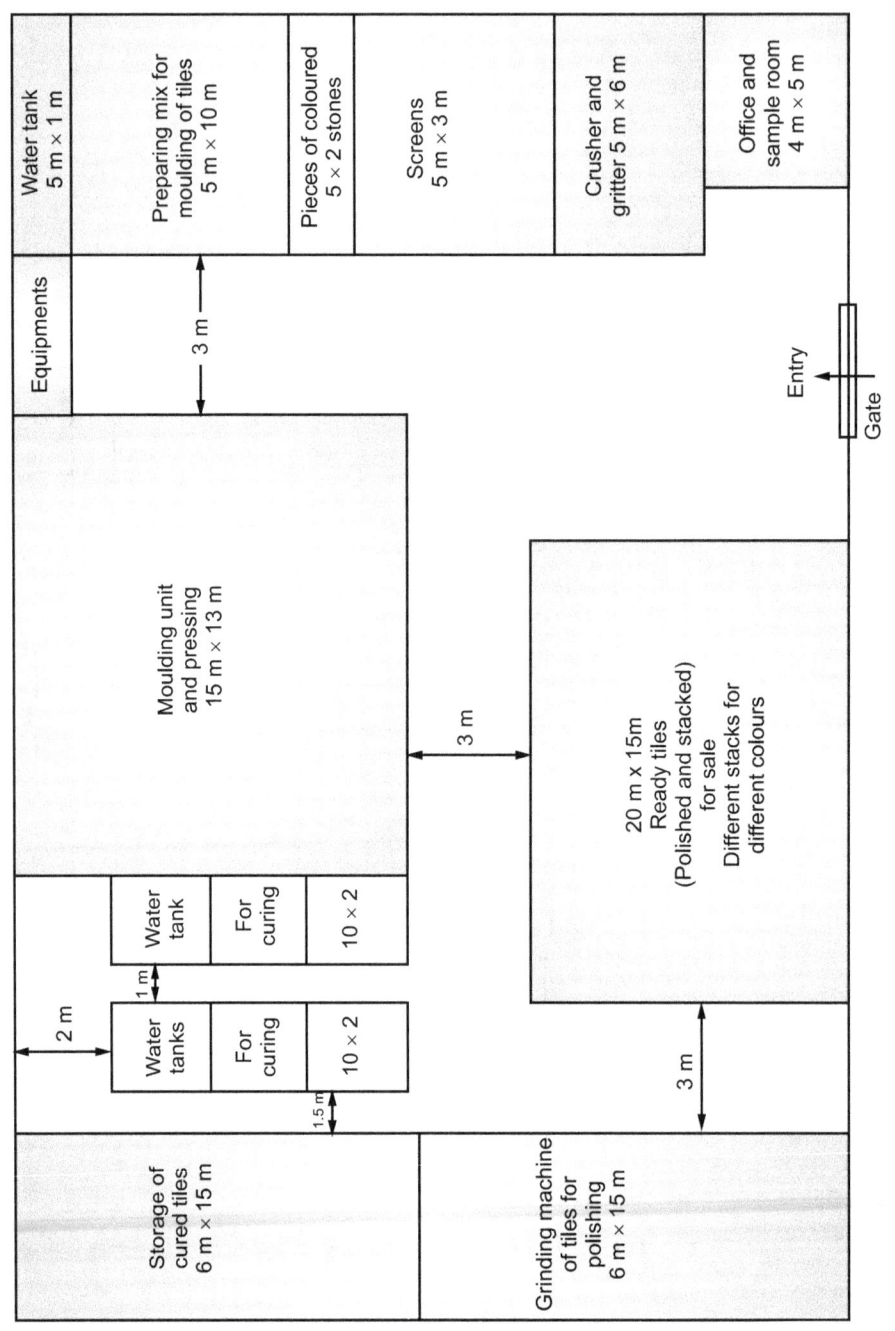

Fig. 10.4: Details of tile manufacturing unit

10.1.1 Data Required for Steel Fabrication Shop

Units required	Sizes
1. Storage of iron and steel rods, bars, pipes etc.	4 m × 3.5 m
2. Gauge to measure thickness of steel flats	1 m × 1 m
3. Bending machine installation	3 m × 2 m
4. Steel cutting unit	3 m × 2 m
5. Welding shop (a) Gas welding; (b) Electric arc welding.	10 m × 6 m
6. Office	4 m × 3 m
7. Staff room	4 m × 3 m
8. Sanitary accommodation for staff	3 m × 2 m

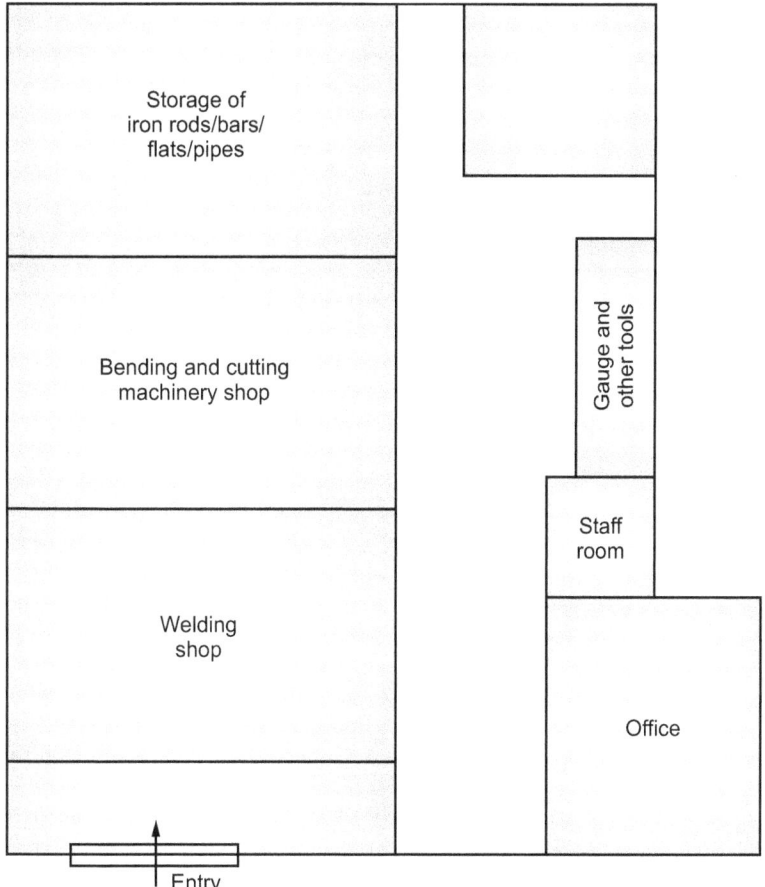

Fig. 10.5: A fabrication shop

10.1.2 Data Required for Vehicle Service Centre

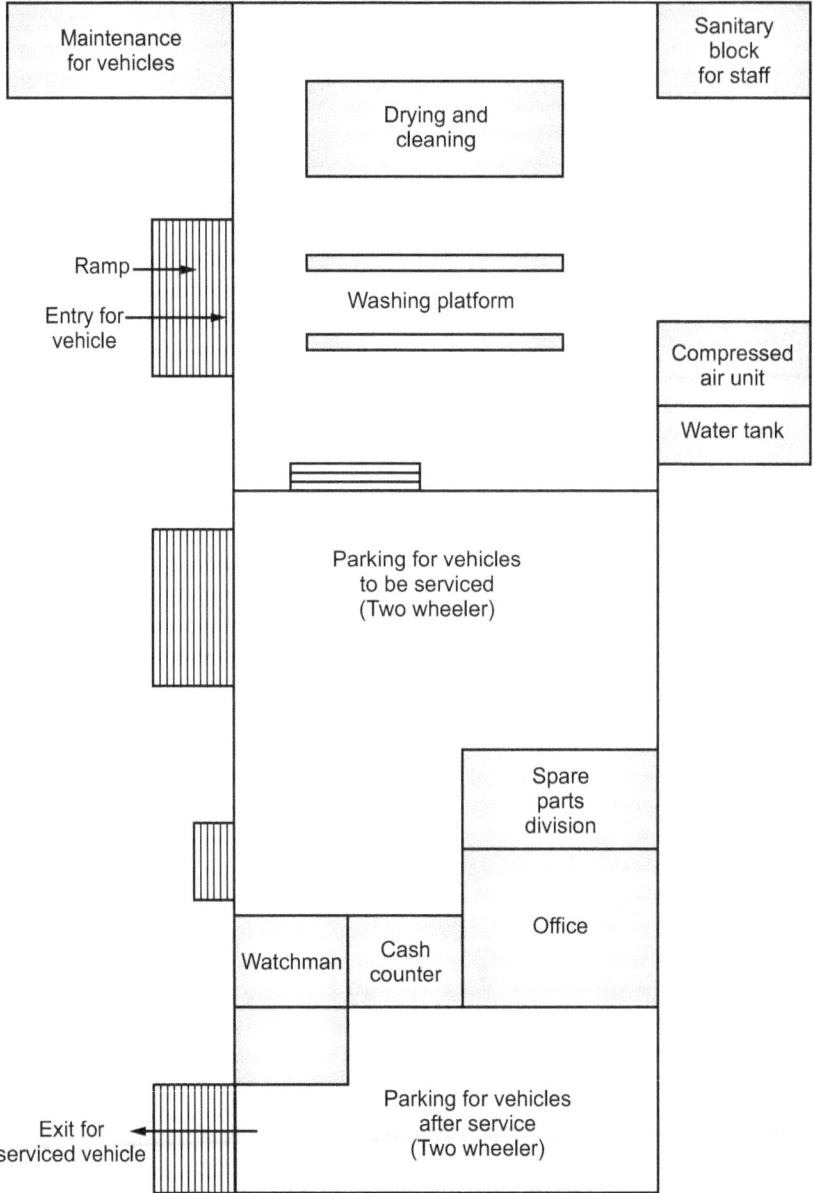

Fig. 10.6: Vehicle service centre

1. Office and cash counter.
2. Space for vehicles for servicing.

3. Space for vehicles service, i.e. maintenance, tool room, oiling, washing, cleaning etc.
4. Spare parts division.
5. Space for vehicles after servicing.
6. Delivery.

Sizes: For 25 vehicles a service centre can be provided with:
1. Office: 4 m × 3 m.
2. Cash counter: 2 m × 2 m.
3. Space for vehicles for service, i.e. entry and parking: 20 m × 6 m.
4. Servicing division: Washing - 3 m × 3 m;
   Drying, Cleaning - 4 m × 3 m;
   Oiling and Maintenance - 4 m × 3 m;
   Spare parts division - 5 m × 3 m.
5. Compressed air unit: 3 m × 2 m.
6. Parking of vehicles after service: 20 m × 6 m.
7. Delivery room with counter: 3 m × 3 m.

10.1.3 Data Required for P.V.C. Pipe Unit

P.V.C. pipes are most commonly used now-a-days in various chemical industries and food processing industries. These are popularly used in sewer pipes and in low pressure water supply pipes. General requirements are similar to other small scale industry.

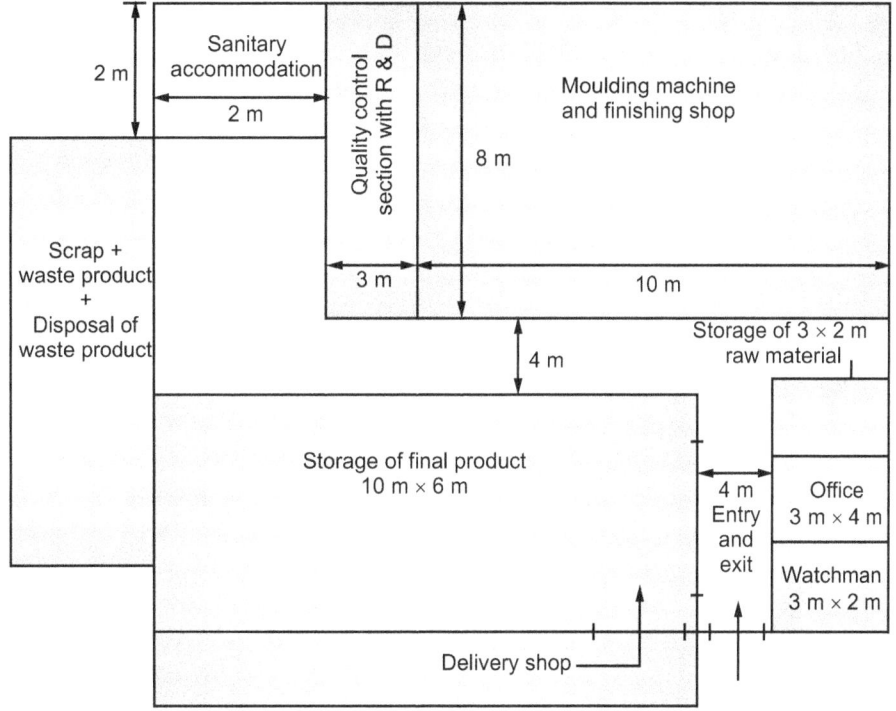

Fig. 10.7

Manufacturing of these pipes require:
1. Raw material (polyethylene, poly propylene etc.)
2. Crusher.
3. Injection moulding machine.
4. Moulds of required diameter and shape.
5. Finishing, cutting, machine shop.
6. Quality control section.

10.1.4 Prestressed Concrete Pole Factory

Units required for a pole factory are:

1. **Raw Material Storage:**
   (a) Cement
   (b) Steel
   (c) Sand
   (d) Aggregate
   (e) Water
   (f) Oil or grease to apply on forms.

   These are stored at their appropriate places.

2. **Batching Plant (Measurement of Materials):**
   (a) Cement stored in godowns is batched or taken in proper proportion by weight.
   (b) Steel is batched by weight according to bar bending schedule (details of reinforcement).
   (c) Water is batched by volume.
   (d) Sand and aggregate are batched by weight.

   For a pole factory, a conveyor system is preferred as an automatic batching plant.

3. **Mixing Plants:** Raw materials of concrete (cement, sand, aggregate, water) are mixed in proportion by concrete mixers. Continuous type of mixers may be used for this factory.

4. **Placing Concrete in Forms:** Before placing concrete in forms, a nominal reinforcement is arranged in wooden form work or steel form work. Now a fresh concrete is placed in forms and compacted by using vibrators.

5. **Curing:** After the forms are removed, curing process is done for hardening of cement concrete.

Now poles are ready to use as electric poles or fencing poles etc.

Process layout is as below for this factory.

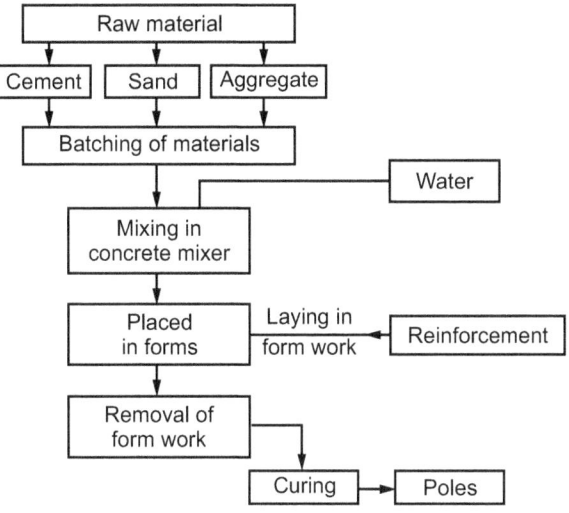

Fig. 10.8

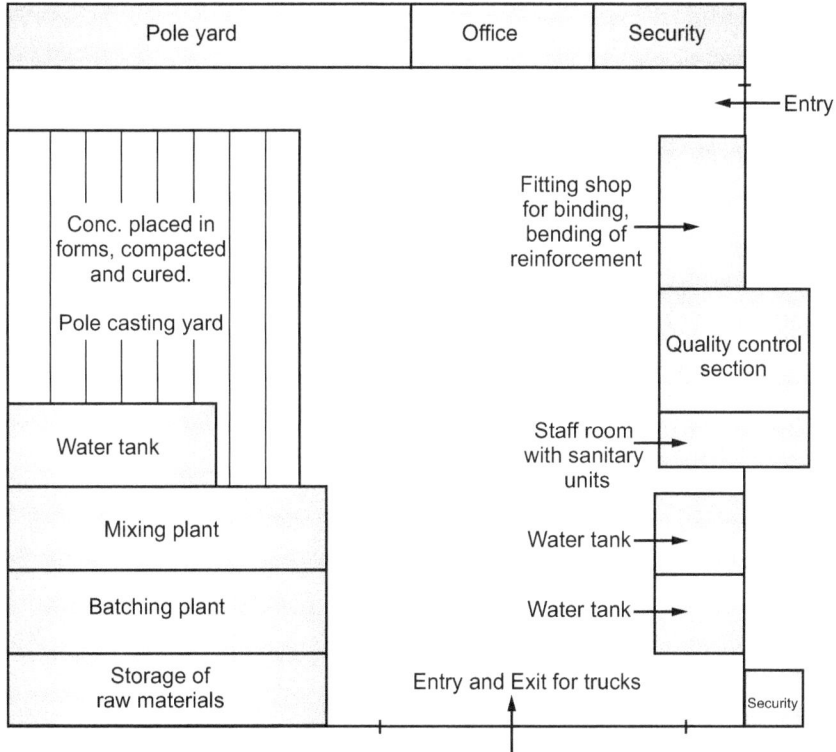

Fig. 10.9: A typical layout of a pole factory

10.2 GENERAL BUILDINGS

(A) Post Office:

Following units in a general post office should be considered.

Entrance and moving space	30 m²
Public dealing counters	Height 1.6 m – 1.8 m, width 0.7 m – 0.95 m
Post master's room	15 m²
Working area for other staff	30 m²
Post separation room	30 m²
Safe custedy area for cash	9.5 m²
Entertainment room	12 m²
Water room and Toilet	7.5 m²

1. Two entrances have been provided; one main entrance for all the visitors and one service entrance for employees.
2. Entrance to post master's office should be such that it is easily accessible by both outsiders as well as employees.
3. The public dealing counters separate the waiting space from the working and post separation space.

(B) Health Club or a Club House:

Entrance	1.2 m wide
Changing room	9.5 m² (separate for gents/ladies)
Gymnasium	4.5 m × 4 m
Indoor game area	4 m × 5 m (each game) i.e. Table tenis, billiard etc.
Store room	2.75 m × 3 m
Parking area	

Sanitary Blocks:

Description	Male	Female
W.C.	1 for 25	1 for 15
Urinals	1 for 6 – 20	—
	2 for 21 – 45	
	3 for 46 – 70	
	4 for 71 – 100	
	1 for 25	1 for 25

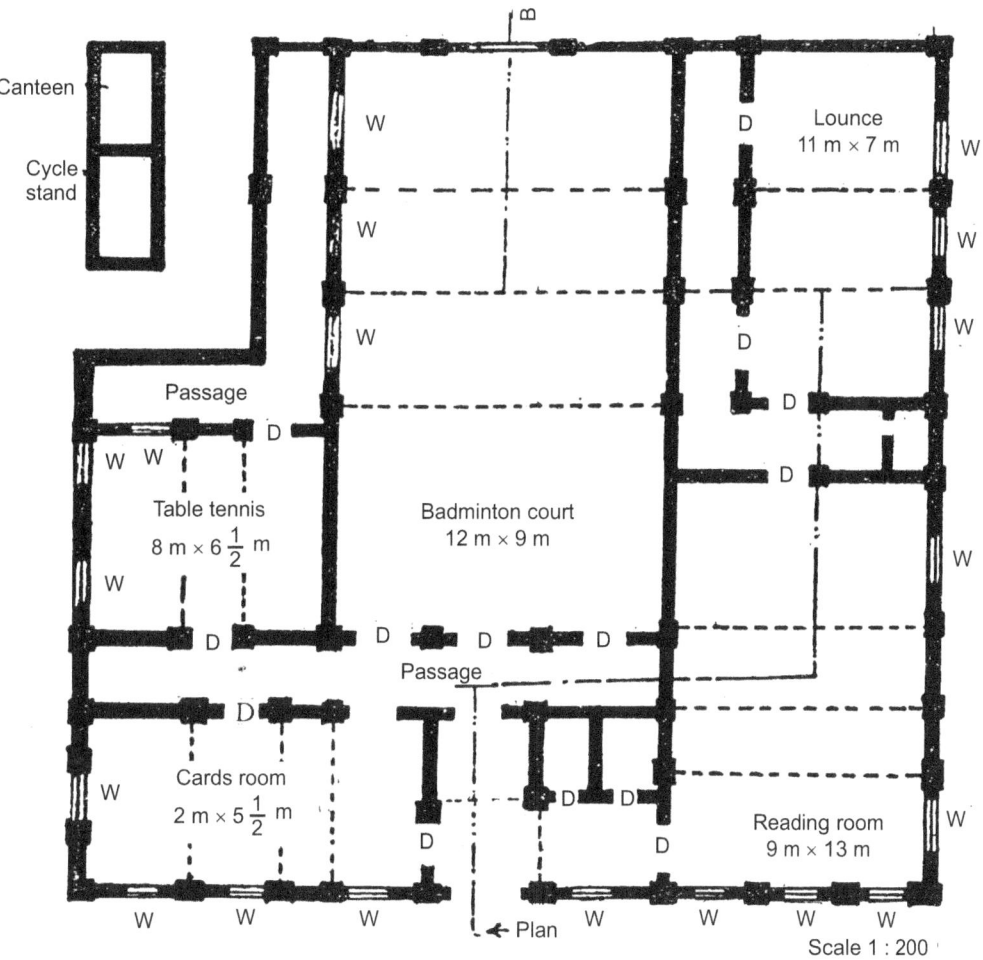

Fig. 10.10: Community centre

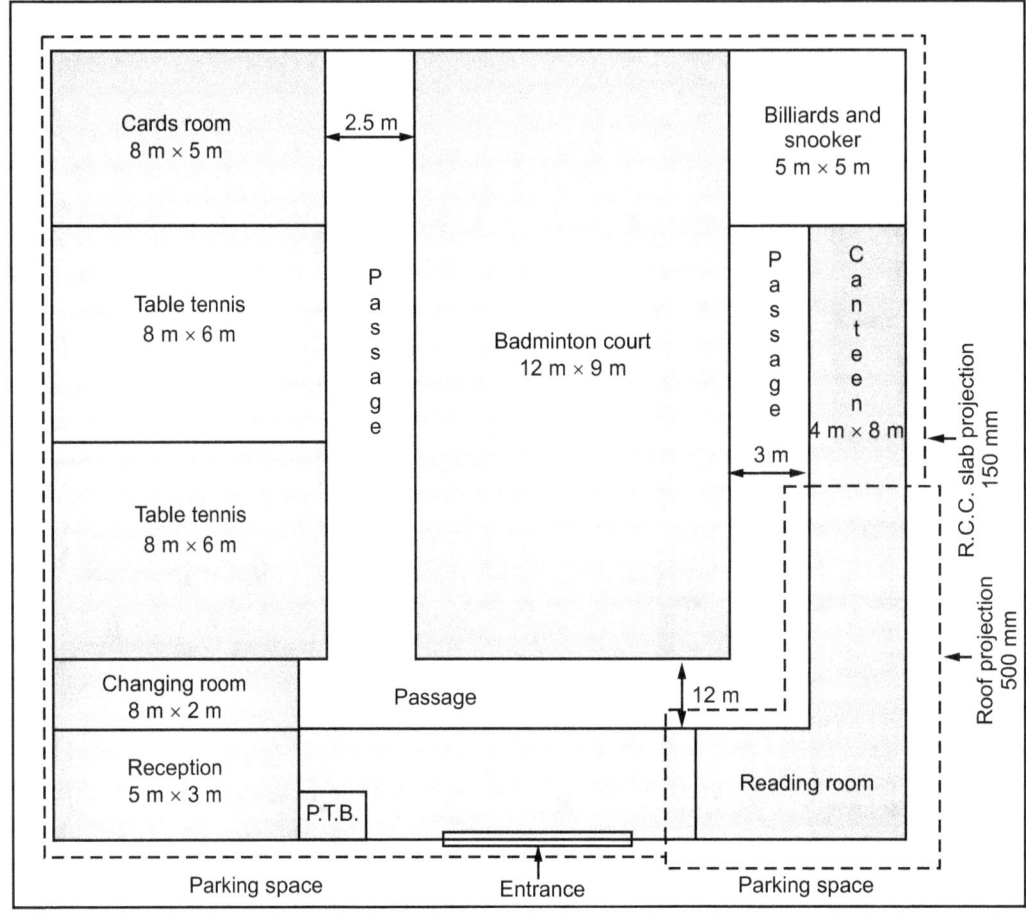

Fig. 10.11: Line Plan of a Community Centre (not to the scale)

(C) Marriage Halls:

The various units in a marriage halls may be provided as follows:

Entrance
Parking area
Kitchen   15 – 20 m²
Dining area
Store room   12 – 15 m²
Administrative office   12 m²
Auditorium   1.1 m² / person
Rooms for visitors   4 m × 3 m (each)
To be provided according to requirement.
Circulation space   1.8 m wide passages

Sanitary Blocks:

Description	Male	Female
WC	1 for 100 upto 400 and above 400, 1 for every additional 250	1 for 100 upto 200 and above 200, 1 for every additional 100
Urinals	1 for 50	—
Wash basins	1 for 200	1 for 200

(D) Banks:

The various units in a bank with their approximate sizes are as follows:

Parking area	
Entrance cum waiting space	30 m²
Counters	4 m² each with height 1.6 m, – 1.8 m width 0.4 m – 0.8 m
Working area for other staff	20 m²
Branch Managers cabin	12 m²
Cashier cabin	5 m²
Store room	12 m²
Safe Deposit lockers cum cash room	15 m²
Water and Toilet room	7.5 m²

The banks designed is a similar manner as post office, same principles may be followed in planning a bank.

(E) Lodge:

A lodge is a place where people reside for one or two days during traveling. Only provisions like sleeping arrangements are to be made. Also in some cases pantry and small canteen facilities that could only serve tea and breakfast could be provided.

The area required various units can be as follows:

Office	12 m²
Entrance	2 m wide
Rooms	
(i) Single occupancy	9.5 m²/head
(ii) Double occupancy	7.5 m²/head
Pantry	2.75 m × 3 m
Store	2 m × 3 m
Kitchen	2.75 m × 3 m

Sanitary Provisions:

Description	Male	Female
WC	1 for 10	1 for 8
Bath	1 for 10	1 for 10
Urinals	1 for 25	—
Wash basins	1 for 10	1 for 10

(F) Factory Building with an Administrative Block:
Main factory
Office and administration block.
Store for raw material.
Store for finished goods.
Canteen.
Laboratory / Quality control Department.
Circulation space.   1.5 m to 2.0 m in width

Sanitary Blocks:

Description	Male	Female
W.C.	1 for 15	1 for 15
Urinals	1 for 6 – 20 2 for 21 – 45 3 for 46 – 70 4 for 71 – 100	–
Wash basin	1 for 25	1 for 25

1. The sizes of a factory may depend on the requirement and type of the product to be manufactured.
2. In case of a factory buildings care should be taken to leave sufficient space for circulations as it may be needed for shifting of materials also.
3. The administrative block may be planned according to requirements.
4. Departments and divisions having related functions should be located in their proper relation so that the internal circulation is compact.
5. Uniform type of furniture and equipment provides greater flexibility and uniformity in appearance.
6. Generally offices are provided on each side of a central corridors.

10.3 GENERAL GUIDELINES AND SOME COMMON UNITS WHICH ARE NEEDED IN PUBLIC BUILDINGS

Some of the common units required in all types of public buildings are:

1. **Sanitary Blocks:** The sanitary blocks includes bath rooms, bed rooms, wash hand basins and urinals. The number to provided in each building various according to the requirements. Common sizes adopted as a general guidelines are as follows:

   Bath rooms   1.2 m × 2.1 m, 1.9 m × 2.7 m
   Water closet   0.9 m × 1.2 m, 1.0 × 1.2 m
   Urinals   0.9 m × 0.75 m

2. **Circulation:** Various units are connected together by passages, corridors and verandahs. Vertical circulation can be effected by the stair and lifts.
   Common sizes adopted are as follows:
   Passage / corridor   1 – 3.0 m
   Verandah   width 1.8 – 3.5 m
   Stairs   width 1.2 m (min.)
   Riser   150 – 170 mm
   Tread   300 – 325 mm
   Landing   1 – 1.8 m wide
   Head room   1.8 m (min.)
   Floor height   2.7 m – 6 m

3. **Entrance or Reception:** Each public buildings, requires space to be provided at the entrance. The area that shall be provided at the main entry point will very slightly with the number of occupants that might enter at a time. But in any case, width of an entrance shall not be less than 2.75 m.
   General sizes to be provided can be as follows:
   3 m × 6 m   4 m × 5 m
   3.5 m × 7 m   4.5 m × 6 m
   3.75 m × 8 m   6 m × 7.5 m
                     7 m × 8.0 m

4. **Parking Space, Garages and Cycle Stands:** Open parking space is essential around any type of building the area of an parking to be provided for any public building will depend on the type of a building and number of persons visiting the building. In calculation of such area some assumptions visitor and accordingly it should be designed.

Area Required:

Vehicle	Area required
Cars	20 m^2 / vehicle
Scooters and Motorcycles	3 m^2 / vehicle
Cycles	1.2 m^2 / vehicle
Buses	60 m^2 / bus

General Guidelines for Furniture Sizes of Various Units:

A building is not complete if the necessary furniture is not provided. Whatever may be the function of the buildings and activity inside its various areas, we need furniture.
Sizes of furniture to be provided at various places are as below:

Office table   - 1.8 × 0.9 × 0.75 m
Subordinate officer - 1.5 × 0.9 × 0.75 m
Clerk table   - 1.35 × 0.75 × 0.75 m
Chair with arms   - 0.45 × 0.05 × 0.45 m
Cupboards   - 1.10 × 0.50 × 1.8 m
Stands for books   - 1.8 × 0.45 × 2.1 m
                       1.1 × 0.45 × 1.35 m

Space Left Around Furniture:
1. 50 cm length of a desk be provided in a school per student.
2. The width required from the front edge of desk to rear edge or back of the seat is about 0.85 to 0.90 m.
3. The gangway between desks should not be less than 40 cm in width preferably 45 cm.
4. At least 15 cm gap should be left between wall and a desk.
   The table to be provided in a library or a canteen shall be of a such a size that 4 to 6 persons are seated.

Approximate Sizes of Furniture:
1. Twin sofa or Chair   - 0.75 m × 1.3 m
2. Office chair or small chair   - 0.45 m × 0.45 m
3. Small arm chair   - 0.65 m × 0.45 m
4. Club chair   - 0.75 m × 0.9 m or 0.65 m × 0.75 m
5. Writing table   - 1.35 m × 0.75 m
6. Small desk   - 1.20 m × 0.60 m
7. Cafee table   - 1 m diameter
8. Bridge table   - 0.9 m × 0.9 m
9. Single bed   - 0.9 m × 2.0 m
10. Double bed   - 1.35 m – 1.4 m × 2 – 2.1 m
11. Divan or setter   - 0.75 m × 1.65 m
12. Dressing stool   - 0.45 m × 0.38 m
13. Chest for drawers   - 0.60 m × 0.38 m
14. Bed side table   - 0.60 m × 0.30 m
15. Small dressing table   - 0.45 m × 0.90 m

IMPORTANT POINTS

- Types of buildings.
- Points to be considered for planning:
  (a) Covered under residential
  (b) Educational buildings
  (c) Institutional buildings
  (d) Assembly buildings
  (e) Business buildings etc.
- General buildings:
  (a) Post office
  (b) Health club
  (c) Marriage halls
  (d) Banks
  (e) Lodge
  (f) Factory building
- General requirements for above mentioned buildings.

QUESTIONS

1. Design a state transport bus terminus for a Taluka place. Make suitable assumptions and mention them clearly. Clearly specify the tails of the following:
   (i) Open space.
   (ii) Waiting space platforms.
   (iii) Offices.
   Draw a line plan to a suitable scale.
   Show a typical furniture arrangement plan for content buildings.

2. It is proposed to construct a Post Office with the following data:
   (i) Entrance-cum-waiting space: 50 sq.m.
   (ii) Public dealing counter (six in numbers): Total 30 sq.m.
   (iii) Working space for other staff 35 sq.m.
   (iv) Post master office: 15 sq.m.
   (v) Post separation room: 30 sq.m.
   (vi) Store room: 15 sq.m.
   (vii) Meeting room: 20 sq.m.
   (viii) Sanitary units: As per standards.
   (ix) All passages: 2000 mm wide.
   (x) Assume any additional suitable data, if necessary and mention it clearly with justification.
      (a) Draw a scale 1 : 100 or suitable, Line plan showing location of doors and windows.
      (b) Show line sketches of furniture arrangement.

3. It is proposed to construct a Single-Storeyed Shopping Complex with the following data:
   (1) Entrance: of suitable size.
   (2) Big shops: 4 nos., 30 m² each.
   (3) Small shops: 8 nos., 20 m² each.
   (4) Telephone booths: 2 nos. of suitable size.
   (5) Separate sanitary blocks for ladies and gents.
   (6) Staircase for future expansion.
   (7) All passages 2.5 m wide.
   (8) RCC framed structure.
   (9) Assume additional data if necessary.
   (a) Draw to a scale of 1 : 50 or suitable, line plan with northline.
   (b) Locate all openings and columns.
   (c) Show details of furniture arrangement with dimensions in any one shop.

4. Design a Single-Storeyed Restaurant building on a Highway. The following units are to be provided:

   (1) Entrance and general stationery shop — 45 m²
   (2) Dining hall — 300 m²
   (3) Service — 35 m²
   (4) Kitchen — 45 m²
   (e) Store-room — 18 m²
   (6) Cloak room for keeping baggage — 15 m⁴
   (7) Water closet for gents — 2 nos.
       Water closet for ladies — 2 nos.

   Draw to a scale of 1 : 50 or suitable:
   (a) Line plan showing location of doors and windows.
   (b) Furniture arrangement in the dining hall.

5. It is proposed to construct a PWD Executive Engineer's office with the following data:

   (1) Entrance and waiting — 60 m²
   (2) Head clear — 20 m²
   (3) Administrative office — 100 m²
   (4) Gents' sanitary block — 20 m²
   (5) Executive engineer's office (with attached toilet of suitable size) — 35 m²
   (6) PA to executive engineer (with attached toilet of suitable size) — 20 m²
   (7) Drawing, printing and xeroxing — 40 m²
   (8) Technical assistant — 20 m²
   (9) Records and stationary room — 30 m²
   (10) Ladies room (with attached toilet of suitable size) — 15 m²
   (11) All passages — 3000 mm wide

   Draw to a scale of 1 : 50 or suitable.
   (a) Line plan showing location of doors, widows and northline. (15)
   (b) Write schedule of openings. (2)
   (c) Suggest suitable flooring material for various rooms. (3)

■■■

University Question Papers

March 2014

Time: Four Hours **Max. Marks: 80**

UNIT - I

1. What are the principles of planning of residential building, explain any two with sketches? [8]
2. Explain any two.
   (i) Air conditioning system (ii) Fire protection of building (iii) Building Bye - Laws. [8]
3. Compare one pipe system and two pipe system of plumbing with sketches. [8]

UNIT - II

3. Draw working plans of a single Storeyed Residential building with the given line plan Fig. 1 and data as given below:
   Foundation = 1.6 m deep below G.L., Load bearing structure
   Plinth Height = 500 mm
   Super structure = Bottom of R.C.C. Slab above plinth = 3.60 m
   Parapet = 500 mm High, Brick masonry 300 mm thick in cm 1 : 6
   Doors = standard size as per I.S. Code.
   Windows = 15% of room area
   Assume suitable any other relevant data.
   Draw to scale 1 : 75 or suitable.
4. Detailed ground floor plan. [8]
5. Front Elevation. [8]
6. Section. [8]

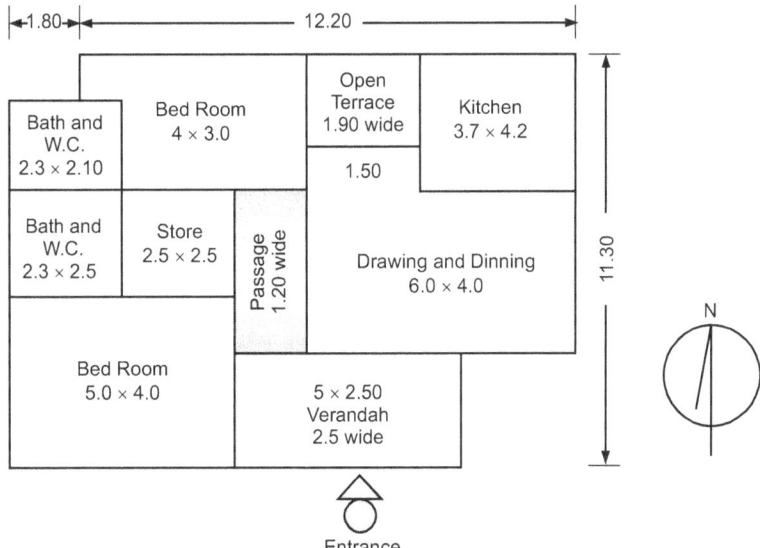

Fig. 1: Line Plan (All Dimensions in m)

UNIT - III

7. Draw a typical floor plan of a flat (three room kitchen) in a apartment with the following data.

   Habitable rooms area = 9.5 m² minimum for one room.
   Two room = 7.5 m² for other room (with minimum width of 2.4 m)
   Kitchen = 5.5 m² (with minimum width of kitchen 1.8 m)
   Bath room = 1.5 m × 1.2 m or 1.8 m² area
   W. C. = 1.1 m²   [8]

8. Fig. 2 shows a plan of entrance steps. Front side of which is touching the picture plane. The observer is standing at 73H (Height of object). Assume suitable eye level above G. L. Draw one point perspective view to a scale of 1 : 20 or suitable. Retain all construction lines. [8]

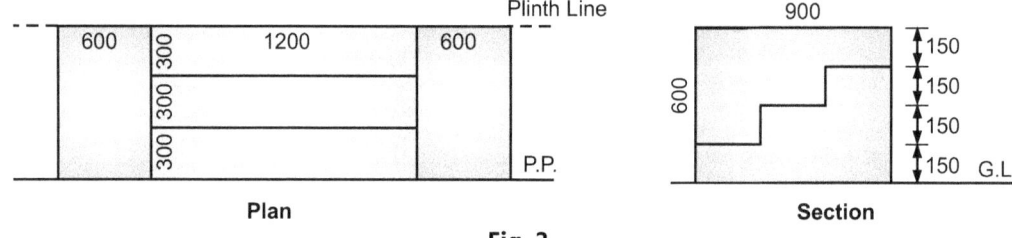

Fig. 2

9. Fig. 3 shows a plan of entrance steps one side of which is inclined at an angle of 30° to the picture plane and touches the same at 'A'. The observer is standing at a distance of 2 m along the central visual ray. Assuming eye level at 1.5 m above G.L. Draw the two points perspective view to a scale of 1 : 20. Retain all construction lines. [8]

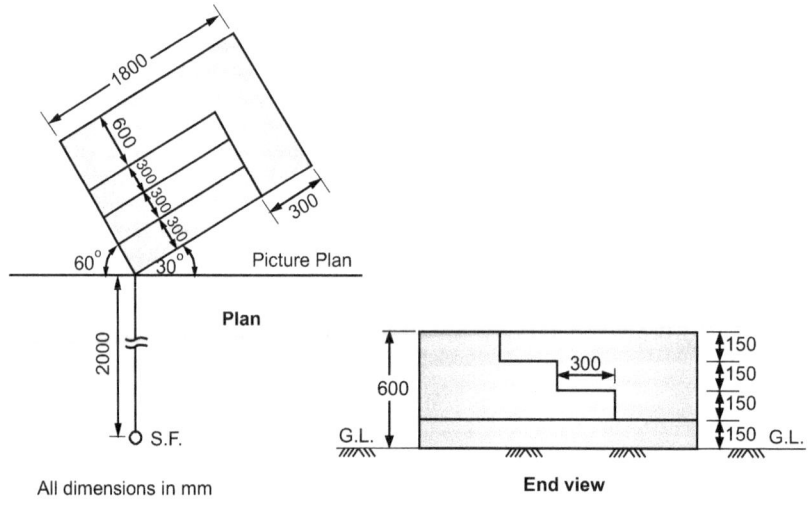

Fig. 3

UNIT - IV

10. Draw to some convenient scale, a line plan of a primary health center constructed in rural area with the following given data.

    (i)   Entrance and waiting space = 3 to 6 m wide
    (ii) Doctor's room = 10 to 12 m^2
    (iii) Examination room = 10 to 12 m^2
    (iv) Operation theatre = 20 to 25 m^2
    (v)   Wards = 8 to 10 m^2 per bed.
    (vi) Medical store = 10 to 12 m^2
    (vii) Laboratory = 15 m^2
    (viii) Sanitary block. **[8]**

11. Draw line plan of a library building with the following given data to some convenient scale.

    (i)   Entrance and moving area = 1.8 m wide (minimum)
    (ii) Librarian's room = 9 m^2 (minimum)
    (iii) Sections in library
          Reference books = 20 to 60 m^2
          Book section = 20 to 60 m^2
          Magazines and Newspapers = 3 m wide (minimum)
          Stacking space = 20 m^2
    (iv) Circulation
    (v)   Parking space and cycle stand
    (vi) Sanitary block. **[8]**

12. Draw line plan of a hostel building with the following given data to suitable scale.

    (i)   Entrance = 3 m wide
    (ii) Rooms: Single = 3 m × 3.1 m Double = 3.5 m × 4 m
    (iii) Circulation
    (iv) Recreation Hall = 2 to 3 m^2/head
    (v)   Dining Hall = 3 to 4 m^2/head

(vi) Kitchen = 2.75 m × 3 m

(vii) Pantry = 2 m × 3 m

(viii) Store = 2.75 m × 3 m

(ix) Public telephone

(x) Sanitary block. [8]

UNIT - V

The various units in a bank with their approximate sizes are as follows:

Entrances cum waiting space = 30 m^2

Counters 4 m^2 with width 0.4 to 0.8 m

Working area for other staff = 20 m^2

Branch managers cabin = 5 m^2

Stare room = 12 m^2

Safe deposit lockers cum cash room = 15 m^2

Water and Toilet room = 7.5 m^2

13. Draw plan of bank building with above given data with suitable scale showing doors and windows. [8]
14. Draw elevation of above drawn plan of Bank building with suitable heights. [8]
15. Prepare schedule of Doors and windows in above drawn Bank building and suitable site plan for it. [8]

October 2014

Time: Four Hours Max. Marks: 80

UNIT - I

1. (a) (i) Explain any one type of principle of planning of residential building, with sketch.

    (ii) What do you understand by floor area ratio (F.A.R.), explain. [8]

   (b) Write short notes on any two:

    (i) Ventilation.

    (ii) A.C. system.

    (iii) Fire protection of building. [8]

   (c) Explain the difference between one point and two point plumbing system with sketch. [8]

UNIT - II

2. Fig. 1 shows a line plan of residential building. Assume suitable data if required and draw any two of the following.

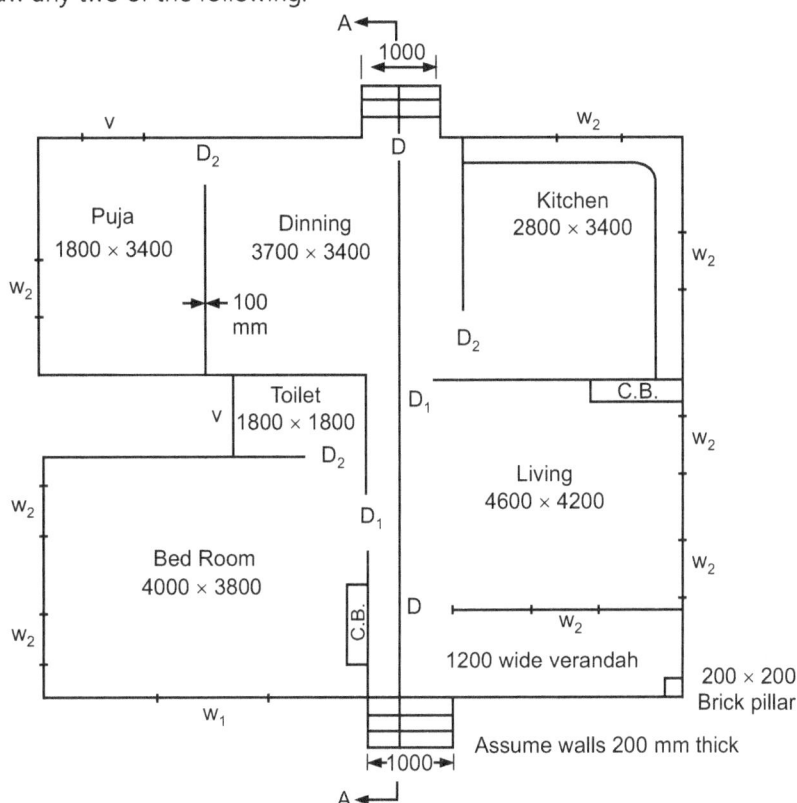

Fig. 1: Line diagram

   (a) Detailed plan. [8]
   (b) Elevation and schedule of openings. [8]
   (c) Section through 'AA'. [8]

UNIT - III

3. (a) Draw a typical ownership flat in an apartment with the following data line plan only, with minimum dimensions:

   Living room = 9.5 m², 3 m minimum width

   Bed rooms (Two) = 9.5 m² minimum for each room with minimum width 2.4 m.

   Kitchen = 5.5 m² with minimum width of 1.8 m.

   Bath rooms = 2.8 m² with minimum width of 1.2 m.

   W.C. = 1.1 m². [8]

(b) The Fig. 2 shows the plan and elevation of an object. It is inclined at a angle of 30° to the picture plan and touches the picture plane at 'A'. The observer is standing at a distance of 3.0 m from picture plane along the central visual ray. Assuming eye level at 2.0 m above ground level, draw the perspective view to a suitable scale. [8]

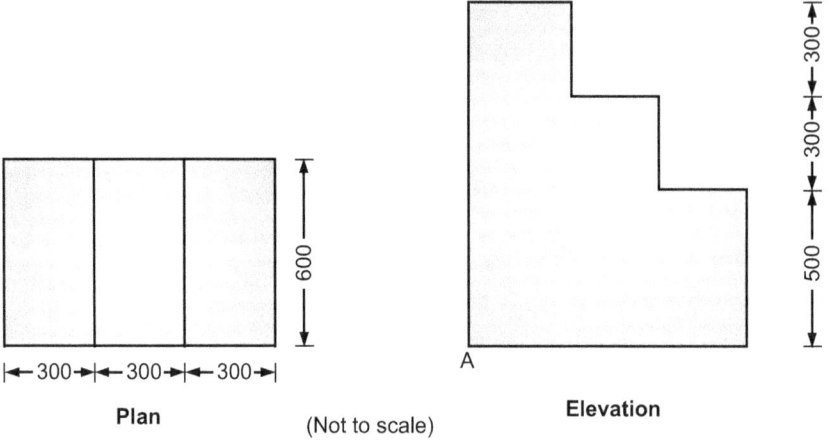

Fig. 2

(c) The Fig. 3, shows the plan and elevation of an object. It is inclined at an angle of 30° degrees to the picture plane and touches the P.P. at 'B'. The observer is standing at a distance of 2.5 m from the P.P. along central visual ray. Assuming eye level at 1.80 m above ground level, draw the perspective view to a suitable scale. [8]

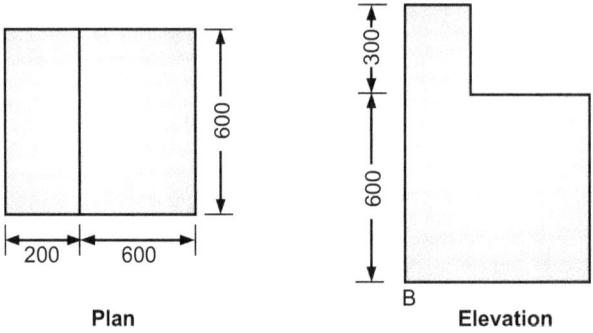

Fig. 3

UNIT - IV

4. (a) Draw a line plan of school building for 8 class rooms with 40 students in each class room. Area required for one student 1.2 m². Also there must be a head masters room, staff room office and sanitary block, staircase, verandah etc. of suitable sizes. The building is single storied R.C.C. framed structure type. Assume suitable additional data and scale. [8]

(b) Draw a line plan of Dispensary with the data given below:
   (i) Entrance and waiting space = 2 m wide (minimum)
   (ii) Doctor's room = 2.75 m × 4 m.
   (iii) Examination / dressing room = 3 m × 4 m.
   (iv) Operation / dressing room = 3 m × 4 m.
   (v) Sanitary block.
   (vi) Store room = 2.75 m × 3 m.
   (vii) Compounder's space = 2 m wide (minimum)
   (viii) Circulation space.
   Assume suitable additional data and scale. [8]

(c) Draw a line plan of a Library with the data as follows:
   (i) Entrance = 1.8 m wide (minimum).
   (ii) Delivery counter.
   (iii) Librarian's room = 9 m^2 minimum.
   (iv) Sections in Library =
      Reference books - Area = 20 m^2 – 60 m^2
      Book section – Area = 20 m^2 – 60 m^2
      Magazines and News papers = 3 m wide (minimum)
      Staking space = 20 m^2.
   (v) Circulation
   (vi) Sanitary block.
   Assume suitable data if required and relevant scale. [8]

UNIT - V

5. (a) A line plan of a post office building is given in Fig. 4. Draw to a suitable scale with required data assumed, if required.
   (a) Detailed plan. [8]
   (b) Elevation with door window schedule. [8]
   (c) Section 'AA'. [8]

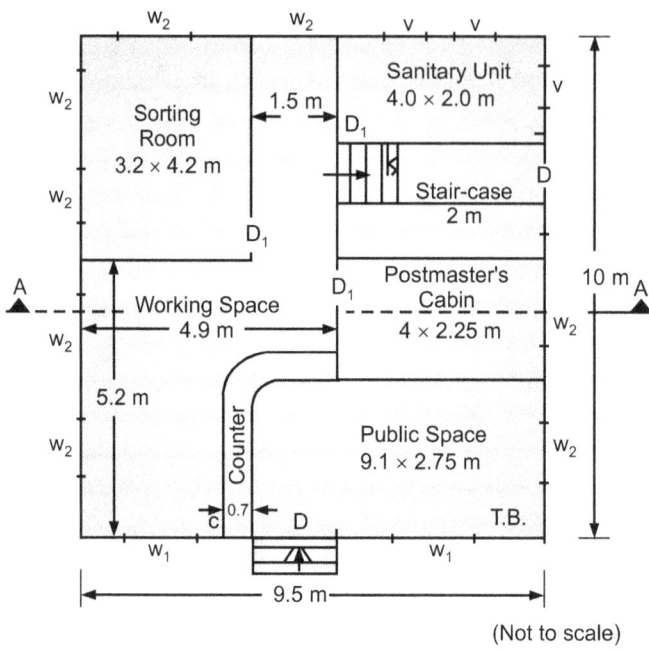

Fig. 4: Typical Plan of a Post office (Not to scale)

Wall thickness 0.20 m.

D and W - Doors and Windows.

T. B. - Telephone Booth.

■■■
March 2015

Time: Four Hours   **Max. Marks: 80**

UNIT - I

1. (a) Explain the term:
   - (i) Building bye laws and its necessity.
   - (ii) Systems of ventilation. [8]

   (b) Explain the term:
   - (i) Necessity of air conditioning.
   - (ii) Fire load. [8]

   (c) Explain the term:
   - (i) Requirements for different building services.
   - (ii) One pipe and two pipe system. [8]

UNIT – II

2. Planning of residential building single storeyed, flat roof type load beating structure with detail drawing (Refer Fig. 1) and other data given below:
   (i) Foundation is at 1000 mm depth.
   (ii) Sill height = 800 mm.
   (iii) Ceiling height = 3000 mm.
   (iv) Thickness of slab = 120 mm.
   (v) Rise = 160 mm, Tread = 250 mm and width 01 stairs = 1300
   (vi) Chajja projection = 750 mm.
   (vii) Slab projection = 150 mm.
   (viii) UCR masonry in cm (1.6) in plinth and foundation.
   (ix) BBM in cm (1.6) 300 thick for masonry wall
   (x) Provide doors and windows suitably.
   Draw to a scale of 1 : 100 assuming any other data
   (a) Draw detailed plan of Fig. 1. [8]
   (b) Front Elevation showing all details of Fig. 1. [8]
   (c) Section along A'A' with all details. [8]

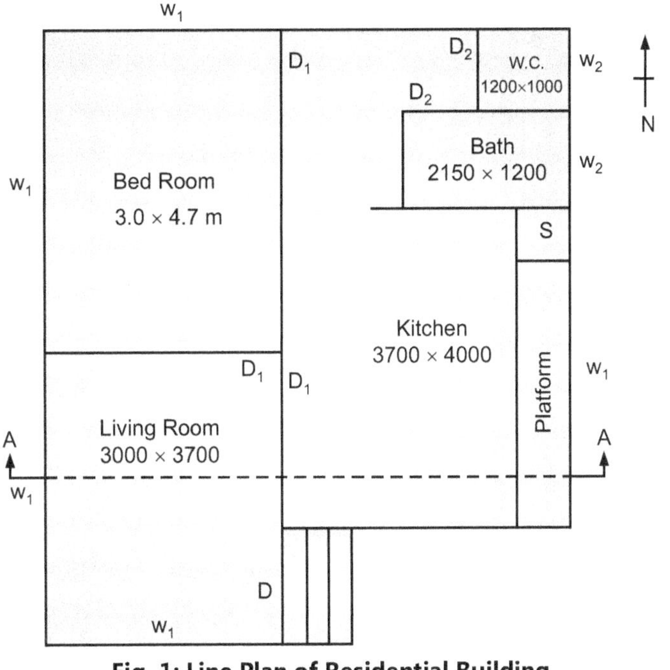

Fig. 1: Line Plan of Residential Building

UNIT – III

3. Planning and designing of apartment house (Flat) having framed structure only form given data.
   (i) Size of plot – 25 m × 30 m.
   (ii) Permissible built up area on each floor 1/3 of plot area.
   (iii) Draw a scale of 1 : 100 assuming all necessary data.

(a) Draw Typical floor plan of flat (Detailed) showing column position. [8]
(b) Detail Elevation of the above typical floor plan assuming all standard details. [8]
(c) The Fig. 2 shows the plan and elevation of an object it is inclined at a angle of 30° to picture plane (B). The observer is standing at a distance of 3.0 m from picture plane along central visual ray. Assuming eye level a 2.0 m above G.L. Draw the perspective view to suitable scale. [8]

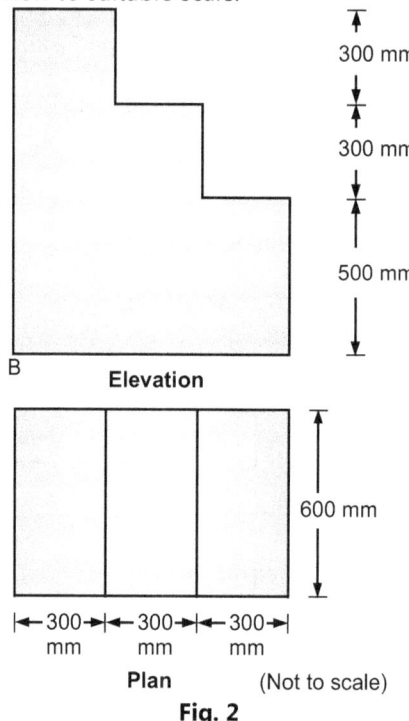

Fig. 2

UNIT – IV

4. (a) Draw a line plan of hostel building for 40 students double seated with all requirements with scale of 1 : 100 (Frame structure only). [8]
   (b) Showing the detail furniture arrangement of one room. [8]
   (c) Showing detail site plan of the hostel building. [8]

UNIT – V

5. (a) Draw a line plan of bank building with all requirements with scale of 1 : 100 (Frame structure only). [8]
   (b) Showing the detail schedule of Doors and windows of bank building. [8]
   (c) Showing parking plan of the Bank building. [8]

www.ingramcontent.com/pod-product-compliance
Lightning Source LLC
Chambersburg PA
CBHW080439230426
43662CB00015B/2319